GEORGE WASHINGTON'S SECRET SPY WAR

Also by John A. Nagy

Dr. Benjamin Church, Spy

Spies in the Continental Capital

Invisible Ink

Rebellion in the Ranks

GEORGE WASHINGTON'S SECRET SPY WAR

The Making of America's First Spymaster

John A. Nagy

ST. MARTIN'S PRESS ☲ NEW YORK

GEORGE WASHINGTON'S SECRET SPY WAR.
Copyright © 2016 by John A. Nagy. All rights reserved.
Printed in the United States of America.
For information, address St. Martin's Press,
175 Fifth Avenue, New York, N.Y. 10010.

www.stmartins.com

The Library of Congress Cataloging-in-Publication
Data is available upon request.

ISBN 978-1-250-09681-4 (hardcover)
ISBN 978-1-250-09682-1 (e-book)

Our books may be purchased in bulk for promotional,
educational, or business use. Please contact your
local bookseller or the Macmillan Corporate and
Premium Sales Department at 1-800-221-7945,
extension 5442, or by e-mail at MacmillanSpecial
Markets@macmillan.com.

First Edition: September 2016

10 9 8 7 6 5 4 3 2 1

To Ida Marie Nagy, my wife,
for all these years of enormous amounts
of patience and encouragement
to write the books

CONTENTS

GEORGE WASHINGTON'S SECRET SPY WAR

INTRODUCTION

"There is nothing more necessary than good intelligence to frustrate a designing enemy, and nothing that requires greater pains to obtain."

GEORGE WASHINGTON TO ROBERT HUNTER MORRIS,
JANUARY 1, 1756.[1]

George Washington has been dead for over two hundred years and one would think that nothing new could be written about him, that everything has been discovered and observed under the microscope, but I have found that there is one key aspect of his extraordinary life and career that to this day has remained little explored. He was America's first spymaster. And his skill as a spymaster provided for the opportunity to win the American Revolution and independence from Great Britain.

Washington took a disorderly, hygiene-deficient, ill-equipped, ill-behaved rabble that could not march or fire in unison and defeated the best-disciplined, best-equipped, and best-trained army of its day. When he resigned as commander in chief of the Continental Army, King George III of England called him "the greatest character of his age." Unlike some other founding fathers, he is neither forgotten nor has his impact dimmed despite the passage of time. Every year millions of people from around the world make a pilgrimage to his Mount Vernon home to learn more about him. The demand for information about this multifaceted man has recently spawned a new major library, the Fred W. Smith National Library for the Study of George Washington, which opened in 2013 in Mount Vernon, Virginia. The library raised $106 million from private sources for the study of Washington's life, achievements, and character. The quest for knowledge of the man burns brighter today than ever.

George Washington was a Virginia farmer who became America's first and the eighteenth century's greatest spymaster. This will be the first book to focus on this vital component of his military leadership. To the extent that his spycraft is written about in previous books, it is most often about the usual topics of Nathan Hale, the inept spy; Benedict Arnold, the traitor; and the Culper Spy Ring, Washington's fourth and overcredited spy ring. There are a number of books on these subjects that are available.

Over the last twenty-four years I have discovered hundreds of spies who went behind enemy lines to gather intelligence during the American Revolution and returned to the American side. Previously I have published the names of 160 such spies, many of whom were completely unknown. There are some spies in this book that are now revealed for the first time.

George Washington did not come completely unskilled in this extremely important facet of warfare to the American Revolution; that is, he was not totally ignorant of spy craft as some would have you believe. His first steps in the field of espionage began as a young man during the French and Indian War.

During that war, despite his young age he quickly realized that the French were encouraging his Indian allies to turn away from him and become their allies. He discovered that the French were sending spies to find out all they could about him and the strength and disposition of his Virginia forces. He took great delight in sending the French spies back to their handlers with false information. He also recognized that he needed intelligence of what the slippery French were planning so that he could prepare for what was to come. He needed his own spies to gather the intelligence he wanted and required. He recruited spies to go into the French fort at the Forks of the Ohio to bring back the condition of the fort and the status of its men. He even did some espionage himself at Fort Le Boeuf. He knew he had to be on the lookout for French deceptions. He provided code words so that his spies were not fooled by false messengers claiming to have been sent by him.

Not everything went his way. He signed a document in French, a language he could not read, that said he had "assassinated" an emissary of France while he was on a peaceful mission to the British. Washington insisted that not only this word but other portions of the capitulation document had been mistranslated. It was a wet document signed in the rain in the Allegheny wilderness. It was a document that set the world on fire and brought on the Seven Years' War, known as the French and Indian War in North America.

Although he routinely cautioned his staff on the need for secrecy in conducting secret service activities, not everyone listened. He had spies—such as George Higday—who were captured by the British because of the carelessness of their case agent, Benjamin Tallmadge. When Washington received Tallmadge's letter of July 3 informing him of the loss of his correspondence in a skirmish, Washington wrote back that the person who was in the most danger was George Higday, who lived on or near the North River not far from the Bowery in New York City. "I wish you could endeavor to give him the speediest notice of what has happened. My anxiety on his account is great. If he is really the man he has been represented to be, he will in all probability fall a sacrifice."[2] As Washington had predicted, Higday was arrested on July 13 and placed in the provost, the military jail.

From the provost Higday wrote a desperate letter to General Henry Clinton informing him that about three or four weeks prior he had taken three American officers across the Hudson River to New Jersey.

> On going over their discourse was what a fine thing it might be for me to fetch information over for Washington that he would make me rich in so doing accordingly I being left by God and his divine protection to myself [he yielded to the temptation and he went with the American officers to General George Washington] and offered the above proposals but he was afraid to enter [into agreement] but said he would consider on it. And did not countenance me much & had some Congress money & thought to buy a cow on time with it—the money was so bad I could not buy one so I returned home for which reason I suppose he hath sent this letter that now is taken— Now I did not think even they would write to me for Washington said my name was in the black book for being a friend to government and would not trust me.[3]

On August 28, 1780, Higday was listed on the British provost report for New York as an inhabitant of the city who was placed in the provost by the commander in chief, General Clinton. It indicated he had spent 507 nights in jail without being charged with a crime.[4] He was an example of what could happen to spies due to American carelessness even if they were only suspected.

In the eighteenth century every general was expected to develop and run his own intelligence-gathering operation. Every lieutenant colonel and colonel with ambition to advance in rank to general needed to study his commander's methods for conducting intelligence gathering if they had not already mastered them. It was on-the-job training. Washington worked during the French and Indian War under British Major General Edward Braddock, commander of all British forces in North America. He would have known Braddock's cipher and how it was used.

Espionage was a skill set upon which Washington heavily depended during the Revolution. For someone who supposedly never told a lie, he routinely used deception to his advantage whenever he could and was constantly on guard for deceptions the British were playing against him.[5] When Brigadier General Philemon Dickinson of the New Jersey Militia suggested a deception in New York, Washington, who was in Pennsylvania, wholeheartedly embraced the idea with childlike glee. He immediately ordered the coordination of troops, devising several strokes around New York City to confirm the deception.

He took special care to make sure his secret service people knew the information that he wanted to ensure he received the intelligence he needed. He arranged for his spies to use the cover of being smugglers of foodstuffs to the British. He never had much in the way of hard currency to pay his spies and they would not take Continental currency as payment. He allowed them to return from the enemy lines with contraband. Some either made too many trips or abused the privilege and became known publicly as a source of smuggled goods. They became so obvious and obnoxious that they were arrested by the local authorities. Washington realized that he had to get the governor of New Jersey involved to protect his spies since they could not publicly defend themselves in court. If they announced in court that they were American spies, they could not be used again, as word would get to the British. Not protecting their spies would hamper finding a replacement.

Washington was active in trying new procedures. He tried to use a standardized questionnaire in interrogating deserters. It did not produce the results he wanted and I have not been able to identify it being used again. He provided the sympathetic ink stain used in invisible writing to Elias Dayton and Benjamin Tallmadge for use by their spies. Sympathetic ink is a liquid which becomes invisible soon after writing. It can later be made visible only by the application of a second liquid which causes a chemical reaction. When more sympathetic ink was needed, he instructed Deputy Quartermaster General Lieutenant Colonel Udny Hay to assist James Jay in building a laboratory to manufacture the "medicine," as they called it, in their correspondence.

Being the obvious underdog, he used espionage to level the playing field and then exploit it to the best advantage possible. After several mutinies in 1781, his assessment of the army's condition was desperate. The campaign goal for the year was to attack New York but it required the French navy to control the waters around York Island (Manhattan Island). The French navy changed their destination in North America from Upper New

York Bay to Chesapeake Bay. Washington now had to change the objective. He had to move the American and French armies to Virginia as fast as possible to coordinate with the French navy to attack British General Charles Cornwallis's army encamped at Yorktown before he could escape to North Carolina or be evacuated by the British navy. He needed to get past the British army in New York without being delayed by having to fight his way across New Jersey. He conjured up all his deception and espionage skills to accomplish this task. The procedure he employed is today known as a Deception Battle Plan and has been copied and used most notably in the twentieth century with the 1944 Allied landing at Normandy in World War II and the U.S. Operation Desert Storm against Iraq in 1991.

One

FRENCH LESSONS

Once again George Washington ventured into the wilderness. It was October 1753 and he would be going deeper into the wilderness than he had ever gone before. He would be journeying into the disputed lands. Both England and France claimed the territory west of the Allegheny Ridge known as the Ohio Country. He was in his early twenties. He stood six feet three inches tall, weighed around 175 pounds, and suffered from a slight case of amblyopia or "wandering eye."[1] He was the adjutant of the northern district of the Virginia militia. He had striven several years to obtain this position.

King George's War between the British and the French and their Indian allies, which was the North American phase of the War of the Austrian Succession (1744–1748), was over. It was fought between the northern British settlements in North America and the colony of New France. The Treaty of Aix-la-Chapelle restored all colonial borders to their prewar status. The war, however, failed to resolve the territorial disputes between Britain, France, and their colonies in North America.

Born in Glasgow, Scotland, Lieutenant Governor Robert Dinwiddie of Virginia had been in office only two years when in
1753, he learned that the French had built Fort Presque Isle near
present-day Erie, Pennsylvania, and Fort Le Boeuf, which was
about fifteen miles south of Lake Erie. The forts threatened
Virginia's interests in the Ohio Valley. Dinwiddie was looking to
send an emissary to the French in the Ohio Country to tell
them they had to leave British soil. Washington, who was only
twenty-one years old, volunteered to deliver the demand as
well as spy on the French to determine their military capabilities in the region. There would not have been many (and may
have not been any) other suitors for the position. Dinwiddie accepted his offer despite Washington's young age.[2]

When George was fourteen years old, his older half brother,
Lawrence, whom he admired, encouraged him to look to the
sea for adventure and a career in the British navy.[3] Mary Ball
Washington, his domineering widowed mother, upon discovering his plan, humored him at first but then put an end to those
dreams.[4] Lawrence hired a professional surveyor to teach George
the trade. It suited his talents, as he was proficient in mathematics and had a fondness for the outdoors. Augustine Washington, George's father, died on April 12, 1743, at age forty-nine
when George was eleven years old. One of the possessions he
left was a complete set of surveyor's instruments. Surveying
was a good career path for a young man in which to rise in
Virginia society. As more people arrived, more lands needed to
be surveyed. It ensured there would be work and was a good
source of income. It was a career that also allowed an observant
surveyor, like George, to identify the choice lands to buy for
himself, and he took advantage of the opportunities open to
him in real estate.

With Augustine's death, Lawrence inherited the 2,500-acre estate on Little Hunting Creek, which he renamed Mount Vernon in honor of British Vice Admiral Edward Vernon.[5] He married Ann Fairfax, eldest daughter of Colonel William Fairfax, who lived four miles down the Potomac River at Belvoir Plantation. It was a social coup for the Washingtons, as the Fairfax family was one of the most powerful in Virginia. They controlled the Fairfax Grant of 5,282,000 acres in the Northern Neck of Virginia between the Rappahannock and Potomac Rivers.[6] Lord Thomas Fairfax, the absentee proprietor of the Northern Neck, visited the colony in 1746 and moved there in 1747 to stay.[7] He initially stayed at Belvoir Plantation. In 1752, Lord Fairfax, a life-long bachelor, permanently moved to Greenway Court, near White Post, Clarke County, Virginia, where he died in 1781.

William Fairfax, cousin of Lord Thomas Fairfax, served as agent for the vast landholding. He appointed his son George William Fairfax, who was twenty-four years old, to sell the lease-holds in Lord Fairfax's western lands of the Fairfax Grant.[8] In March of 1748, Washington accompanied his neighbor George William Fairfax across the Blue Ridge Mountains into the Virginia frontier of the Shenandoah Valley.[9]

Washington put quill to paper and recorded a diary of his first adventure into the wilderness. He called it "A Journal of My Journey over the Mountains." It was a journey through the forest of chestnut, oak, pine, and sugar maple trees; of sleeping under the stars; traveling over the primitive rutted paths that served as roads; and navigating engorged whitewater streams in the driving rain. He slept on bearskins under the stars or in smoky tents. It was a new world to him, to which he adjusted remarkably quickly. It showed his ability to adapt to changing situations. He would put this skill to great use during the Revolution when he had to change his strategy for conducting his military campaigns after the fall of New York City and most of New Jersey to the British.

The surveying party stayed with a Captain Isaac Pennington at his lodging at present-day Berryville, Virginia.[10] Saying it lacked the comforts to which George had been accustomed is a major understatement. After eating supper he was led to a room where he undressed and got into a rustic bed, discovering it to be "nothing but a little straw, matted together without sheets or anything else, but only one threadbare blanket with double its weight of vermin, such as lice, fleas, etc." As soon as the light bearer left the room, he shot out of the bed, brushed off his body an immeasurable number of critters, and put on his clothes. When the surveying party arrived at Fredericktown (now known as Winchester, Virginia), he got a feather bed with clean sheets, which was more to his liking. He said he fumigated the lice he had picked up along the way.

Washington's performance in the field impressed William Fairfax, the proprietor, who secured him a commission as surveyor for the College of William and Mary in Williamsburg. In 1749 he received the patronage appointment as surveyor for the newly formed Culpeper County.

Lawrence Washington held the post of adjutant general with the rank of major of the Virginia militia. When he died in 1752, Lieutenant Governor Robert Dinwiddie and the Virginia House of Burgesses decided to divide the post into four positions. George immediately campaigned for the post of the Northern District, which included Mount Vernon and Belvoir Plantation. He was instead given the position of adjutant of the Southern District with the rank of major in the Virginia militia, a less desirable post. George was told by William Nelson that he was third in line for the position of adjutant of the Northern District.[11] When the Northern District became vacant again, he succeeded in getting appointed to the position in November 1753. He appears to have obtained the position because of his knowledge of the western lands of the Fairfax Grant from surveying them, having impressed William Fairfax, who held a position of importance in Virginia, and few if any wanted the job. He was described as "a youth of great sobriety, diligence, and fidelity."[12]

Land west of the Allegheny Ridge and into the Ohio Valley was disputed between the French and the British colonies of Pennsylvania and Virginia. All three claimed it belonged to them. Lieutenant Governor Dinwiddie discovered that the French, England's archenemy, had built their forts in the Ohio Country; he saw it as a French invasion threatening Virginia's interests in the area. It threatened the Ohio Company, a land venture with a claim to a half-million acres of frontier land, of which the portly Dinwiddie was a stockholder, thus putting his personal fortune at risk. Washington was to lead an expedition to warn the French to withdraw and deliver a letter from Dinwiddie to the French commandant at Fort Le Boeuf. The letter requested that the bearer be sent back with a reply. It called for a peaceful departure of French forces from the lands upon the Ohio River in the western parts of the colony of Virginia.[13] Washington began planning for his expedition, and while in Fredericksburg he enlisted Jacob Van Braam, a Dutchman, as his French interpreter.[14] Two weeks later he enlisted Christopher Gist, a skilled guide.[15]

Washington and his party set out in mid-November. This time he would be traveling beyond the Fairfax Stone, which was marked on November 13, 1746, with an "FX." It indicated the source of the Potomac River and the end of Lord Fairfax's grant.

He recalled that he traveled 250 miles through an uninhabited wilderness country covered in a sheet of white and ice to within fifteen miles of Lake Erie to reach Fort Le Boeuf. The weather was excessively bad for travel through the impenetrable forests, but they pushed on. They found some relief when they were taken into the rustic cabin of John Fraser, a fur trader, at the junction of the Monongahela River and Turtle Creek at present-day Braddock, Pennsylvania.[16] The Monongahela was impassible for their horses because of the rain and snow. Some of the baggage was removed from their packhorses and taken north downstream by canoe. They continued moving north and reached the Forks of the Ohio, now known as Pittsburgh. The Allegheny River was a frigid, fast-flowing obstacle. Washington, however, was an expert horseman. Relying on his skill and his horse, he was able to traverse the dangerous river. One misstep by his horse, or an error in judgment on his part, could have easily thrown him into the frigid waters. Others were more cautious as they dismounted and crossed the icy waters by canoe. One of Washington's assignments was to evaluate locations for forts, and in his report he gave his approval for a fort at the Forks of the Ohio, as it had command of both rivers.

Continuing eighteen miles westward from the Forks, they arrived at Logstown on the north bank of the Ohio River (near present-day Ambridge, Pennsylvania), where George met with the sachems of the Six Nations to enlist their support of his mission by providing him with an escort. He met Chief Shingas of the Delaware Indians.[17] At a parley at Logstown, he interrogated four French deserters. He was able to extract from them confirmation of the current suspicion in Williamsburg that the French had plans to connect their Louisiana and Canadian lands, thereby blocking the British from extending their control inland from the east coast.

Indian leader Tanacharison was in his fifties and was known as Half King. He returned to Logstown on November 25 from a hunting trip.[18] He had a strong hatred of the French. He claimed they had killed, cooked, and eaten his father. He also believed the British were there to trade with the Indians while the French wanted their land.[19] The Indians provided Washington with just four of their number as escorts. Washington suspected that the Indians were not as strongly on the British side as he had hoped or had been led to believe.

The party traveled north for five days in unrelenting rain. Soaked to the bone and slowed by their wet clothes, they reached Venango (which is today the city of Franklin), at the juncture of the Allegheny River and French Creek. There they met French Captain Philippe Thomas de Joncaire.[20] He invited Washington to have dinner with him and some French officers. The alcohol flowed freely and the French officers drank their fill. Once inebriated they lost their inhibitions. They bragged about taking control of the Ohio Country and they divulged the locations of the French forts in the area. The next day the French were hungover but still had their wits about them as they got Washington's Indians so falling-down drunk they became too intoxicated to continue their journey with Washington. Joncaire had outmaneuvered the inexperienced Washington, who now had to delay his trip.

After three days' delay at Venango, the expedition was ready to continue. He had not only lost time but he now had French monitors traveling with him. Joncaire, an experienced political agent for New France, would have sent an advance notice of

Washington's expedition to Fort Le Boeuf. The group ventured north despite the bad weather for the forty-mile journey to the fort.

They had to navigate a multitude of streams and swamps. Shortly after beginning their journey, the weather changed to freezing rain and snow. The top of the snow gained a crusty cover of ice. The rain on top of the crusty snow turned it slippery. Each step was agonizing as they either crunched through the crusted snow or slid across its surface.

The temperature continued its downward fall and it had now turned bitterly cold. The kind of cold that goes right to the bone. The party's progress had slowed considerably. It was moving way too slow for the impatient Washington. He and Gist pushed on alone, leaving the rest of the expedition to meet them at Fort Le Boeuf. The two of them traveled an incredible eighteen miles in one day in absolutely horrendous conditions. It was the dark of night of December 11 when after 5 p.m. he and Gist reached the fort.[21] Fort Le Boeuf was a primitive assemblage of four buildings constructed of planks and covered with bark to keep out the cold, rain, and snow.

The next morning he was received by Jacques Legardeur de Saint-Pierre, commandant,[22] a gray-haired elderly man with one eye and with "much the air of a soldier."[23] Washington delivered the sealed letter, which contained the message telling the French to pack up their belongings and leave. Saint-Pierre requested several days to prepare his response.

While Washington was waiting at Fort Le Boeuf he took on the role of spy. He wrote in his diary, "The chief officer retired to hold a Council of War, which gave me an opportunity of taking the dimensions of the fort."[24] Being a surveyor he knew the length of his pace, which made it easy for him to take measurements as he casually walked the fort. He learned firsthand what it would feel like to be a spy. He now knew the anxious fear of being discovered, the tingling feeling under the surface of your skin as your blood pressure rises. It made him aware of what he would be asking so many men, women, and children to do for him in the future during the Revolution. He observed the fort's military capabilities. He had the people who were with him get an exact count of the canoes. He reported 50 birch-bark and 170 pine-bark canoes along French Creek.[25] They were there for use by the French army to move quickly down the river deeper into the Ohio Country.

Saint-Pierre gave Washington his response. He advised that he was not intimidated by the British and had a right to be on French soil. He would arrest any English traders who came upon French territory. "As to the summons you send me to retire. I do not think myself obliged to obey it."[26] Three days later on the 14th, Saint-Pierre gave Washington a letter to deliver to Lieutenant Governor Dinwiddie. The letter instructed Dinwiddie to send his demand to the major general of New France at Quebec City.

Saint-Pierre stocked a canoe with supplies for Washington's return journey. It was only then that he discovered Saint-Pierre during the delay had bribed his Indians with guns and alcohol to stay behind. Washington had been outmaneuvered once again by the rascally French. He thought Saint-Pierre had plotted "every scheme that the devil and man could invent to set our Indians at variance with us to prevent their going till after our departure."[27] He then confronted Half King and accused him of a prodigious betrayal. He was able to convince the Indians to depart with him and Gist.

These experiences with the French caused Washington in the future to go beyond due diligence in providing detailed instructions to his subordinates to ensure they were not outmaneuvered by the enemy as he was. He also learned the value of deception in getting the upper hand.

Washington and his entourage set off for Murthering Town, a Delaware Indian village near present-day Harmony, Pennsylvania. Gist's and Washington's horses gave out and could not travel any farther and had to be abandoned. They then proceeded by canoe. At the first resting place the Indians had killed a bear and would not leave until they consumed every last morsel of the animal. Not willing to wait, and wanting to avoid more delays, Gist and Washington struck out alone.

The cold weather had turned worse. At Murthering Town they picked up some Indians aligned with the French who were going to take them to the Forks of the Ohio. Washington trusted the Indians but Gist was smarter in the ways of the wilderness. The Indians had departed except for one who was carrying Washington's backpack. When they got to a clearing the Indian dashed out in front, turned quickly, and fired his weapon at them but missed. Gist caught the Indian and was about to kill him when Washington pleaded for his life. Gist reluctantly relented. They held him prisoner and released him after dark. Fearing that the Indian would return with others and attack them, they traveled all night to get distance from him.

When they came to the Allegheny River, it was not frozen as they had expected. It was flowing rapidly with bobbing chunks of ice, making any crossing extremely dangerous. They constructed a raft to carry them to the other side. They pushed off from the shore and began their crossing, but the raft became stuck in the ice. Washington tried to free the raft using his barge pole and fell into the water. The river was ten feet deep and ice cold. Hypothermia and frostbite were major concerns as he was having difficulty breathing. He managed to pull himself back on the raft. The raft was now freed from the flowing ice but had become stuck on an island. They spent the night on the frigid island. Overnight the temperature dropped low enough that the river froze solid, and they were able to scramble over the ice to the safety of the other side.

Washington continued his journey south out of the wilderness to the tidewater area of Virginia. He stopped at Belvoir Plantation to entertain the Fairfaxes with the tale of his experiences. After a short stay, he was off to Williamsburg, the capital of the colony. On January 16, 1754, he delivered the sealed response from Saint-Pierre to Lieutenant Governor Dinwiddie, who instructed Washington to turn his journal into a report for the Governor's Council, which was to convene the next day. His journal of his expedition was published in both Virginia and later in England, bringing him fame on both continents. Based on his report and Saint-Pierre's response, Dinwiddie advised the Board of Trade in London that the French intended to militarily occupy the Ohio Country.

The Virginia House of Burgesses awarded Washington £50 for his services. Washington unhappily wrote to his brother Augustine, "I was employed to go on a journey in winter . . . and what did I get by it? My expenses borne!" It was a harsh experience in the ways of politics. He was always a quick learner. During the Revolution he only asked for his expenses to be reimbursed. He kept a journal of his expenses that was rather vague. Less documentation was provided for the larger amounts, raising the opinion in some historians that some of the amounts were embellished.

In January 1754, even before learning of the French refusal, Dinwiddie sent a small force of 100 Virginia militia under the command of Captain William Trent to build a fort at the Forks of the Ohio, where the Allegheny and Monongahela Rivers merge to form the Ohio (present-day Pittsburgh).[28] The French quickly drove off the Virginians and built a larger fort on the site, calling it Fort Duquesne, in honor of the Marquis Ange Duquesne de Menneville, who had recently become the governor general of New France.[29]

A week after Washington's return from Fort Le Boeuf to Williamsburg, Dinwiddie authorized him to raise fifty men from Augusta County and fifty from Frederick County and train them. They were to build a road through the Allegheny wilderness and mountains to the Monongahela. Washington was given orders that provided him enormous latitude in their execution. He was to take a defensive position. However, if the French started harassing any British military positions or civilians, he was allowed to use deadly force. He was to "restrain all such offenders and in case of resistance to make prisoners or kill and destroy them."[30] Dinwiddie gave command of the expedition to Colonel Joshua Fry, a member of the Virginia House of Burgesses.[31] He was thought to be a capable frontiersman and had been to Logstown west of the Forks of the Ohio. Washington served as second in command but was to lead the advance detachment. Fry with his men would rendezvous with him.

The young Lieutenant Colonel Washington attempted to turn the rabble into soldiers. They were from levels of society into which Washington had never ventured and he did not understand them.[32] He reported to Dinwiddie about his recruits and their diversity of character.

> We daily experience the great necessity for clothing the men, as we find the generality of those, who are to be

enlisted, are of those loose, idle persons, that are quite destitute of house, and home, and, I may truly say, many of them of cloths; which last, renders them very incapable of the necessary service, as they must unavoidably be exposed to inclement weather in their marches, &c., and can expect no other than to encounter almost every difficulty, that's incident to a soldier[']s life. There is [sic] many of them without shoes, others want stockings, some are without shirts, and not a few that have scarce a coat, or waistcoat to their backs; in short, they are as illy provided as can well be conceived.[33]

In March of 1754 Dinwiddie received a report of a French raiding party proceeding to the Forks of the Ohio. Dinwiddie was fearful the French would establish their hold on the Forks and prevent the British from establishing their position in the territory. He immediately ordered Washington to take whatever men he had and proceed directly to the Ohio Country. Once there he was to complete the fort at the Forks.

At noon on April 2 he set out from Alexandria to the Forks with two companies of foot, commanded by Captain Peter Hog and Lieutenant Jacob Van Braam, who had been Washington's interpreter at Fort Le Boeuf.[34] They traveled six miles before they encamped. They moved slowly, as they had to carve out a road as they progressed. Along the way they were joined by Dr. Captain Adam Stephen and a detachment of soldiers.[35]

On the 19th, he met an express carrying a letter from Captain Trent demanding a reinforcement with all speed, as he hourly expected a body of 800 French. Washington sent a dispatch to Colonel Fry that he and his men were needed right away. Trent had left Ensign Edward Ward in charge of the construction of the fort while he went for provisions. Shortly thereafter Ward received word that the French were marching on his location. Ward hastily threw up a stockade. On April 27 the French forces under the command of Captain Claude-Pierre Pécaudy de Contrecoeur, numbering 1,000 men and eighteen pieces of artillery, demanded Ward surrender his forces totaling forty-one men.[36] Outnumbered 24 to 1 and facing a battery of artillery, Ward realized that putting up resistance would be suicide so he chose to surrender.[37] Washington received the news of the surrender three weeks later.[38]

On May 11, Washington sent Captain Stephen with a party of twenty-five men to go to Christopher Gist's residence near present-day Mount Braddock, Pennsylvania.[39] Stephen was to find out if there was a French detachment from Fort Duquesne in the area. Washington instructed him that if he came across any Frenchman he was to take him into custody and bring him back to camp. Washington wanted to interrogate the captive himself to ensure that the most complete information was extracted. He was "also desirous to enquire what were the views of the French, what they had done, and what they intended to do, and to collect every thing."[40] He had been tricked twice by the French and was not about to be so again. Stephen encountered heavy rains that sent the mountain streams into swift-flowing rivers cascading over their banks. The ground turned to mud and it slowed his progress. When he arrived near the intersection of the Monongahela and Redstone Creek, he met some Indian traders who informed him that because of the heavy rain Joseph Coulon de Villiers, Sieur de Jumonville found it unsuitable for reconnoitering and took his party back to Fort Duquesne. Jumonville had fought in King George's War (1744–1748). In 1754 he was sent to Fort Duquesne, where he served under his older half brother, Captain Louis Coulon de Villiers. Stephen sent a spy into Fort Duquesne, thirty-seven miles away. Five days later his spy returned and provided detailed information about the fort.[41]

Washington realized that he did not have enough men to attack Fort Duquesne. Half King suggested it would be suitable to advance as far as Redstone Creek. They decided to build a fortification, clear a road wide enough for artillery to pass, and wait for new orders. Captain Trent's men had been released and had now joined Washington, bringing the total under his command to 150,[42] still too small to attack 1,000 French soldiers in a fort.

Washington waited for Colonel Fry and his forces to arrive. He met Captain Ward's agent, who informed him that an additional 400 French soldiers had arrived at the Forks of the Ohio and more were expected. This information was confirmed by several traders.[43]

On the evening of May 17, 1754, two Indians who had left Fort Duquesne five days earlier met up with Washington. He always used intelligence from more than one source to determine the true state of affairs. He interrogated both Indians to find out how the French were proceeding in constructing their fort. It was already breast high with a thickness of twelve feet, which was filled with dirt and stone between two walls. They had removed all the trees around the fort and planted grain where the trees had once been. The Indians believed the French numbered between 600 and 800 with more expected in a few days. They said the French believed they could defy the British.[44]

On the morning of May 24, two Indians had come to Washington from Half King bringing a letter warning that the French army was in the area and to guard against them. He wrote,

"They intend to fall on the first English they meet; they have been on their march these two days."[45] Washington said he personally "examined those two young Indians in the best manner I could, concerning every circumstance, but was not much the better satisfied."[46]

The same day when he arrived at Great Meadow at two in the afternoon, he met a trader who confirmed Half King's information. Later that evening he received another report that the French were at the crossing of the Youghiogheny River about eighteen miles away.[47] He quickly sent out a party of horse soldiers to scout for the enemy. He wanted to know where they were. They returned without discovering them. However, the camp was alarmed at two in the morning under a moonless night lit only by the stars.[48] The sentries fired at the outline of someone in the distance. Unable to determine if it was the enemy or one of their own deserters, the soldiers nervously stayed on their arms till dawn, at 3:55.[49]

On the morning of the 27th, Gist arrived and advised he had seen the tracks of Michel Pépin, also known as La Force, with fifty men about five miles from Washington's camp. With the enemy at his doorstep, Washington immediately detached men under the command of Captain Peter Hog, Lieutenant George Mercer, and Ensign William La Péronie to do reconnaissance to discover if they were getting any closer. With the French in his immediate area Washington wanted to motivate the Indians in his camp against them and ensure they stayed aligned with him. He told the Indians that the French had enquired at Mr. Gist's residence while he was away as to what had become of Half King. Washington using this lie told them the French wanted to kill their chief. It had the desired result. Washington was a quick learner in the art of manipulation. Washington wrote that the Indians offered to accompany him to go after the French, and if they found it true that Half King had been killed, or even insulted by them, one of them would presently carry the news to the Mingo Indians, in order to incite their warriors to fall upon them.[50] One of these young men was sent toward Mr. Gist's; that if he should not find the Half King there, he was to send a message by a Delaware Indian.

About eight at night, Washington received a message sent by Half King that he was on his way to join him. Along the path Half King saw two men and followed them. It led him to a low, obscure place. Half King believed the whole party of the French was hiding there.

Washington was convinced he was about to be attacked by the French. He was not going to be outsmarted again. He immediately assembled forty men and secured his ball and powder at camp under a strong guard. Beneath a heavy rain in a moonless, starless sky that was as dark as pitch, they traveled a path barely wide enough for a man to pass. Several times they wandered off the path for fifteen or twenty minutes before they returned to it. It was so dark they were constantly bumping into trees and each other. They traveled this way all night long. At sunrise on the 28th they arrived at Half King's camp.

A council was held and it was decided on a joint attack against the French. Two Indians were sent to investigate and locate the current enemy position. They found the French had encamped in a rocky glen without taking any precaution against an attack. Washington and Half King were in complete agreement that they should attack. The combined forces marched out of Half King's camp in a single file, Indian style, until they reached the French camp.[51]

Of the engagement, Washington wrote, "We were advanced pretty near to them, as we thought, when they discovered us; whereupon I ordered my company to fire." The battle "only lasted a quarter of an hour, before the enemy was routed."[52]

The French version of the incident is that Jumonville's mission was that of an ambassador, that he was on a peaceful mission to carry an ultimatum to the English forces to leave the Ohio Country, when he was attacked at seven in the morning. The French version claims that Jumonville's party only consisted of eight men. Washington's report was that his forces killed ten, wounded one, and took twenty-one prisoners. In a letter to his brother Augustine, he wrote that "there were twelve [Frenchmen] killed."[53] The twenty-one captured included Monsieurs La Force, Drouillon, together with two cadets (Boucherville and Dusablé), who were sent under guard to Lieutenant Governor Dinwiddie at Winchester.[54] Washington added a postscript: "I fortunately escaped without a wound, tho' the right wing where I stood was exposed to and received all the enemy's fire and was the part where the man was killed and the rest wounded. I can with truth assure you, I heard bullets whistle and believe me there was something charming in the sound." When George II heard the statement, he remarked, "He would not say so, if he had been used to hear many."[55]

Exactly what happened to Jumonville is unclear. Washington wrote, "We killed Mr. de Jumonville, the Commander of that Party, as also nine others." That Jumonville was wounded in the battle is certain. According to some accounts, Jumonville lay dying on the ground clutching some papers he implored his lieutenant colonel to read. The papers were either given to Washington or read to him. While this was transpiring, an Indian, by some accounts Half King, murdered Jumonville while he lay helpless on the ground. He crushed his skull with his tomahawk and then washed his hands in Jumonville's brain.

The French report says that he was killed while the message he brought ordering the English to leave was being read. The French report read, "The Indians who were present when the thing was done, say, that Mr. de Jumonville was killed by a musket-shot in the head, whilst they were reading the summons."[56]

The Indians scalped the dead, and took most of the weapons. After the battle Washington said that he marched with the prisoners to Half King's camp. The French had raised the greatest suspicion by their actions. Half King was of the opinion their intentions were evil. Washington wrote that after leaving the Indian camp:

At that time they [the French] informed me that they had been sent with a summons to order me to depart. A plausible pretense to discover our camp, and to obtain the knowledge of our forces and our situation! It was so clear that they were come to reconnoiter what we were, that I admired at their assurance, when they told me they were come as an embassy; for their instructions mentioned that they should get what knowledge they could of the roads, rivers, and of all the country as far as Potowmack [sic]. And instead of coming as an embassador, publicly, and in an open manner, they [the French] came secretly, and sought after the most hidden retreats, more like deserters than embassadors in such retreat they incamped, and remained hid for whole days together, and that, no more than five miles from us: From thence they sent spies to reconnoiter our camp; after this was done, they went back two miles, from whence they sent the two messengers spoken of in the instruction, to acquaint M. de Contrecour of the place we were at, and of our disposition, that he might send his detachments to inforce the summons as soon as it should be given.[57] . . . They say they called to us as soon as they had discovered us; which is an absolute falsehood, for I was then marching at the head of the company going towards them, and can positively affirm, that, when they first saw us, they ran to their arms, without calling; as I must have heard them, had they so done.[58]

A few days later he would learn from an Indian trader that when Jumonville was sent after him, another detachment was sent toward the lower part of the river. The trader believed they were to kill all the English they should meet.[59]

Washington retreated to Great Meadow. He feared that when the French heard of the defeat they would retaliate in force from Fort Duquesne. He built a small circular stockade of logs that he called Fort Necessity.[60] On the 6th, Gist brought word of the death of Colonel Fry. He had fallen off his horse and died from his injuries. The death of Fry left Washington in full command of the expedition, a position Dinwiddie would make official.[61] On the 10th, word came that the French were on the march toward Fort Necessity. Washington immediately sent out some scouts, who brought in nine French deserters. Trying some subterfuge, Washington had them copy a letter he wrote to their friends in the French army at Fort Duquesne who they thought would desert.[62] Over the next few days came conflicting information on the number of French and their location. News came that confirmed the French fort at the Forks of the Ohio was completed.

A council was held with several Indian tribes. Having previously underestimated the chicanery of the French, Washington had become very suspicious of those he did not know. He realized some of the Indians were sent as spies by the French. They were inquisitive and asked too many questions. They wanted to know what route Washington would take to the fort and when he expected to get there. Washington decided that two could play the game, a game he would play many times during the Revolution. He provided them with false information to take back to the French. He stopped work on widening a trail into a road and told the spies they would travel through the woods. He told them he was waiting for reinforcements and artillery. After the spies left, construction on the road to Redstone Creek was recommenced.[63]

He persuaded Kaquehuston, a Delaware Indian, to carry the letter the French deserters had written to Fort Duquesne.[64] He gave specific instructions on how and what he should observe at the fort. Washington's sources told him that the French were encamped outside and could not keep a strict guard. After Kaquehuston left, Washington sent an Irish-born frontier trader named George Croghan as a spy to the French fort with detailed instructions on what intelligence he was to collect.[65] Again Washington did not trust the information brought back by one spy. Whenever possible he tried to confirm the first report with intelligence from a second source before taking action.

Monacatootha, an Oneida chief and a staunch ally of the English, had left Fort Duquesne two days earlier.[66] He had seen the arrival of reinforcements and heard of the French plan to attack with 800 soldiers and 400 Indians. The French deserters had been reporting that reinforcements were expected at any time. More bad news was that two of Washington's men had deserted to the French and acquainted them with the size of Washington's men under arms and the lack of food. They had neither meat nor bread for the last six days. They had only one quart of salt and twenty-five head of cattle, most of which were milk cows, for 400 men. The Indians threatened they would leave unless everyone returned to Great Meadow.

A council of war was held at Mr. Gist's residence on June 28. In light of the situation of the enemy coming with three times their number, it was unanimously resolved that it was necessary to immediately return to the fort at Great Meadow and wait for supplies. Because of the lack of horses, their small cannons, known as swivel guns, had to be pulled by the men.[67] They arrived at Fort Necessity on July 1 and found there was almost no food left. Facing the possibility of starvation their Indian allies quietly slipped away. The regiment was too exhausted to move so they took position in the fort.

The French, under the command of Louis Coulon de Villiers, Jumonville's brother, left Fort Duquesne on June 28. Villiers, with hatred and fire in his eyes, was determined to avenge the murder of his brother. They traveled in pirogues up the Monongahela to the mouth of Redstone Creek.[68] By midday on July 1 they had advanced to the area between Redstone Creek and Mount Braddock, where they discovered the road Washington had been building. Villiers chose to camp there for the night. The overcast skies opened and the driving rain seemed like it would never end. On the morning of July 3 he moved his forces toward Fort Necessity. Villiers wrote in his journal, "We marched the whole day in the rain."[69]

The French arrived just before eleven in the morning on July 3 at Fort Necessity. Washington was outnumbered 3 to 1.

Villiers was moving his men to a point of woods that overlooked the fort. If they reached the location, they could fire into every part of the fort. To stop the French advance, Washington was forced to do what he was hoping to make the French do; that is, to attack over an open field. The French Indians made a direct assault on Washington's men. The regulars and two of the fort's cannons fired and took a toll on the Indians. When Washington turned around, to his utter amazement his Virginia Regiment had broken and run into the water-filled trenches in front of the fort for protection. With no one behind him, Washington, standing alone, was forced to retreat. Villiers took possession of the point of woods, which sealed the fate of the fort. Once in position he had his men keep up a continuous fire into the fort.[70]

Fighting continued all day in a driving rain that gained in intensity throughout the afternoon. It was described as "the most tremendous rain that can be conceived." The situation in the fort was deteriorating rapidly. One hundred men were dead. Food supplies were close to gone. The powder and the guns were wet, which caused the guns to foul. There were only two screws in the entire fort to remove the wet charges from the muskets. The ground in the fort had turned into a quagmire. With each step the men took, they sank deeper into the mud. There was a terrible sucking sound as each man tried to pull his boots out of the mud. The men could barely move, much less put up a defense.[71]

After an exhausting day of fighting with little food, wet powder, and no reinforcements, Washington surrendered. The document of surrender is dated July 3, 1754, at eight o'clock at night but it was signed around midnight while it was still raining.

The documents were drawn up in French, a language Washington could not read. He had to depend upon Jacob Van Braam to translate. The problem is that in the opening statement of the document the French claim, "As our intentions have never been to trouble the peace and good harmony subsisting between the two princes in amity, but only to revenge the assassination committed on one of our Officers, bearer of a Summon." In article VII is the phrase "at the Assassination of M. de Jumonville." The surrender document created an embarrassing controversy for Washington and the British.

The French interpreted the signatures of Captain James Mackay and George Washington on the document as an admission that they had "assassinated" an emissary of France while he was on a peaceful mission to the British. Washington insisted that not only this word but other portions of the capitulation had been mistranslated. It was a wet document signed in the rain in the Allegheny wilderness. It was a document that set the world on fire and brought on the Seven Years' War, known as the French and Indian War in North America.

On July 4 at about ten in the morning Washington's forces, with drums beating and flags flying, marched out of Fort Necessity. Van Braam and Captain Robert Stobo remained with the French as hostages in accordance with article VII until the French prisoners were returned. Dr. James Craik, a Scot who served as the expedition's surgeon, stayed with some of the wounded men to nurse them back to health.[72] Washington and his men began the long march back to Wills Creek (present-day Cumberland, Maryland) while the French set Fort Necessity ablaze.

On July 17, 1754, Washington arrived in Williamsburg and reported to Lieutenant Governor Dinwiddie. The outcome of

Washington's mission should have been foreseen, as he was a twenty-two-year-old lieutenant colonel lacking in experience who was given vague instructions and an inadequate militia. The Virginia Regiment was composed of drifters and unemployed townspeople who were poorly clothed, fed, supplied, and trained. Washington's biggest failure was his inability to obtain support from the Indians. It left him with an inferior force in a wilderness opposing a larger force of French and French-aligned Indians.

Dinwiddie was subsequently active in attempting to rally other colonies and the British in defense against the French. The Lords of Trade in London agreed that something had to be done to dislodge the French from the Ohio Country. They sent sixty-year-old Major General Edward Braddock to Virginia with two regiments of foot. The units were called from garrison duty in Ireland. They began boarding the ships in the cold of winter and it took several days to load the troopships. Braddock was an experienced soldier, having served forty years in the British army. He was short, overweight, and a strict disciplinarian.[73]

Using British regulars and friendly Indians, Bradock was expected to follow the same route from Virginia to the Forks of the Ohio used by Washington. Once there he was to destroy Fort Duquesne. The British were going to have other expeditions attack Fort Saint-Frédéric on the west shore of Lake Champlain, Nova Scotia, and the wooden stockade called Fort Niagara.[74] Washington, along with Captain Robert Orme, served as aide-de-camp to Braddock. In that position they would have access to Braddock's cipher key for his enciphered correspondence, as they would have had to decode and transcribe the missives. (See Appendix for the cipher key.)

Captain Stobo, while a hostage at Fort Duquesne, secretly drew a scale map of the fort. On the back of the map he wrote a long letter in which he advised Lieutenant Governor Dinwiddie not to return the French prisoners, and urged that Fort Duquesne be taken that fall. If the French discovered his letter, he would be hanged as a spy. The letter was safely delivered by a friendly Indian. Stobo's drawing was given to General Braddock, probably when he arrived at Alexandria, Virginia.[75]

Braddock's expedition left Alexandria in early April 1754. Braddock had to meet with the colonial governors from Massachusetts, New York, Pennsylvania, and Virginia to coordinate plans for the combined assaults on the French. When he caught up with his expedition they had neither food nor wagons. Despite promises of cooperation from civilian contractors, they did not produce the needed items. Washington learned how much an army's supplies depended on civilian cooperation and goodwill. This tempered his treatment of the civilian population during his command of the Continental Army. He realized that to be successful he would need to learn how to coax politicians, his own officers, and civilians to do his bidding.

When the expedition arrived at Winchester, Virginia, the expected Indian reinforcements were nowhere to be found. They pushed on to Willis Creek and the newly built log palisade of the poorly situated Fort Cumberland, possibly the worst possible location, as the fort was dominated by high ridges from which fire could easily be rained down. The regulars drilled while the militia milled around in their tents. Despite his best efforts Braddock also was unable to secure the cooperation of the Indians at the fort.[76] It meant that his regulars and militia would have to go alone into the wilderness.

Once the expedition of 2,900 men started its journey Braddock realized he had brought too much of everything. His baggage train was going to take a very long time to get over the mountains, some of the steepest slopes in what would become the continental United States. He had wagons repacked, and surplus goods, supplies, and most of the camp followers were sent back to Fort Cumberland. The lighter load helped slightly. However, cannons still had to be raised and lowered over some slopes by block and tackle. The journey was tiring for both man and beast. Men and horses were exhausted and some fell dead where they stood. Realizing that the situation was intolerable, Braddock picked 800 regulars, eight artillery pieces, and thirty wagons to be an advance force. The rest were placed under the command of Colonel Thomas Dunbar of the 48th Regiment of Foot. They were to follow later. On the 24th, the advance force crossed the Youghiogheny River and passed a recently abandoned Indian camp with smoldering campfires and almost 200 bark lean-tos. The French under the command of Captain Contrecoeur had 600 men at Fort Duquesne but also had the support of several hundred Indians. He sent 72 French soldiers, 146 Canadian militia, 36 officers, and 637 Indians under the command of Captain Daniel Liénard de Beaujeu to find and attack Braddock.[77]

Lieutenant Colonel Thomas Gage of the 54th Regiment of Foot led an advance party of 300.[78] They crossed the Monongahela and scattered thirty Indians. Braddock, with fifty regulars and the wagons, crossed the river about two in the afternoon. He had not sent any spies among the French and was relying on Gage's advance detachment for reconnaissance. Gage's advance detachment came under fire from the Indians, who had muskets. In the initial fire Captain Beaujeu was killed and the French faltered. The Indians were undaunted and pushed the attack through the woods and routed the flanking troops. They then turned their attention on the main body. Gage's forces were pushed back into their baggage wagons. With the sounds of the dying filling the air, Braddock tried to rally the regular soldiers but the counterattack failed in the smoke that filled the air and the debris of the battle. The expedition had lost all order and discipline. Braddock, who had four horses shot from under him in the battle, was himself hit by a ball that passed through his arm and lodged in the body. Washington had Braddock's bleeding body placed in a wagon and taken to the other side of the river where Gage had formed a guard. The Indians did not pursue, as they chose to loot the baggage train and scalp the dead and dying.[79]

Before Braddock died on July 13, he ordered Washington to travel to Colonel Dunbar, who was leading the slow-moving baggage train from Fort Cumberland. The instructions were for Dunbar to rush forward medical supplies and food. In the black of night his guide had to dismount several times to determine if they were still on the trail. He finally reached Dunbar on July 10.[80] Rumors were started that wildly exaggerated the situation and some of Dunbar's corps raced back to the perceived safety of Fort Cumberland. Dunbar now inherited the command of the expedition. He decided not to counterattack. He chose instead to destroy his baggage train and take the remaining forces to Fort Cumberland, which they reached on July 22. Two weeks later, he marched his troops to Philadelphia for winter quarters. Horace Walpole stated, "Braddock's defeat still remains in the situation of the longest battle that ever was fought with nobody."[81]

Later that year Washington had to contend with his first mutiny among his Virginia militia. On August 19, 1754, at Alexandria, Virginia, while he was at church, twenty-five militia assembled and, in full view of their officers, left. The mutiny was quickly stopped and they were "imprisoned before the plot came to full height."[82] He would face many more mutinies when he became commander of the Continental Army.

The French influence in the Ohio Country was growing. In England, William Pitt in June 1757 became the secretary of state and started devising new war strategies. Major General Jeffrey Amherst was to attack the French fortress of Louisbourg in Nova Scotia. Brigadier General George Augustus Howe and Major General James Abercrombie would attack Fort Carillon (later renamed Fort Ticonderoga). Brigadier General John Forbes was to attack Fort Duquesne.[83] Forbes on March 20 wrote to Acting Governor John Blair to have the Virginia militia take position at Winchester. He described Washington as "a good and knowing officer in the back country."[84] Washington wrote back, "Permit me to return you my sincere, and hearty thanks for the honor you were pleased to do me in a letter to Mr. President Blair; and to assure you, that to merit a continuance of the good opinion you seem to entertain of me, shall be one of my principal studies; for I have now no ambition that is higher."[85]

Washington had learned from the Braddock expedition that the best way to fight the French Indians was with Indians allied with the British. He urged Forbes to secure Indian allies before venturing into the Ohio Country wilderness. Forbes tried but by September the Indians were still refusing to support the British. Forbes rejected the route taken by Braddock, instead choosing a route across western Pennsylvania. He would build small forts along the way. The last fort was Fort Ligonier, built in September 1758 at Loyalhanna, which was fifty miles from Fort Duquesne. Building the forts would slow his progress but would provide safe havens to which he could retreat in case of an attack. The forts would also be used as supply depots, which would lessen the length of his supply train. During the expedition there was a defeat of Major James Grant of the Highlanders by the French and Indians in front of Fort Duquesne on September 14. The Treaty of Easton, signed in Pennsylvania in October, officially ended the hostilities between the British and the Ohio Indians.[86]

A French raiding party of 200 attacked Loyalhanna (Fort Ligonier) on November 12. During the battle at dusk, through the haze of smoke, Washington led a detachment of Virginians who were part of an exchange of friendly fire. It resulted in American casualties of fourteen dead and twenty-six wounded. However, the British succeeded in driving off the French. With Virginia militia enlistments expiring on November 30 and winter weather soon to make conditions intolerable, Forbes pushed on to the Forks of the Ohio. On November 23, as they were clearing a path through the woods ten miles from Fort Duquesne, they heard a loud explosion in the distance. The next day Forbes sent out a reconnaissance party. When they arrived at Fort Duquesne, it was in ashes. The French force of about 500, having lost their Indian allies and having no reinforcements scheduled to arrive, decided they did not want to oppose Forbes's artillery. They blew up Fort Duquesne leaving only smoldering timbers for the British, and retreated by boat up the Allegheny. The British were now in control of their long-sought prize of the Forks of the Ohio. Forbes then ordered the construction of a new fort, to be called Fort Pitt. He then returned to Philadelphia, where he died on March 11, 1759. Washington returned to Williamsburg in December 1758. He reported news of the victory and resigned his commission as colonel of the 1st Virginia Regiment.[87]

He had learned much during his expeditions to the Ohio Country in dealing with an enemy. He had learned how important espionage was to the success of any mission. Braddock's expedition did not employ any spies, and without intelligence, it was routed. He now knew, "There is nothing more necessary than good intelligence to frustrate a designing enemy, and nothing that requires greater pains to obtain."[88]

Two

DRINKING, FLASHING THE
LADIES, AND GRAVE
ROBBING

After the French and Indian War, England was burdened with paying off the war debt and the expenses for protecting their colonies. They believed that the colonies should pay their fair share of the debt and expense of their defense. Parliament in the 1760s instituted a series of taxes to raise the funds. Members of American colonial society rejected the authority of the British Parliament to tax them without colonial representation in the government. Protests by colonists escalated. In 1773, Boston Tea Party colonists destroyed a consignment of taxed tea from the Parliament-controlled and -favored East India Company. Parliament responded by imposing a series of punitive laws known as Coercive Acts, which were called the Intolerable Acts in the rebelling colonies. In response to the Boston Tea Party, Parliament closed the port of Boston on June 1, 1774, until the East India Company had been reimbursed for the destroyed tea. Patriots in other colonies rallied behind Massachusetts. In late 1774 the Patriots set up their own alternative government to better coordinate their resistance efforts against Great Britain, while other colonists, known as Loyalists, preferred to remain aligned with the British Crown. The Patriots had sent delegates to a Continental Congress in Philadelphia.

Tensions escalated and resulted in an outbreak of fighting between Patriot militia and British regulars at Lexington and Concord on April 19, 1775. It resulted in a disastrous British retreat back to Boston. It was a rout and the British casualties included 70 killed, 182 wounded, and 22 soldiers captured.[1] The Massachusetts Provincial Congress requested that the Continental Congress take on the army besieging Boston. Dr. Joseph Warren, one of the leaders of the rebellion in Massachusetts, wrote, "As the army now collecting from different colonies is for the general defense of the right of America, we w[oul]d beg leave to suggest to y[ou]r consideration the propriety of y[ou]r taking the regulation and general direction of it, that the operations may more effectually answer the purposes designed."[2] It was a case of passing the buck or in this case the pound. Massachusetts could not afford the expense of feeding, equipping, and paying the army.

The Continental Congress meeting in Philadelphia at the twenty-two-year-old Georgian-style Pennsylvania State House agreed to support those conducting the siege and surrounding the city of Boston, and for several days was concerned with sending the group gunpowder, men, and money.[3] On June 15, it appointed a Virginian, George Washington, to lead them and turn them into an army.[4] The rustic returns to the battlefield: That would be the British concept of a gentleman farmer from

Virginia who was going to lead the mob of Massachusetts malcontents surrounding Boston.

Many of the men did not have uniforms or any sign of rank. Some brought the only weapon they had on their farm—a pitchfork or shovel—and some had no weapon at all. It was not a cohesive army but a ragtag collection of men with little organization and even less hygiene. Washington had to build a fighting force from this collection of individuals from different states that hated and distrusted each other, some probably more than the British. They had little respect for the military acumen of their officers, since in many cases they voted for their officers, many of whom were elected on the basis of popularity and not their military ability.

Washington took command of the disheveled men at Cambridge, Massachusetts, on July 3, 1775. He was expected to turn them into a functioning army and defeat the greatest military force on the planet, the British army. It would have been a daunting task for even a highly experienced commander. If he was to succeed, he was going to have to call upon every bit of the military skills he had learned during the French and Indian War some twenty years earlier. He was also going to have to adjust from those frontier warfare skills in acquiring and using Indian allies to fighting in the European style of linear warfare.

Washington, upon taking command, had many concerns that needed immediate attention. Many of the problems dealt with the command and control that would be expected. Although there were instances of insubordination, an armed mutiny did not occur until Thompson's Pennsylvania Riflemen mutinied on September 10, 1775.[5] Even considering the unusual situation of an all-militia army, some actions were out of the realm of the expected.

The newly minted soldiers were bathing naked in the Charles River. Considering the general lack of hygiene, bathing was a good thing. However, some naked men would climb up on the bridge crossing the Charles River. The soldiers then flashed their private parts at the ladies as they traveled past. To address this issue, instill discipline, and bring the practice to a quick end, Washington issued the following General Order on August 22:

> The General does not mean to discourage the practice of bathing whilst the weather is warm enough to continue it, but he expressly forbids, any persons doing it, at or near the bridge in Cambridge, where it has been observed and complained of, that many men, lost to all sense of decency and common modesty, are running about naked upon the bridge, whilst passengers, and even ladies of the first fashion in the neighborhood, are passing over it, as if they meant to glory in their shame:— The Guards and Centries [*sic*] at the Bridge, are to put a stop to this practice for the future.[6]

Soldiers in any army at any point in history always seem to find a way to get alcohol in some form to quench their thirst. The unruly Continental Army besieging Boston was not exempt from the practice. Allowing drunken soldiers was not an efficient or acceptable way to run an army. In an attempt to maintain order and control and to cut down on the number of violators, Washington issued this General Order:

> Whereas a number of pretended sutlers utterly disregarding the good of the service, sell liquor to every one

indiscriminately, to the utter subversion of all order and good government; the troops being continually debauched, which causes them to neglect their duty, and to be guilty of all those crimes which a vicious, ill habit naturally produces. To prevent such evils from spreading in the camp: no person is for the future to presume to sell any stores, or liquor to the troops, unless he be first appointed sutler to some regiment, by the colonel or officer commanding the same, who will immediately punish such sutler for any transgression of the rules and orders he is directed to observe; And if any person, not regularly authorized and appointed, shall presume to sell liquor, or stores to the troops in the camp: It is recommended to the brigadier general, to issue an order for securing their persons and effects. The delinquent to be punished at the discretion of a general court martial and his effects to be applied for the refreshment of the fatiguemen, and out guards belonging to the brigade.[7]

General courts-martial were awarding confiscated alcohol to the fatiguemen, the soldiers assigned to building fortifications, cutting wood, hauling water, and digging latrines. It also included the outguards. This practice certainly encouraged them to vigorously enforce the rules and search out violators.

Another serious issue that required Washington's immediate attention was the grave robbing of American soldiers to steal salable items. He had to issue a General Order to stop this repulsive practice:

Complaint has been made to the general; that the body of a soldier of Col[onel] [Benjamin] Woodbridge's [Massachusetts] Regiment has been taken from his grave by persons unknown; The general and the friends of the deceased, are desirous of all the information that can be given, of the perpetrators of this abominable crime, that he, or they, may be made an example, to deter others from committing so wicked and shameful an offence.[8]

July 2 was a day of plentiful rains, which made the morning of the 3rd exceedingly pleasant, but it warmed up by noon, wrote Ezekiel Price.[9] It was on this day of July 3, 1775, that George Washington, under an elm tree on the Cambridge common, took command of the Continental Army.[10]

Just a few days before, two American spies in the besieged city of Boston had been arrested by British authorities, thereby losing to the American cause two operatives in the city. The first, John Leach, was stopped on the street a few doors from his house on June 29 at 3 p.m. by Major Cane and Joshua Loring Jr.[11] He was taken to his house where Major Cane demanded the keys to his desk. He then searched all the papers and drawings he could find. Leach was then arrested and taken to the Queen Street Jail. Twenty minutes later Cane and Loring brought in the second of the spies, James Lovell, to the jail after searching his papers.[12] Papers were found on the body of Dr. Joseph Warren after the Battle of Bunker Hill that incriminated Lovell.

The two spies had shared a room with Peter Edes, son of Benjamin Edes, co-owner of the *Boston Gazette* and *Country Journal*. The next day Cane took Leach's drawings and showed them to General Gage. Leach recounted in his journal that they were held in the jail surrounded by a "scene of oaths, curses, debauchery, and the most horrid blasphemy, committed by the Provost

Marshal, his deputy and soldiers, who were our guard, soldier prisoners, and sundry soldier women, confined for thefts, &c. We had some of the vilest women for our neighbors; some placed over our heads, and some in rooms each side of us; they acted such scenes as was shocking to nature, and used language, horrible to hear; as if it came from the very suburbs of hell."[13] In addition to this deplorable living arrangement, they were provided only bread and water till the end of August.[14]

Leach and Lovell did not know with what crime they were going to be charged. On the evening of the 17th, they were informed that the next day there would be a Garrison Court of Inquiry at the Concert Hall at the intersection of Hanover and Queen Streets. It would not be until the 19th that Lovell was charged with "being a spy and giving intelligence to the rebels." Leach was charged with "being a spy, and suspected of taking plans," that is, for making drawings of British military fortifications.[15]

Captain Richard Symes of the 52nd Regiment of Foot was called as a witness for the prosecution and incorrectly identified Leach and Lovell.[16] Having been forbidden to carry letters to her husband, Sarah Leach, on August 13, smuggled a note to her husband rolled up in the foot of a stocking.[17] Leach was finally released when two people stood bond for him and he promised not to leave the city.[18] Lovell was exchanged for Colonel Philip Skene in November 1776.

Washington inherited some spies who were already working inside Boston. From his experience in the French and Indian War he knew how valuable these spies could be in providing information on what the British were doing and planning in the city. He was smart enough to continue their operation. Some of the American spies he inherited were Goodwin and Enoch Hopkins, ferrymen. In 1775 Enoch Hopkins operated a ferry from the North End of Boston to Charlestown.[19] Goodwin's ferry went from Charlestown to Chelsea and was called the Winnisimmet ferry (spellings varied). The Winnisimmet ferry continued to operate at least through October 1775. Once the British took Charlestown on June 17, they controlled the travel between that peninsula and Boston.[20] Hopkins and Goodwin were described "as bad rebels as any. . . . I have seen them bring men over in disguise and they are up in town every opportunity they have gathering what intelligence they can and when they return communicate it to the rebels the other side."[21]

Washington needed to know what the enemy was doing in Boston so he could be prepared for any British military attacks. He did not want a trap to be sprung on him by the enemy, as had happened to General Braddock in the French and Indian War. He advised Congress, "I have not been able from any intelligence I have received, to form any certain judgment of the future operations of the enemy." His sources were telling him the British were expecting "an attack from us and are principally engaged in preparing against it." He had ordered "all the whale boats for many miles along the coast to be collected and some of them are employed every night to watch the motion of the enemy by water, in order to guard as much as possible against any surprise." He told Congress that one of his pressing duties was gaining intelligence of the enemy.[22] His solution, just like at the Forks of the Ohio, was to get spies operating behind enemy lines to provide the needed information.

Washington's first initiative with espionage in Boston happened shortly thereafter. An unidentified person had undertaken the dangerous assignment "to go into the town of Boston; to establish a secret correspondence for the purpose of conveying intelligence of the enemy's movements and designs."[23]

Washington needed to make arrangements for the movement of the correspondence. On July 28 he had Colonel Joseph Reed, his military secretary, write to Lieutenant Colonel Loammi Baldwin.[24] The letter informed of the plan Washington wanted Baldwin to execute in order to provide constant intelligence from Boston. Baldwin was instructed to tell no one about the operation and to destroy Reed's letter once he knew its contents. He was warned that the people in Boston depended upon him and his secrecy for their safety. He was to give the same warning of the need for secrecy to his contacts.

Reed sent Baldwin several letters of which at least one was written by Dr. Benjamin Church Jr. Baldwin was to provide the letters to Andrew Tewksbury, who lived about four miles distant toward Shirley Point.[25] Tewksbury was to give the letters to a waterman who was to deliver them to John Carnes on Orange Street (now Washington Street).[26] Carnes at his grocery store sold cloth, shoes, stockings, penknives, notions, and other goods. He was to return the answers to the questions and provide additional information of what was happening in Boston by the same route. Baldwin was to forward the responses by an express rider to Washington at the Continental Army headquarters in Cambridge.[27] The ring initially worked, as Baldwin advised Washington that he had heard from "Mr. J_ C_ [John Carnes], the Grocer" on the 14th and was expecting to get more information by the 16th.[28]

Ezekiel Price wrote in his diary on Sunday, August 20, "This morning a woman got out of Boston, who brought a letter from Parson [John] Carnes, which mentioned that the regulars in Boston intended to come out this night or to-morrow night, —in consequence of which, preparations were making in the several American encampments to receive them."[29] If the rumor mill was identifying Carnes as an intelligencer for the Continental Army, it may have reached the British spies in the American camps.[30]

Dr. Church, who wrote a letter that was sent to Carnes, was well-known as a high Son of Liberty in Massachusetts. He was a member of the Massachusetts Provincial Congress representing Boston and a member—and in some cases, chairman—of its committees. He was a member of most of Boston's pro-revolutionary organizations. With Dr. Warren having been killed at the Battle of Bunker Hill, and with John and Samuel Adams and John Hancock in Philadelphia, Dr. Church was left as the most influential political leader of the revolutionary movement still in Massachusetts. However, he had been working as a British spy before Washington's arrival in Massachusetts.

Dr. Church certainly would have told the British of Carnes being an American spy. The British could only accuse Carnes of the suspicion of conspiring with the Americans outside Boston. If they gave out too much detail of what they knew, they would have exposed their own spy, Dr. Church. They may have based their actions on the careless handling of Carnes's name as reported by Ezekiel Price. Whatever reason the British used for their claim, they were able to prevent Carnes from reporting any additional information by banishing him from the city. Washington's first spy ring produced little intelligence and had a very short life. The concept was good but the execution was poor. Washington would do much better in operating spy rings later in the war.

Washington's agent who went into the city to establish operatives to provide the intelligence he desperately needed was not always successful. He received a response from an unknown person who may have been an attorney in Boston dated August 14 who declined to get involved as a spy for Washington.[31]

After the first response on July 14 from John Carnes, a grocer and retired minister in the south part of Boston to be the intelligencer for the Continental Army, Washington made payment to the unnamed agent for the mission. He wrote in his expense book that he paid $333.33 "to enduce him to go into the town of Boston, to establish a secret correspondent for the purpose of conveying intelligence of the enemy's movements and designs."[32] He took the precaution not to write in his expense notebook on July 15 the name of the person who had accomplished this extremely important and necessary task to protect the person's identity. He added the following note: "The names of the persons who are employed within the enemy's lines, or who may fall within their power cannot be inserted."[33]

Washington was desperate to get intelligence on the British plans. On August 8, 1775, in a letter to the New York legislature from his headquarters at Cambridge, he wrote, "I have been endeavoring, by every means in my power, to discover the future intentions of our enemy here."[34]

Sometimes you just get lucky and the intelligence falls in your lap. Dr. John Connolly was forced to flee with his servant of two years, William Cowley, from his residence in Pittsburgh for the tidewater area of Virginia. Connolly had dreams of raising an army in the west. They traveled to Portsmouth, Virginia, to see Lord Dunmore. They stayed with Lord Dunmore for fourteen days in August on his ship, the *Royal William*. After discussing Dr. Connolly's plans, Dunmore sent Connolly with some dispatches on his tender *Arundel* to General Thomas Gage in Boston to get approval of Connolly's plan.[35]

After their arrival in Boston, Cowley slipped out of the city and made it to the American lines. He told of Dr. Connolly's plan to raise an army in the west and attack Fort Pitt at the Forks of the Ohio. Cowley agreed to return to the city and remain in Connolly's service for the purpose of collecting as much intelligence as he could. Connolly and Cowley stayed in Boston for a total of ten days and then Connolly planned to return to Virginia and meet again with Lord Dunmore. When Cowley realized Connolly planned to leave Boston, he made his escape to the safety of the American lines. He completed a deposition on October 12, 1775, before Abraham Fuller, a justice of the peace for Middlesex County, Massachusetts.[36] Once Washington was convinced the statements in the deposition were true, he transmitted the document to the Continental Congress.[37]

Another method of obtaining intelligence used some local fishermen. Who devised the plan to use the cover of fishermen to get a spy into and out of Boston is unknown. Peter Force, in his book *American Archives,* wrote that the fishermen were as "equally as bad [as the ferrymen], for they will get a pass from the Admiral for a boat and perhaps four men, they will take three fisher-men and one rebel, and as soon as they get below they will land the rebel and take another on board, so he comes up in the stead of him that they carried down, and sees and hears what he can, and then returns the same way that he came."[38]

Washington's actual operation involved three fishermen's who obtained a permit to fish dated September 15, 1775, from British Admiral Samuel Graves, Vice Admiral of the White and commander of His Majesty's Ships at Boston.[39] The permit allowed William Colfleet, Thomas Maples, and Edmund Saunders to fish in an open boat with the liberty to get their bait at Governor's Island, which was owned by the Winthrop family.[40] The

British, who were in need of food supplies, were happy to provide the permit. Upon their return with their catch, the fishermen were to sell their fish in Boston. The way the American intelligence system worked was they would take two fishermen and one spy when bringing their catch to the city. Upon landing at a pier in Boston, the fishermen would be involved with selling their fish and most probably selling some other items they brought and buying items to sell behind the American lines to make some money on the side. Spies who operated on a frequent basis tended to use the cover of being a smuggler throughout the war. Washington allowed his spies to bring smuggled merchandise to sell behind American lines. Since he had limited resources to pay his spies, it was a form of compensation.

While the fish were being peddled, the spy would go into the city and gather his intelligence. The spy would return to the boat and then leave with the fishermen. They most likely used Governor's Island, then in the middle of Boston Harbor, as a home base to switch spies and fishermen since they had an unrestricted pass to be there. The spy would then make his way to his contact behind American lines.[41]

Washington also had to be concerned with British spies operating in the American camps and the intelligence they were sending back to British headquarters. Between June 20 and September 26 a total of 1,018 passes were issued for slightly more than 16 percent of the population to leave Boston.[42] How many were spies for the British is unknown but certainly some were.

British General Gage was sending spies out since the beginning of the year. Among General Gage's papers is a spy letter dated May 13, 1775, that advised, "They intend shortly to fortify Bunkers [sic] and Dorchester Hills." A month later Gage brought about the Battle of Bunker Hill. However, things do not always go as planned. The British army had its logistical problems at Bunker Hill; they took 12-pound balls for 6-pound cannons. The reason for this "blunder of the oversized balls sprung from the dotage of an officer of rank in the corps, who spends his whole time in dallying with the schoolmaster's daughters. God knows he is old enough—he is no Sampson—yet he must have his Dalilah [*sic*]."[43] During the siege Gage ordered his spies to find out what was happening in the siege lines around Boston. One of his spies submitted a report in August that indicated the spy had been able to get this information from Captain Richard Dodge, one of the guards at Chelsea, who was very talkative.[44]

After the Battle of Bunker Hill, the thirty-nine-year-old Lemuel Cox, a Boston native, was caught going into British-occupied Boston twice and possibly a third time. He definitely was arousing suspicion. In November, General Washington had General Horatio Gates send Lemuel Cox to James Otis at the Council of Massachusetts headquarters and advised Otis that Cox was believed to be a British spy. Gates informed Otis that a Captain Forster would inform them of Cox's actions. Gates wrote, "His [Cox] distant removal from the camp will at least be absolutely necessary."[45] On December 29 Cox was imprisoned at Ipswich, Massachusetts, about thirty miles northeast of Boston.[46]

A Mrs. Cooke had been sent into the American camps at Cambridge, Mystic, and Roxbury, Massachusetts. In her deposition she told of the locations of provision and powder magazines, the general distrust of General Charles Lee by the soldiers, the problem of exchanging paper money, and the sickness in the camps. At General Lee's headquarters at Mystic she was questioned about her presence in camp. She claimed to be trying to find her husband and was told that he was registering the names of all the deserters.

While in the American camps she spoke in Gaelic to the Irish riflemen and was interviewed by a Captain Savage. She believed she was suspected of being a spy. She had overheard conversations of Colonels Paterson and Read discussing troop movements. She reported that forty barrels of gunpowder arrived from Rhode Island on the 24th. She decided to leave the siege camps and intended to go to Rhode Island but got on the wrong road and found herself at Newbury and from there went to Portsmouth but had missed the governor. She then went on to Lexington where she was arrested. The selectmen of the town examined her and sent her to the Massachusetts Provincial Congress at Watertown where she was again examined. They then sent her to General Washington. He ordered that she be taken by a flag of truce to the British at Charlestown.[47]

Washington's biggest disappointment came from Dr. Benjamin Church Jr. He was one of the political leaders of the revolutionary movement in Massachusetts. He was a member of almost every committee and the chairman of some of them. He had so impressed the Continental Congress during a visit that they selected him to be the first director of the Continental Army's Medical Department.

He had also been playing both sides. He had been on the British payroll and was being paid quarterly. He regularly was sending information to British headquarters since his election to the Massachusetts Provincial Congress in February 1775. He had used a courier who hid his messages in the channel meant for the drawstring of his britches. The courier journeyed across the harbor to Boston using the custom houseboat. When the Americans had stopped the boat from operating, Dr. Church was in a dilemma. He had to determine a new method to get his reports to British headquarters. If he did not report he would not be paid.

His solution was to use the HMS *Rose*, a twenty-gun frigate anchored in Newport, Rhode Island.[48] In 1774 the *Rose*, under the command of James Wallace, was sent to Narragansett Bay in Rhode Island to put an end to the very lucrative practice of smuggling. Dr. Church wrote a letter in cipher to his brother-in-law in care of British Major Cane. He entrusted the letter to Mary Butler, his mistress and a prostitute in Boston, who was pregnant with his child. She was to take the letter to the captain of the British warship at Newport. She carried the letter between her leg and her stocking. The captain was a drunk and she could not get the letter to him on the ship. She instead gave the ciphered letter to Godfrey Wenwood, her ex-husband, to deliver. He was a well-known baker in Newport. Anxious to get her out of town, he agreed to deliver the letter. Since he could not read the ciphered letter, he decided not to deliver it.

A short time later Mary sent Wenwood a letter asking why the letter had not been delivered. Realizing Mary was in contact with someone in British-held Boston, he took the letter to the lieutenant governor of Rhode Island. He in turn sent him to Rhode Island–native American General Nathanael Greene at Cambridge. Greene brought the letter to Washington's attention. He had Mary arrested. Sixty-year-old Major General Israel Putnam, popularly known as "Old Put," brought her to the Continental Army headquarters in Cambridge on his horse. The two of them made a hilarious sight. Pregnant Mary was hanging on to the crupper, the rope from the back of a saddle that goes under the horse's tail and back to the saddle. The story is told that when Washington saw Butler hanging off the back of Putnam's horse, he laughed. It's one of the rare recorded instances of Washington laughing during the war.

Under interrogation and threats of punishment, she eventually cracked and identified Dr. Church as the source. He was placed under house arrest. Washington had Church's ciphered letter translated. Using frequency analysis, two groups of decoders arrived at the same message. Certain letters (ETAOIN) and pairs (TH, ER, ON, and AN) of letters are used more often in a correspondence. Also in the eighteenth-century alphabet, the letters "I" and "J," as well as "U" and "V," are interchangeable. Some alphabets contain the ampersand "&" as an extra letter. By analyzing the frequency of letters and pairs of letters appearing in a document and replacing them with the standard alphabet letters, the secret message can be revealed.

It was decided that Church was guilty of treason. The newly passed military code did not sufficiently provide for cases of treason: the strongest punishment that a court-martial could render was thirty-nine lashes. However, nothing said when the punishment had to be given. Church was sent to jail in Connecticut for several years waiting for his thirty-nine lashes.

That Dr. Church, the head of the Continental Army's Medical Department, was corresponding with the enemy was a great shock to Washington and others. His discovery as a traitor was inconceivable to John Adams. He had been a patient of Dr. Church. He had given Adams his small pox vaccination, and, when in Philadelphia, he treated his eye problems. John had written his wife, Abigail, that the lotion Dr. Church had given him "has helped my eyes so much that I hope you will hear from me oftener than you have done."[49] He had trusted him and been betrayed.

Washington had found that due to a misunderstanding in reporting on the amount of gunpowder, the amount available was in short supply. He informed the generals at a war council on August 3 at the Cambridge headquarters. The report indicated there were approximately ninety barrels of powder in the magazines at Cambridge and Roxbury. A suggestion was put forward to make an attempt with 300 men on the British magazine in Halifax. This was not acted upon. The other suggestion was to get supplies from the neighboring provinces of Connecticut, New Hampshire, and Rhode Island.[50]

The next day Washington wrote to Congress, "But on ordering a new supply of cartridges yesterday, I was informed to my very great astonishment, that there was no more than 36 Bbbls. [barrels] in the Massachusetts store, which added to the stock of Rhode Island, New Hampshire and Connecticut makes 9940 lb. not more than 9 cartridges a man."

He checked into what caused such a monumental deficiency: "The Committee of Supplies, not being sufficiently acquainted with the nature of a return or misapprehending my request, sent in an account of all the ammunition which had been collected by the Province [of Massachusetts], so that the report included not only what was on hand but what had been spent." He went to the speaker of the House of Representatives to obtain a supply from the neighboring towns, "in such a manner as might prevent our poverty from being known. As it is a secret of too much consequence to be devulgd[sic], even to the General Court." He was afraid the British would find out how desperate the situation was. He was going to write to the governors of Connecticut, New Hampshire, and Rhode Island "urging in the most forcible terms the necessity of an immediate supply if in their power. I need not enlarge on our melancholy situation it is sufficient to say that the existence of the army and Salvation of the country depends upon some thing being done for our relief both speedy and effectual and that our situation be kept a profound secret."[51]

The story is told that Washington had barrels of sand marked "gunpowder" and placed in the military powder magazines. It makes a great deception story. However, I have not been able to find any period documents to back it up. There is no direct evidence of a disinformation campaign involving gunpowder. Mrs. Cooke, the British spy, had reported that forty tons, or over 880 barrels, of gunpowder had arrived from Rhode Island. With this large supply the Americans would certainly be able to maintain the siege. Or were some—or even all—of the 880 barrels filled with sand?

Elias Boudinot of Elizabeth, New Jersey, wrote in his journal:

When our Army lay before Boston in 1775 our powder was so nearly expended that General Washington told me that he had not more than eight rounds a man, although he had then near fourteen miles of line to guard, and that he dare not give an evening or morning gun. In this situation one of the Committee of Safety for Massachusetts, who was privy to the whole secret, deserted and went over to General Gage, and discovered our poverty to him. The fact was so incredible that General Gage treated it as a stratagem of war, and the informant as a spy, or coming with the express purpose of deceiving him and drawing his army into a snare, by which means we were saved from having our quarters beaten up.[52]

The Americans under the command of Ethan Allen and Benedict Arnold captured Fort Ticonderoga on May 10, 1775. Washington had twenty-five-year-old General Henry Knox bring cannons from the fort all the way across snow-covered Massachusetts to the siege lines surrounding Boston.[53] By placing the cannons upon Dorchester Heights overlooking the city and the harbor, Washington made the British occupation of Boston untenable. From Dorchester Heights the Continental Army could fire down on the city and the ships in the harbor. Because of the angle, the British cannons were unable to fire up on the Americans. The British were forced to evacuate Boston on March 17, 1776, and left for Nova Scotia. The colonists were now in control of Massachusetts but British troops would soon regroup and return. New York with its large harbor was the most likely destination. The British would be able to employ their overwhelming naval superiority there.

Three

~

DESPERATE TIMES

These are the times that try men's souls. The summer soldier and the sunshine patriot will, in this crisis, shrink from the service of their country; but he that stands by it now, deserves the love and thanks of man and woman. Tyranny, like hell, is not easily conquered, yet we have this consolation with us, that the harder the conflict, the more glorious the triumph. What we obtain too cheaply, we esteem too lightly."[1] Thomas Paine wrote these famous words to rally American resolve during the darkest hours of the war. In the beginning of the summer of 1776 the situation looked so promising for the Americans but by fall it had sunk to the deepest, darkest depths of despair.

In the spring the British army and navy were forced by the American cannons on Dorchester Heights to retreat from Boston to Nova Scotia. The summer had started with the Continental Army in control of the thirteen rebelling colonies. The British in North America controlled Canada, Nova Scotia, and East and West Florida.

Washington knew that after Boston the scene of action

would be moving to New York. The Continental Army upon its arrival at New York started cutting down trees and building its defenses where streets met the water's edge. As the soldiers arrived in the city many of its inhabitants fled. In March of 1776, Andrew Elliot said that you cannot picture a more distressed place than New York City, which was crowded with armed men who were not interested in saving the city but in keeping it from the British army.[2] During the summer of 1776, Washington had the Continental Army stationed in New York City, Brooklyn, and northern New Jersey.

The British were making preparations to attack New York with its enormous harbor. At New York they could use their overwhelming naval superiority to command the situation. When the British arrived they landed unopposed on Staten Island on July 2. Washington's intelligence assets were telling him that General William Howe's force was between 9,000 and 10,000. By the end of July 1776, the British had assembled an army of 32,000 British and Hessian soldiers on Staten Island. "Hessians" is the term given to the approximately 30,000 soldiers rented by the British government from the rulers of several small German states for service in the American Revolution. They were from Anhalt-Zerbst, Ansbach-Bayreuth, Brunswick, Hesse-Cassel, Hesse-Hanau, and Waldeck. They came as entire military units commanded by their own officers. They wore their existing uniforms and fought under their own German flags.

The British quickly used up all the fresh meat on the island. They then turned to eating horse meat.[3] Throughout the entire war, Washington was always aggressively checking on British food supplies and the type of food and forage that was placed aboard their ships. It provided him with a good indicator to determine the condition of the enemy's army and a forecast of events to come. He would always ask his spies to discover if the men had been given precooked rations or rations to cook themselves. Precooked rations indicated to Washington that an attack or expedition was imminent because the men would not have time to prepare and eat the meal. If they were given rations to cook, they would be staying in camp long enough to cook and eat their meal.

The British, having eaten all the cattle, goats, and sheep, needed to leave Staten Island quickly. It could no longer support them as they soon would exhaust the supply of horses available as food. They started making preparations to break out and find a fresh food supply. Several alternatives were available to them. They had enough ships that they could move their army wherever they wanted in the New York area. Because of all the possibilities, no one knew where they were going. Washington and his officers wondered if they would attack in New Jersey, and if so, where: Paulus Hook, Elizabeth, Perth Amboy? The coast of New Jersey (present-day Monmouth and Ocean counties) was not a viable option because it would require the ships to cross the tricky sandbars at Sandy Hook and take the ships away from New York City, which was the obvious objective of the campaign.

Would they make their move directly on New York City or would it be Brooklyn with its abundance of farms? Washington desperately needed to know where and quickly so he could set his defense. He could not adequately defend so many locations over such a wide-ranging area against a British attack. Washington was urgently searching for intelligence from everywhere. He knew, as everyone else did, that the British army was not going to stay on Staten Island for very long, and the fighting, the spilling of blood, and the dying would soon begin.

With so many enemy soldiers in such a small area as Staten Island, which is only fifty-eight square miles, it was difficult to get people to go there as a spy. It seemed like the soldiers were bivouacked in almost every house on the island. It was almost a certainty that a spy, who was not familiar with Staten Island would soon be discovered and then hanged.

Washington sent Brigadier General Hugh Mercer to take overall command of American forces in New Jersey.[4] Governor William Livingston of New Jersey advised that he had no intelligence of the British operations from the previous night.[5] He counseled Mercer that he was not having a problem getting people willing to be guides "but as to spies I am greatly discouraged."[6] On July 14, Mercer reported that he had not been able to procure any intelligence from Staten Island. From Perth Amboy, opposite to the west of the southern tip of Staten Island, he could see two enemy regiments but they had taken no new actions. "No person has yet come over to us nor is it easy to find one of our friends duly qualified as needy to undertake the business as a spy on the island."[7] Mercer advised that he was able to get the assistance of Captain John Mercereau in bringing intelligence from Staten Island on the evening of the 15th.[8] Mercereau operated a stage line between New York and Philadelphia. His extended family and friends were from Staten Island. "He under took the service very cheerfully—told he could go very secretly to his brother-in-law's who it seems resides back in the woods, remote from the parties [of soldiers] along shore." He left and got to the house of his brother-in-law and sister when they were alone. He was told there was a soldier in every house near the shore. He returned with an intelligence report on July 16. The intelligence he brought back was that the British had fortified their position with 600 to 700 soldiers at the New Blazing Star on the west side of Staten Island.[9] It was the exact spot where the Americans had planned to attack. This was the start of the Mercereau Spy Ring, which continued in operation until at least 1780.

With the British and Hessians landing on Staten Island, Congress formed a committee to devise a plan to encourage the Hessian mercenaries to desert. The committee gave its report on August 14.[10] Benjamin Franklin wrote to General Horatio Gates, adjutant general for the Continental Army, that "the Congress being advised that there was a probability that Hessians might be induced to quit the British service by offers of land, came to two resolves for this purpose, which, being translated into German and are printed are sent to Staten Island, to be distributed, if practicable, among those people."[11] John Hancock on August 16 sent Washington a copy of the resolve of Congress of the 14th.[12] It stated:

> [S]tates will receive all such foreigners who shall leave the armies of his Britannic majesty in America, and shall choose to become members of any of these states; that they shall be protected in the free exercise of their respective religions, and be invested with the rights, privileges and immunities of natives, as established by the laws of these states; and, moreover, that this Congress will provide, for every such person, 50 acres of unappropriated lands in some of these states, to be held by him and his heirs in absolute property.[13]

That the foregoing resolution be committed to the committee, who brought in the report, and that they be directed to have it translated into German, and to take proper measures to have it communicated to the foreign troops. In the meanwhile that this be kept secret.[14]

The plan called for a spy to travel across the Arthur Kill from New Jersey to Staten Island to deliver the documents. Although the plan was not of Washington's initiative and he was in New York, he definitely did what he could to support it. Christopher Ludwick, a native-born German and resident of Philadelphia, was given a mission to infiltrate the Hessian camp on Staten Island and distribute the German handbills prepared by the Continental Congress and aimed at encouraging desertion.[15] Joseph Reed, Washington's secretary at the Continental Army headquarters in New York City, wrote on August 19 in an unsealed letter to Governor Livingston of New Jersey requesting assistance with this project. It told of Ludwick's mission and asked Livingston to provide any assistance he could for its success. After reading the letter, Livingston was to give it to Ludwick, who would then identify himself and his mission to Joshua Mercereau. Reed stated Ludwick "puts his life in his hands in order to serve the interests of America."[16] The letter did not provide further instructions but implies that Mercereau, who knew the area, would take Ludwick across the Arthur Kill to Staten Island and to the Hessian camps and back.

Washington reported to Hancock, "The papers designed for the foreign troops, have been put into several channels, in order that they might be conveyed to them, and from the information I had yesterday, I have reason to believe many have fallen into their hands."[17] Since Washington referred to several channels worked in this secret black operations mission, it appears that several members of the Mercereau Spy Ring were involved. Mercereau identified one of the people operating with him and his family at this time as Abraham Egbert of Staten Island.[18] A Lawrence Mascoll was paid on August 23 for going to Staten Island to obtain information and might have also been another channel to which Washington referred.[19]

In a letter to Hugh Mercer dated August 23, 1776, from Elizabeth Town, Livingston stated that Ludwick got over safely the previous night, which would have been the evening of August 22. It would have been with Mercereau as his guide. Livingston wrote that Ludwick was disappointed at the results.[20] The Hessian brigade of Colonel von Donop had already boarded ships and started landing on Long Island on the 22nd.

Washington reported to John Hancock, president of Congress, on August 29 at half past four in the morning about Ludwick's lack of success: "As to the encouragement to the Hessian officers, I wish it may have the desired effect, perhaps it might have been better, had the offer been sooner made."[21] Some of the leaflets, which were dated August 14, did reach their objective. Some of them had been received by members of Colonel Friedrich Wilhelm, Freiherr von Lossberg's brigade on Staten Island.[22]

The rumor among the British on Staten Island in early August of 1776 was that they expected the Americans were going to burn New York City so as to leave nothing for them.[23] As the Americans advanced onto Long Island, the actions of Colonel Edward Hand of the 1st Continental Infantry, 1st Pennsylvania Regiment reinforced the rumor. While Hand retreated before the British on August 22, he burned several parcels of wheat that he believed would fall into the enemy's hands.[24]

British forces of approximately 22,000 men gave the Continental Army a crushing rout on August 27 in Brooklyn. Washington was pinned with his back to the East River and the British to his front. During the course of the evening John Glover and his Massachusetts Marbleheaders moved the Continental Army from Brooklyn across the East River to New York. With the rising sun the British found their quarry had slipped the noose and escaped.

Washington was desperate. He needed to know what the British planned to do. He wanted the men to be aggressive in their tactics. He told Generals William Heath and Clinton, "As every thing, in a manner, depends upon obtaining intelligence of the enemy[']s motions, I do most earnestly entreat you and Gen[era]l Clinton to exert yourselves to accomplish this most desirable end. Leave no stone unturn[e]d, nor do not stick at expense to bring this to pass, as I never was more uneasy than on Acc[oun]t of my want of knowledge on this score."[25]

Washington as usual gave specific instructions to his generals of exactly what he wanted done. He did not leave anything to chance. He continued:

> Keep besides this precaution, constant lookouts (with good Glasses) on some commanding heights that looks well on to the other shore (and especially into the bays, where boats can be concealed) that they may observe more particularly in the evening if there be any uncommon movements—much will depend upon early Intelligence, and meeting the enemy before they can intrich [*sic*]. I should much approve of small harassing parties, stealing as it were, over in the night, as they might keep the Enemy alarm[e]d and more than probably bring off

a prisoner from whom some valuable intelligenc[e] may be obtain[e]d.[26]

The British dealt the Continental Army a series of defeats. The American losses were staggering. The surrender of Fort Washington at the northern end of York (Manhattan) Island on November 16 was the climax to the British capture of the island. The American losses were 54 killed, 100 wounded, and a whopping 2,858 captured.[27] The British were now in complete control of York Island.

All the deserted houses of the rebels in New York City were confiscated and marked "GR," which is the Latin form of "King George," as property of the government for use by the occupying forces.[28] On September 20, 1776, in New York City there was a great fire that the British believed was started by the Sons of Liberty. According to the eyewitness account of John Joseph Henry, an American prisoner aboard the HMS *Pearl*, it began at 12:30 a.m. in the Fighting Cocks Tavern, near Whitehall Slip. It was an establishment of the lower sort. Some believe it was also a brothel. Its patrons were considered some of the city's most disreputable residents. The fire was fanned by winds southwest of the city and the flames leaped from one structure to another. It quickly was out of control. The fire raged up Broad Street to Beaver, to Broadway, and raced up Broadway all the way to King's College (now known as Columbia University) on Park Place, where the open spaces stopped the fire. By some accounts the fire destroyed 560 houses as well as a church.[29] A quarter of the city now lay in ruins. The red-light district, which was located between Trinity Church on the south and King's College on the north, was in ashes; only the basements of the wooden shacks survived. It was known as the "Holy Ground" because most of the property was owned by Trinity Church. The residents placed canvas tarps over the basements and continued to conduct their business of gambling, drinking, and prostitution. The area was now known as "Canvas Town" and was even more rowdy than before.

The rumor was the fires were started by left-behind agents and a squad of forty men led by a colonel who had come to New York City from Paulus Hook, New Jersey. There was no shortage of rumors, but proof of arson was hard to come by.

Nine arsonists were caught in the act of assisting the conflagration and were arrested. Some of the others were thrown into the fires they started. "One fanatical rebel, whose wife and five children could not persuade him to refrain from this murderous arson, mortally injured his wife with a knife when she tried to extinguish the fire with buckets of water. The man was seized by some sailors, stabbed to death, and then hung by his feet in front of his own home. He was left hanging there until the 20th at four o'clock in the afternoon."[30] Abraham Patten, an American spy, in a gallows confession on June 6, 1777, admitted to having been one of the those who set the fire.[31] Since Major General James Robertson expected the rebels to try to burn the rest of the city, he issued a proclamation on January 13 that instituted a fire watch.[32]

The question arises: Did Washington order the burning of New York City? There is neither direct proof nor documents that he made such an order. Washington wrote to Hancock from the Heights of Harlem on September 22, 1776, that he had "not been informed how the accident happened nor received any certain account of the damage."[33] He wrote Jonathan Trumbull that he did not know how the fire started but that an aide-de-camp of General Howe informed Colonel Reed "that several of our countrymen had been punished with various deaths on account of it; some by hanging, others by burning, etc., alleging that they were apprehended when committing the facts."[34]

A Captain Van Dyke was arrested on suspicion of aiding and abetting the arson. He claimed he was cut off from his unit during the American army's retreat of the city. He took refuge in a home in the city and was employed by the women of the house. He claimed to have surrendered to Colonel George Brewerton of De Lancey's Brigade.[35] He denied that he said anything on the subject of the fire.[36] British Major General James Robertson, on February 10, 1778, told Colonel Elias Boudinot, American commissary general of prisoners, that Van Dyke could not be exchanged without the approval of General Howe, as there was evidence of his being concerned in burning the town.[37]

Nathan Hale, a twenty-one-year-old Yale graduate, had volunteered to go on a dangerous spy mission from Connecticut to New York. There is no evidence that Washington had ever met him. Washington, with his attention to detail, would have provided him with guidance to trust no one. Hale's cover story was that he was an out-of-work schoolteacher looking for a job at the beginning of the school year. However, no cover story was provided as to why he was no longer in the Continental Army, which would have raised suspicions of his departure in camp.

Consider Tiffany, a Tory British supporter and storekeeper from Barkhamstead, Connecticut, who provided history with an account of the capture of Hale:

[Robert Rogers] detected several American officers, that were sent to Long Island as spies, especially Captain Hale, who was improved in disguise, to find whether the

Long Island inhabitants were friends to America or not.
Colonel Rogers having for some days, observed Captain
Hale, and suspected that he was an enemy in disguise;
and to convince himself, Rogers thought of trying the
same method, he quickly altered his own habit, with
which he made Capt[ain] Hale a visit at his quarters,
where the Colonel fell into some discourse concerning
the war, intimating the trouble of his mind, in his being
detained on an island, where the inhabitants sided with
the Britains [Britons] against the American Colonies, intimating withal, that he himself was upon the business
of spying out the inclination of the people and motion
of the British troops. This intrigue, not being suspected
by the Capt[ain], made him believe that he had found a
good friend, and one that could be trusted with the secrecy of the business he was engaged in; and after the
Colonel's drinking a health to the Congress: informs
Rogers of the business and intent. The Colonel, finding
out the truth of the matter, invited Captain Hale to dine
with him the next day at his quarters, unto which he
agreed. The time being come, Capt[ain] Hale repaired to
the place agreed on, where he met his pretended friend,
with three or four men of the same stamp, and after being refreshed, began the same conversation as hath been
already mentioned. But in the height of their conversation, a company of soldiers surrounded the house, and
by orders from the commander, seized Capt[ain] Hale in
an instant. But denying his name, and the business he
came upon, he was ordered to New York. But before he
was carried far, several persons knew him and called

him by name; upon this he was hanged as a spy, some say, without being brought before a court martial.[38]

This happened at the same time as the great fire, and General Howe wanted revenge. He ordered Hale's execution without a trial. While the city was still burning, Nathan Hale was hanged at 11 a.m. on September 22 at the Park of Artillery, which was next to the Dove Tavern (at modern-day 66th Street and Third Avenue).

Washington and his army had been chased out of New York and then across the Hudson River into New Jersey. Spies operate best between two stationary positions. They need a fixed position to return with their information if it is to be timely. The armies at this time were moving too quickly for spies to operate successfully. The situation was too fluid, as the British were chasing the retreating American army across New Jersey.

The British army was controlling more territory every day and Washington could do nothing to stop them. While the Continental Army was moving south across New Jersey, Washington had all the boats near Trenton rounded up. When the Americans reached Trenton, they were weary, ragged, and well-nigh disheartened. Washington's flotilla moved the men across the Delaware to the safety of Pennsylvania. Howe's army entered Trenton with music playing like a grand parade of a conquering army. When they went down to the riverbank, they found there were no boats on the New Jersey side. The British army was now in control of most of New Jersey.

Washington's morale was sinking just like that of his army. Washington wrote, "When I reflect upon these things, they fill me with much concern, knowing that General [William]

Howe has a number of troops cantoned in the towns bordering on and near the Delaware [River], his intentions to pass as soon as the ice is sufficiently formed, to invade Pennsylvania, and to possess himself of Philadelphia, if possible. To guard against his designs, and the execution of them; shall employ my every exertion, but how is this to be done?" Washington's conclusions of Howe's intention to go to Philadelphia were confirmed by intercepting a letter with a message written in invisible ink. One of his aides-de-camp exposed the invisible writing when he held the document near the fireplace. Washington was familiar with invisible ink from a 1763 encyclopedia, published in London by the Society of Gentlemen, which was in his personal library at Mount Vernon.[39]

Desperate to know what the enemy was going to do, Washington set his staff to procure the much-needed information, He gave Colonel John Cadwalader of the Pennsylvania militia the authority to employ and pay spies to gather intelligence. On the morning of the 14th Cadwalader sent someone to Mount Holly, New Jersey, who provided the location of the enemy positions on the New Jersey side of the Delaware, south of Trenton. This spy also reported that the Hessians south of Trenton had five brass fieldpieces.

Washington sent instructions to William Alexander, Lord Stirling, on December 14, 1776:

[C]ast about to find out some person who can be engaged to cross the river as a spy, that we may, if possible, obtain some knowledge of the enemy's situation, movements, and intention; particular enquiry to be made by the person sent if any preparations are making to cross the river; whether any boats are building, and where; whether any are coming across land from [New] Brunswick; whether any great collection of horses are made, and for what purpose &c. Expense must not be spared in procuring such intelligence, and will readily be paid by me. We are in a neighborhood of very disaffected people, equal care therefore should be taken that one of these persons do not undertake the business in order to betray us.[40]

Many people believe that John Honeyman of Griggstown, Somerset County, New Jersey, was the spy who was sent into Trenton to gather information on Colonel Johan Gottlieb Rail's forces encamped in the town. Washington always tried to get information from two or more sources to reduce the risk of being deceived by the enemy, a practice he would keep throughout the war. A source of information on Trenton and Bordentown came from an unidentified "half idiot youth." Because of his condition the enemy allowed him to wander about everywhere, but he had sufficient intelligence to return to Washington with very accurate reports of what he saw.[41]

Washington was perplexed by the British movements. Before he moved the army into Pennsylvania, he had all the boats and vessels brought to the Pennsylvania side or destroyed from Philadelphia upward for seventy miles. By guarding the fords he had foiled their attempts to cross. However, from some late movement of theirs, Washington was in doubt whether they were moving off to settle into winter quarters or whether General Howe was making a feint to get him to lower his guard.[42]

On the 18th he wrote to his brother John A. Washington about how bad his situation was:

I have no doubt but that General Howe will still make an attempt upon Philadelphia this winter. I see nothing to oppose him a fortnight hence, as the time of all the troops, except those of Virginia (reduced almost to nothing,) and Smallwood's Regiment of Maryland, (equally as bad) will expire in less than that time. In a word my dear sir, if every nerve is not strain[e]d to recruit the new army with all possible expedition, I think the game is pretty near up, owing, in a great measure, to the insidious arts of the enemy, and disaffection of the colonies before mentioned [New Jersey, New York, and Pennsylvania], but principally to the accursed policy of short inlistments [*sic*], and placing too great a dependence on the militia.[43]

The fall had drawn into winter, the traditional time for armies to go into an encampment to heal their wounds, restock, and prepare for a new campaigning season in the spring. Howe apparently changed his plans and decided against conducting a winter campaign to conquer Philadelphia that year and chose to wait for spring. He set his army across New Jersey at several locations.

Washington's situation was fraught with peril. He had an army that was going home in a few days. His spies told him there were 1,500 Hessians and a troop of British Light Horse at Trenton backed up by additional forces at Burlington, Bordentown, and Princeton. The enemy was anticipated to be at his doorstep as soon as the Delaware River froze, which was expected to happen quickly. Washington had to trust the intelligence he had received.

He devised a plan for the army to divide into three units and cross the Delaware at three locations on the night of December 25, 1776. General James Ewing was to cross and block the road to the south out of Trenton. Colonel John Cadwalader was to cross near the Bristol Ferry and attack or at least distract Colonel von Donop's men, who were south of Trenton supporting the Hessians. Colonel Samuel Griffin, on orders from General Washington, had already crossed the Delaware with 600 men and marched to Mount Holly.[44] Washington was trying to draw the enemy farther apart and away from the river. He wanted them to be unable to come to the aid of the army at Trenton. The Hessians had heard rumors that there were 3,000 American soldiers at Mount Holly. They could not allow a large American force to remain there, as they could attack their advance positions at Bordentown and Burlington.

Washington was not the only commander using spies. The Hessians sent spies into Mount Holly to determine the size of the American forces there. Bazilla Haines, a resident of Bordentown, was sent to obtain intelligence of the rebels. He arrived on the evening of December 21 and lodged in the rebel camp. He estimated that there were fewer than 800 American soldiers. He saw what he thought were two 3-pound fieldpieces at St. Andrew's Church on Iron Works Hill.[45] Colonel Griffin arrested Daniel Bancroft as a spy and sent him to a Philadelphia jail.[46]

Von Donop, with 2,000 Hessians and British regulars, had been lured twelve miles farther south and was unable to support Colonel Rail's forces at Trenton. The Hessians, after forcing the Americans to retreat, settled in Mount Holly for the night, making merry over confiscated alcohol from the taverns, wine from the basement of Aaron Smith's house and shop (present-day 84 High Street), and whiskey from the house of James Clothier.[47]

Von Donop spent the evening enjoying the company of a lady who had been married to a doctor.

Because of the ice-choked Delaware River, General James Ewing was not able to get across. Cadwalader, however, was able to get his men across but not his artillery, and so abandoned the mission and returned to Pennsylvania. Washington and his army crossed the ice-clogged Delaware. They headed south to the Hessians in Trenton. The army train stretched for nearly a mile with all the cannons, horses, wagons, and soldiers. The weather grew worse. Washington rode up and down the column urging his men to carry on. Some men were without shoes and left a trail of bloody footprints in the snow.

Washington split his forces in attacking Trenton. General John Sullivan and his division went by the river road. Washington and General Nathanael Greene went inland and would attack from the high ground to the north of the town. The Americans had lost the cover of darkness but not the element of surprise. Shortly after eight o'clock on the morning of December 26, 1776, Washington attacked, personally leading the middle of three columns through the snow. The Continental Army's artillery fired. The Hessians' drums started beating, urgently summoning their soldiers to assemble. Three Hessian regiments ran from their quarters, quickly forming ranks. As they grouped, the Continental Army advanced and overpowered the German mercenaries. Rall was mortally wounded. Without their commander, Rall's regiment was confused and disoriented and chaotically retreated to an orchard east of Trenton where they were forced to surrender. A large number of Hessians had escaped by retreating over the Assunpink Creek Bridge where General Ewing's forces were to have been.

Washington's gamble worked and yielded a crucial strategic and material victory. In one hour of fighting, the Continental Army captured nearly 900 Hessian officers and men as well as a large supply of bayonets, cannons, muskets, swords, and other military supplies. The Patriot cause was invigorated. The victory pushed the morale of the troops to new heights. After the battle, Washington had the army with its prisoners return to the safety of Pennsylvania.

Four

~

POOLS OF BLOOD

Washington was always concerned about spies. They were a constant problem except when the armies were on the move. He knew he could not stop all of them, so feeding them false information was his next best defense. With that in mind on December 12, 1776, he told Colonel John Cadwalader[1] of the Philadelphia Associators of the Pennsylvania militia, "Keep a good look out for spies; endeavor to magnify your numbers as much as possible."[2] It was a ploy he would use over and over again in creating false troop information, inflating the size and giving the wrong location of his forces for spies to discover and take back to enemy headquarters.

Washington in December of 1776 was desperate to know what the British were doing. Spare no pains or expense to get intelligence of the enemy's intentions, Washington told Cadwalader. He had also told General James Ewing, "Spare no pains nor cost to gain information of the enemy's movements and designs. Whatever sums you pay to obtain this end I will cheerfully refund."[3] He also advised Brigadier General Philemon

Dickinson to spare no pains or expense to obtain intelligence, and all promises he made or monies advanced would be acknowledged and paid.[4] Three days later Washington was still desperate for information and again was encouraging Cadwalader to get intelligence of the enemy's intentions.[5]

Dickinson, who was at Yardley's farm in Bucks County, Pennsylvania, advised Washington on the 21st of the information he was able to collect from two people who had come out of New Jersey on what was going on in New Brunswick, and from a person from Crosswicks regarding boats at Lewis's Mill.[6] A slave from Trenton told of boats being built a mile from town. Dickinson told Washington he was going to increase the amount he was offering to $15 or $20 for someone to go as a spy to Trenton and return. "People here are fearful of the inhabitants betraying them."[7] On the 24th he was able to secure someone to take the risks and he got him across the river into New Jersey. He was due back the next morning, at which time he was going to be provided with a horse to get to Washington.[8]

On the morning of December 31, 1776, while at Crosswicks, one of Cadwalader's spies, who was identified only as "a very intelligent young gentleman," had just returned from the British camp at Princeton some sixteen miles distant. He identified the number and locations of British and Hessian forces in the town. He said "there were about five thousand men, consisting of Hessians and British troops—about the same number of each. . . . He conversed with some of the officers, and lodged last night with them." As part of a disinformation campaign, Washington had previously instructed that the numbers of American troops were to be magnified. The spy complied with these instructions by saying that Washington had 16,000 men. However, they would not believe that Washington had more than 5,000 or 6,000. The spy reported, "They parade every morning an hour before day [break]—and some nights lie on their arms—An attack has been expected for several nights past—the men are much fatigued, and until last night [were] in want of provisions—when a very considerable number of wagons arrived with provisions from [New] Brunswick." He provided a crucial piece of information: the enemy was not expecting an attack from the east, as there were "no sentries on the back or east side of the town" facing the water, thus leaving the town unguarded. The spy also provided enough detailed information for a map, which was made by Cadwalader, showing the enemy's positions at Princeton.[9]

Washington and the army recrossed the ice-choked Delaware and returned to New Jersey on December 29. The artillery was unable to cross till the 31st due to the ice. When assembled at Trenton, Washington's forces numbered 6,000 men and forty cannons. However, enlistments were expiring and soldiers would be going home. The army was going to evaporate before his eyes. Washington appealed to his men to stay in service for some promised bonus money. On December 31, Robert Morris in Philadelphia sent Washington the sum of 410 Spanish milled dollars, 2 English crowns, 10½ English shillings, and one half a French crown, amounting to 155 pounds, 9 shillings, 6 pence in Pennsylvania currency, or 124 pounds, 7 shillings, 8 pence lawful money, which is the value in gold and silver. Buoyed by the combination of victory at Trenton and money from Morris, most men stayed.

After Washington's victory at Trenton, British General Cornwallis returned to New Jersey from New York City. He assembled a force of 8,000 at Princeton, leaving 1,200 at Princeton under the command of Lieutenant Colonel Charles Mawhood of the 17th Regiment of Foot. On January 2, he took his remaining forces, which included twenty-eight cannons, and marched toward Trenton and Washington's army. When he reached Maidenhead (now Lawrenceville), he detached Colonel Alexander Leslie of the 64th Regiment of Foot with 1,500 men. He ordered them to stay there until the next morning. As soon as Washington heard that Cornwallis was on his way to attack him, he detached men to skirmish with the approaching British forces in a delaying action. Due to the American resistance it was not until late in the day when the British army finally reached Trenton. It was the second time in eight days that the Americans would engage the enemy.

The Americans were encamped on the east side of a bridge across the Assunpink Creek. The British advanced in solid columns onto the bridge. The Americans fired in unison and the British fell back. The British regrouped and charged the bridge again. This time the Americans fired a cannon into the redcoats and they fell back once more. After regrouping they moved onto the bridge. This time the American cannons fired antipersonnel canister shot, which is like a shotgun blast of small pellets. The bridge was littered with the dead. A soldier described the scene: "The bridge looked red as blood, with their killed and wounded and their red coats."[10] The firing and the killing continued till sunset when Cornwallis called off the attack. He planned to take the bridge the next morning and then crush Washington and the Continental Army. Both sides were exhausted and the soldiers on both sides were ordered to rest.

It was brought to Washington's attention that the British could cross the creek farther down at Philip's Ford and turn his flank. He would have been caught between the British forces and the Delaware River. It would have been a repeat of the Battle of Long Island. This time he could not escape by crossing the

Delaware, as he had crossed the East River before, as his vessels were farther upstream. He did not have the time for them to be brought to his rescue. Later the British quietly, under the cover of darkness, began moving 2,000 men in the woods into position to cross Philip's Ford in the morning.

Washington had received Cadwalader's spy's intelligence on the enemy situation at Princeton. The unknown spy provided great detail of the British fortifications. This would be the rare occasion that Washington acted on a single spy's intelligence, as there was no time to get corroborating intelligence. Because of the desperate situation, he could not stand pat. He had to do something or be destroyed.

He hurriedly called a council of war. It was decided to slip away during the night and surprise the British at Princeton. The Continental Army's military and personal baggage was sent south to Burlington. The artillery was wrapped in heavy cloth to quiet the noise. Five hundred soldiers were left at Trenton with two cannons. Some were assigned to tend the campfires to keep them burning. Others were to make noise digging with picks and shovels to convince the British that the American army was going to make a stand and was reinforcing its position preparing for the British attack at Philip's Ford. The soldiers who were left as a distraction were to sneak away during the night and catch up to the Continental Army before dawn. The army, as silently as possible, slipped away beginning at 2 a.m. while the British watched the light from the American campfires. For some of the men it would be their third night march in a row in the cold and extreme darkness. They were slowed by the task of getting the artillery over stumps in the frozen, rutted road. After crossing the new bridge, Washington split the army into two units just as when he approached Trenton a week earlier.

Unfortunately, just like a week earlier, they were arriving later than intended and lost the cover of darkness.

Thirty-four-year-old Rhode Islander General Nathanael Greene took the smaller column of soldiers and went west to take control of the main road from Princeton to Trenton. They were to keep the enemy at Princeton from escaping and block any reinforcements coming to the aid of those at Princeton. General John Sullivan of New Hampshire commanded the main body of the army of 5,000 men. They went to the right along the Saw Mill Road.

Cornwallis had ordered forty-seven-year-old Lieutenant Colonel Charles Mawhood to bring the 17th and 55th British Regiments of Foot along with some artillery to Trenton to join his army in the morning. Mawhood marched out from Princeton at about five in the morning. While on the march he sighted the main American army under General Sullivan. He immediately sent a rider to warn the 40th Regiment of Foot in Princeton of the advancing Americans.

Mawhood decided to attack with 450 men the main American army. Brigadier General Hugh Mercer's 1,500 men of Greene's division made the first contact with Mawhood's men in William Clark's orchard. Lieutenant William John Hale of the 45th Regiment of Foot wrote that the American volley was "a heavy discharge, which brought down seven of my platoon at once, the rest being recruits, gave way." He continues, "I rallied them with much difficulty, and brought them forward with bayonets."[11] The two sides matched volley for volley. Pools of blood glistened on the ice-covered field. Mawhood saw an opportunity and ordered a bayonet charge against the American riflemen, who did not have bayonets. Brigadier General Mercer's horse was hit and down Mercer went as he ordered a retreat. His men safely retreated but Mercer fell into British hands. He fought with his sword and was bayoneted many times and would die several days later. His men retreated right into Colonel John Cadwalader's Pennsylvania Associators as they were trying to deploy. Washington came on the field and rallied the men, riding on a white horse within seventy-five feet of the British line. He made a very easy target but somehow came through the battle without a scratch. More American units came onto the field, some with bayonets drawn.

The British fired a volley that went over the heads of the Americans. Washington with the army under control then ordered a platoon to fire as it marched forward. Washington was turning their flank and was about to attack the British rear as well as the front and flank. The circle was closing. The British decided their only course of action was either to fight and be cut to pieces or retreat through the only way still available. Mawhood sent the artillery back to Princeton in an effort to save them. The 55th Regiment of Foot took up position south of the town at a place called Frog Hollow. They were outnumbered 10 to 1. They did some delaying actions, falling back to new defensive positions. This bought the British some time to remove as much of their supplies and artillery out of Princeton as possible and take them to safety in New Brunswick. When the American army was within fifty or sixty feet of the British defenses and ready to charge, a British officer with a white handkerchief on the point of his sword asked for a truce in order to surrender. General Sullivan accepted his surrender.

Some of the British forces that were in the town took shelter in Nassau Hall, which was the main building for the College of New Jersey (now Princeton). Alexander Hamilton had some cannons brought to the front of Nassau Hall and fired at the building. When some Americans broke open the front door, the British waved a white flag through one of the windows and surrendered. The Americans had defeated the British regulars and were now in control of the town. As soon as Cornwallis realized the Americans had slipped away during the night, were now behind him, and he was in an unsupported position, he and his troops headed back to Princeton.

The British payroll chest of £70,000 lay just sixteen miles up the road in New Brunswick guarded by a skeleton force. It was a great prize but Washington's men were exhausted. Some had not had any rest for two nights and a day. From the best intelligence Washington was able to get, the British were so alarmed at the possibility of an attack at New Brunswick that they immediately marched there without halting at Princeton. This allowed Washington to take his men unmolested another thirty miles past New Brunswick to the safety of an encampment in the Watchung Mountains in and around Morristown.

The increase in the morale of the public and the troops was meteoric. The mood went from the despair of expecting Philadelphia to fall to the British juggernaut, which had ridden roughshod over New York and New Jersey, to euphoria over the two American victories. William Hooper, a Continental congressman from North Carolina, best described the change in the public morale and the heady confidence in Washington and the Continental Army after the victories at the Battle of Trenton over the Hessians and the Battle of Princeton over the British.[12] He told Robert Morris:

I congratulate you upon the new face which our affairs have assumed in the Jersies [New Jersey], under every difficulty that a military genius could possibly have to struggle with, General Washington sometimes almost without an army, at best one composed of raw undisciplined troops, impatient [with] command and vastly inferior in numbers to the enemy's has been able to check a victorious army, with everything that could afford a probability of success, thundering at the gates of the Capital of America [Philadelphia], to change their course and is now pursuing them in turn to the only spot which they have possession of in America [New York City]—Will posterity believe the tail [*sic*]? When it shall be consistent with the policy to give the history of that man from his first introduction into our service, how often America has been rescued from ruin by the mere strength of his Genius, conduct, and courage, encountering every obstacle that want of money, men, arms, ammunition, could throw in his way; an Impartial world will say with you that he is the Greatest man on Earth.

Misfortunes are the Elements in which he shines. They are the ground work on which his picture appears to the greatest advantage. He rises superior to them all, they serve as foils to his fortitude and as stimulants to bring into view those great qualities which in the serenity of his life his great modesty keeps concealed. I could fill the side in his praise, but any thing I can say cannot equal his merits or raise your idea of him.[13]

Washington, upon his arrival at Morristown, decided to use misdirection to give the British something to keep them busy. He always tried to control the game whenever possible rather than react to the British moves. He contacted Major General William Heath at Peekskill, New York. He instructed him: "[Y]ou should move down towards New York [City] with a considerable force, as if you have design upon the city. That being an object of great importance, the enemy will be reduced to the necessity of withdrawing a considerable part of their force from the Jerseys, if not the whole, to secure the city."[14]

He knew the British would have their spies looking for any information to take back to the army headquarters at Captain Archibald Kennedy's home at 1 Broadway in New York City.[15] Washington decided to use some deception to his advantage.

Elias Boudinot was working with Washington on intelligence and deception. He wrote in his journal about how diligently and ingeniously Washington tried to deceive British General Howe as to the size of the Continental Army. Most generals in the eighteenth century would have consolidated their troops for the army's protection. "Washington distributed them [his soldiers] by 2 and 3 in a house, all along the main roads round Morris Town for miles, so that the general expectation among the country people was, that we were 4000 strong."[16]

Just as Washington had expected, General Howe sent spies to the American camp at Morristown and Jockey Hollow. One of the spies was a New York merchant well known to the American encampment. He told about how badly he had been treated by the British; therefore, he decided to desert from them. Boudinot did not believe the merchant's story and considered him a spy. He conveyed his suspicions to Washington, who agreed with Boudinot's assessment.

Washington had found the victim for his strategy of deception. He instructed his adjutant general, Colonel Joseph Reed, to prepare troop returns from every brigadier general on the number of soldiers in each brigade. The combined reports indicated the army consisted of 12,000 men. The reports were placed in the pigeonholes in a desk. The adjutant was introduced to the merchant and, as instructed, offered the merchant to lodge with him. They had supper alone and, as planned, at about nine o'clock an orderly servant informed him that General Washington needed to see him immediately. The adjutant made his apology for leaving his dinner companion and departed. The merchant was left alone at the desk with the troop returns for about a half hour. As was hoped he made a copy of the documents. The next morning, as anticipated, the merchant left the American camp and went back to New York City.

British General Howe wholly believed the intelligence the merchant provided. Howe was convinced that if he attacked the Americans he would face a much stronger resistance than the Americans could really muster. Lieutenant Colonel William Luce of the 3rd New Jersey Volunteers, a Loyalist unit under the command of Brigadier General Cortlandt Skinner, was captured by the Americans at Elizabeth Town and brought to Morristown. Being an officer he was given a parole, permitting him to reside with a family who was not in favor of the Revolution. (A parole, short for *parole d'honneur*, was a promise from a prisoner of war that if he was released from jail he would not take up arms or carry out any military acts until he was exchanged.) He was able to obtain very accurate information on the status of the Americans as to artillery, sickness, and strength. He broke his parole and went to New York. When he reported the information he collected to General Howe, he was not believed. Luce was shocked as Howe showed him the copies of the American army returns taken from the adjutant's desk. Howe accused Luce of being an American spy and was going to have him hanged. Luce made his escape and was "mortified and chagrined with having broken his parole and at the last disappointed and treated with contempt and great severity."[17]

Washington's deceptions bought the army time to heal its wounds, recruit soldiers to replace those lost, and prepare for the spring campaign. Alexander Hamilton described the state of affairs as an "extraordinary spectacle of a powerful army [the British] straightened within narrow limits by the phantom of a military force and never permitted to transgress limits with impunity."[18]

Washington assigned hard-drinking forty-four-year-old Brigadier General William Maxwell to oversee the area from Perth Amboy to Newark. He was born in Ulster and was nicknamed Scotch Willie. During the French and Indian War he served in General Edward Braddock's expedition at the same time as Washington. Washington instructed him to be cautious of Loyalists who would swear allegiance to America but would be sending information to the British. He was to keep a military detachment in Newark and Elizabeth for the purpose of obtaining information on the enemy's activities. Scottish-born Adam Stephen, now a major general, was also assigned to obtain intelligence from both the British post at New Brunswick and in New York City. Stephen received $200 of the scarce money for paying informers.

Soon after he arrived in New Jersey with his troops in late 1776, Stephen began submitting intelligence as he had done during the French and Indian War.[19] Stephen advised General William Alexander (Lord Stirling) via a letter dated January 8, 1777, that from "my man from New York, he had received information on General Howe's intended march to Philadelphia."[20]

His information was so late as to be useless. It appeared that Stephen's man from New York was really a double agent who was feeding him information that was outdated and would provide no advantage.

In an April 14 letter, Stephen claimed to have contacts in New York City and on Staten Island and at Bergen and Paulus Hook in New Jersey. On April 23, he wrote to Washington that he had received intelligence that the British planned "A certain conquest of America" before October [1777]. It was said by the British that General Howe would be in Philadelphia by May 1.[21]

Not all of the generals were as vigilant as Washington at ensuring the veracity of the intelligence they collected. As we have seen, Washington made every effort to check the information from one source with that of at least one or more sources. Both Generals Maxwell and Stephen in early 1777 were duped into believing erroneous information. Maxwell described the situation to Stephen: "We have a very difficult card to play [and] we have often to act by the moon or twialight [sic] and leave the world to judge of it in clear sunshine."[22]

Washington was trying to recruit spies to go into New York City. Who should be a spy? What Washington thought can be found in a letter written later by Alexander Hamilton on his behalf advising General Nathanael Greene that he recommended the person selected to be a spy should not be an officer but someone shrewd and a trusted country person who is familiar with the place.[23]

Once Washington reached Morristown he set his intelligence gathering in motion. Colonel Joseph Reed spent $238 for secret services on January 25, 1777, but did not leave a record to whom he made the payment.

On February 4, Washington at Morristown instructed William Alexander, Lord Stirling, to go to Basking Ridge and take command of the troops there and to "use every means in your power to obtain intelligence from the enemy which may possibly be better effected by engaging some of those people who have obtained protections, to go in under pretense of asking advice than by any other means."[24]

William Duer was born in Devon, England, in 1743. He inherited plantations in the Caribbean and moved to New York in the early 1770s. He became a successful merchant dealing primarily in lumber. He became a member of the New York Provincial Congress and the New York Senate in 1777. Duer, on January 28 from Westchester County, had recommended Nathaniel Sackett to Washington:[25]

> I beg Leave to introduce to your Excellency's Acquaintance Mr. Sacket[t], a member of the Convention of the State, a Man of Honor, and of firm Attachment to the American Cause. He will communicate to your Excellency some Measures taken by him, and myself which if properly prosecuted may be of infinite Utility to the present military Operations—I have therefore recommended it to him to wait on you in person in hopes that some Systematical Plan may be adopted, and prosecuted for facilitating your Manoeuvres against the British army. To say more in a Letter, might be imprudent; I shall therefore content myself with observing that Mr. Sacket[t] is (As I know by experience) a Person of Intrigue, and Secrecy well calculated to prosecute such Measures as you shall think conducive to give Success to your generous Exertions in the Cause of America.[26]

Washington acknowledged receipt of Duer's letter, which was delivered by Sackett. He advised that Sackett told him of their plan "for forwarding military operations on your side" of the Hudson River. Washington liked the intelligence-gathering plan and "most sincerely wish had been carried into execution."[27]

Washington understood the possibility of his mail being intercepted, which would expose the plan to the enemy. In his letter of February 3 to Duer he wrote, "I shall say but little to you by way of letter, as I shall communicate my sentiments in a confidential manner to Mr. Sacket[t]."[28]

The very next action, which was on the same day as the intelligence assignment to Lord Stirling, Washington tasked Sackett with "obtaining the earliest and best intelligence of the designs of the enemy." He was going to be paid $50 per calendar month for his expenses and a warrant upon the paymaster general for $500 for those he had to employ in this business, and was to report the expenditures to Washington.[29] He also assigned Benjamin Tallmadge of the 2nd Continental Light Dragoons to assist Sackett.

On February 20, General Greene advised that he could not devise a better plan of gaining intelligence than the one Washington was proposing, adding, "but I hope the old channel of intelligence is not yet shut up."[30] He most likely was referring to restarting the Mercereau Spy Ring operating between New Jersey and Staten Island.

Duer enclosed abstracts of two letters written to Nathaniel Sackett on February 25, 1777, that contain accounts of Loyalist activities on Long Island. The first letter, from Captain John Davis of the 2nd Company, 4th Battalion, 4th New York Regiment, was an intelligence report that Davis received from a Lieutenant Nathaniel Conkling of the 2nd Company and a refugee from Long Island. The report indicated that Edmund Fanning, Captain Frederick Hudson, and other officers went to the east end of Long Island to enlist recruits. Because of the poor response, Fanning planned to return in four weeks. The report also provided information from a letter to a Corporal Jarvis from his wife at Huntington, Long Island, which told of three companies of Tories stationed at that place (but not a man to the eastward). Davis swore that he got the information from a person whose truth and veracity he believed he could depend upon.

The second letter to Sackett was from a "Mr Talmage," who was probably Benjamin Tallmadge. He advised he had "received intelligence from Long Island by one [Major] John Clark [Jr.] that there were no troops at Setauket [on Long Island Sound] but part of two companies at Huntington and one company at Oyster Bay—That the said Clark saw the companies at Huntington that the militia of Suffolk County was ordered to meet on the 16th Feb[ruar]y in order to be drafted for the ministerial service but that they were determined not to serve, however if their services were insisted upon; they were determined to make their escape in time."[31] Little is known of Clark's activities before the Philadelphia campaign in the fall of 1777. It is said he had, during the campaign around Trenton, a hand in the management of some of the secret service activities. He had been an aide to Major General Nathanael Greene, and was then major of the 2nd Pennsylvania Battalion of the Flying Camp. On June 1, 1777, $984 was expended for secret service activities to date and it is supposed that some of that amount would have gone to Clark for his expenses.[32]

Washington was anxious to get intelligence of the enemy's operations. He wrote to Duer, "I am glad Mr. S. [Sackett] plan is nearly completed and I am persuaded the benefits result[in]g from it will be great. The sooner it can be executed the more beneficial it will be."[33]

On April 7, Sackett was at John Suffern's tavern at Suffern, New York, when he wrote up a status report of his activities to Washington. After he had received the appointment he went to New York and began his assignment. At first it was difficult securing agents, but then he had a person referred to him who was well-educated, a good surveyor, and perfect for the assignment. On March 7 he was able to insert him behind enemy lines by crossing over through the English Neighborhood of Bergen Township, Bergen County, New Jersey. This person was to make his way to New York City, rent a room, and secure a permit to go into the country to bring back poultry to sell. The plan was for him to make two trips a week. It was now a month and Sackett had not heard from this person.

When he returned from the English Neighborhood, he found two men of well-known attachment to the American cause who were honest, sensible, and intriguing. They have agreed to go in to the enemy and reside there. He had proposed that one reside at New Brunswick and the other at Perth Amboy. One of the men had associated with well-known Tories. William Bayard, who lived in New York, wrote to him urging him to come to New York. His leaving was delayed so he could get a smallpox inoculation. He finally left on April 4 to get inoculated. Sackett wrote that in order to establish his alibi with the enemy, he gave him permission to enlist eight or ten men to take with him when he went to the British. The other man was inoculated and returned the day before yesterday. He was now among the principle Tories near the enemy lines in order to get letters of recommendation. He was expected back the next day.

Sackett also wrote that he employed a Hessian who had lived in the country for almost forty years. He or a substitute was to talk the Hessians into deserting. They were to meet on April 10. He asked Washington where best to send him.

"The week before last he sent in a woman who was the wife of a man who had gone to the enemy." He posed as a secret friend to King and Country to gain the woman's trust. The woman complained vociferously that the Patriots had confiscated her grain for the use of the army. He advised her to complain to General Howe in New York, which she did. She left New York on March 28 and came back disappointed but advised "there is a large number of flat-bottomed boats in New York the harbor of which are intended for an expedition to Philadelphia."[34]

Washington responded the next day that the Hessian should be sent to New Brunswick. He provided guidance based upon his experience: "The good effect of intelligence may be lost if it is not speedily transmitted—this should be strongly impressed upon the persons imployed [sic] as it also should be to avoid false intelligence and building too much upon reports alone—A comparison of circumstances should be had, and much pains take[n to a]void erroneous acc[oun]ts."[35]

Some of the plans backfired and Sackett's services were discontinued. Sackett gives us some clues as to what happened but not the whole story. On May 23, 1789, while trying to solicit a federal appointment from the recently inaugurated President Washington,[36] Sackett wrote to the president, "Sir, you will be pleased to recollect the business you allotted me in the beginning of the year 1777. In consequence of which I spent many stormy nights on the lines to carry it into effect, after I had gone through all those dangers that awaited me in getting a regular plan laid, and was beginning to carry it on with every appearance of success, the [New] Jersey men falling in love with his horse the doctor narrowly escaped with his life, and the whole scheme was frustrate[d]."[37]

Major General Adam Stephen wrote to Washington on April 23, 1777, and advised that they should be on the watch for Thomas Long, a British spy, who was on his way from Rahway, New Jersey, where he taught school, to Philadelphia. His nickname was "Bunk Eye" for his prominent eyes. Washington advised Congress that he did "not put intire [sic] confidence in the whole" of Stephen's intelligence report, but Long should be apprehended.[38]

Thomas Long was an Englishman who stood five feet six inches tall, was over forty years old, had a fair complexion, and wore white clothes. He apparently escaped detection and completed his spying mission to Philadelphia until the New Jersey Militia apprehended him on November 1, 1779, while he was hiding in a barn near Rahway.[39] Colonel Moses Jacques of the militia presided over Long's court-martial. Long was found without weapons and was convicted as a spy and ordered to be hanged. Ellis Throp was drafted to be the executioner. William Hadar, a native of Hunterdon County, New Jersey, who was with the militia when Long was caught, and Henry Williams witnessed Long's hanging on Thursday, November 4, at Kinsey's Corner near Rahway.[40] An American newspaper account of the day referred to Long as "a villain noted for his cruelties to many of our prisoners."[41] Loyalist John Smith Hatfield of Elizabeth Town, a British guide and spy, claimed that before Long was hanged, his fingers and toes were chopped off.[42]

Some imaginative individuals wanted Long's hanging to be a warning to Loyalists. They exhumed his body at night and propped it on its feet with a pail on its head against the door of

Tory Richard Cozen's house. The plan was that when Cozen opened his door in the morning, Long's body would be standing there to greet him. The spot where Long was hanged was near Cozen's garden and sixty-five to eighty-five feet from his window. During the extreme cold that night, Long's body froze stiff. When Cozen opened his door, Long's body, with the pail on his head, fell into Cozen's house as planned.[43]

Washington in a letter dated April 23, 1777, to Hancock advised that he had asked Major General Adam Stephen to hire persons to go to New Brunswick and New York City. In April 1777, Stephen received $200 for use in paying informers.[44] General Greene mentions that intelligence was received on April 26 from New Brunswick and New York that the British would take the field by June 1.[45] However, the spy was probably deceived, as the information reported that a bridge of boats at New York was complete and part of it was said to be at New Brunswick.[46] Colonel Oliver Spencer, of one of the sixteen additional Continental regiments, helped Stephen to secure correspondence with New York and Staten Island.[47]

Although there is no proof that Abraham Patten was the spy General Stephen had in New Brunswick and New York in response to Washington's request, he is the only one known to have worked in both locations at this time. Quartermaster Carl Bauer of the Hessian Platte Grenadier Battalion wrote that Abraham Patten was "a rebel captain who had lived in [New] Brunswick for some time as a spy, and during that time passed himself off as a merchant."[48] Captain Alexander Graydon of the 3rd Pennsylvania Regiment wrote in his memoirs that Patten had been communicating with General Washington from New York City but did not explain how. According to Graydon, Patten had "generally resided at New York, under the disguise of a zealous royalist, had been indiscreet enough to unbosom himself very fully to Major [Otho H.] Williams." Graydon believed that Patten had informed Washington that General Howe's objective would not be a strike up the Hudson River but to Philadelphia.[49]

A few weeks after the discussion with Major Williams, Patten was at New Brunswick and tried to bribe an English grenadier to desert and carry four letters to Generals Washington and Putnam with the promise of 50 guineas. The grenadier turned the letters over to General Cornwallis. The letters gave information respecting the city of New Brunswick and a plan to set fire to all the magazines in the city on the king's birthday, June 4. "He would not accuse any as his accomplices, but it is said [he] acknowledged at the gallows that he was a principal in setting fire to New York." Between 11 a.m. and noon on June 6, 1777, he was executed as an American spy in New Brunswick.[50] Quartermaster Carl Bauer wrote that when Patten "came to the ladder and was about to climb it he pulled the white hood over his eyes and said, 'I die for Liberty.' "[51] This statement was backed up by Lieutenant Johann Heinrich von Bardeleben of the Regiment von Donop, who reported the statement as "I die for Liberty, and do it gladly, because my cause is just."[52] Captain Lieutenant John Peebles of the 42nd Royal Highlanders wrote in his diary that "the spy Patoun [sic] was hanged to day" and that the 2nd Battalion Grenadiers had just lost six or eight men who deserted to the rebels.[53]

On June 13, Washington wrote to Congress concerning Patten's execution, saying that "his family well deserves the generous notice of Congress. He conducted himself with great fidelity to our cause rendering services and has fallen a sacrifice in promoting her interest. Perhaps a public act of generosity, considering the character he was in, might not be so eligible as a private donation."[54]

We think of Washington as always being perfect. It was not always the case. One such instance was when Washington forgot the fictitious name he was to use in writing to Sackett and had to ask him to refresh his memory.[55]

Major General Israel Putnam at Princeton on February 18, 1777, advised Washington that Thomas Lewis Woodward Jr. had come from Staten Island about three weeks earlier and had made a request for a pass to go back to the British. He was the son of Anthony Woodward Sr., a Quaker from Upper Freehold, Monmouth County, New Jersey, who in 1776 abandoned his large landholdings to join the British army. Based upon the papers Woodward had with him and what he said, Putnam believed "him a very proper object for the gallows, but defer the matter till I know your pleasure."[56]

Washington instructed Putnam to hold a court of inquiry of Thomas Lewis Woodward Jr. as a suspected spy, to determine if he came under the definition of a spy, and if so, then to treat him as such. "I wish, however, that circumstances may be duly attended to, and not too much vigor used on those occasions, unless upon persons evidently of that stamp, 'tis bad policy."[57]

In operating an intelligence network, Washington constantly had to secure money for paying spies. The spies would not accept either Continental or state paper money. Spies always wanted payment in hard currency, gold and silver. Hard currency was perpetually in short supply. Sometimes payments were just a few pounds, as when General Greene was given £7 to pay his informants. As difficult as it was, more money always seemed to be found when truly needed. In May 1777, Major General Benjamin Lincoln was given $450 for arms and secret service.[58]

Washington regularly compared information from one source to another. A standardized set of questions was prepared to compare results. In April 1777 the Continental Army captured a couple of British regulars, Joseph Driver from the 33rd and James Bisset of the 71st Regiments of Foot, at Bonhamtown about seven miles west of Perth Amboy, which at the time was held by the British. A list of twenty-two questions was prepared to ask them, with the opinion of the interviewer added on the accuracy of the answers. The answers to the questions were compared but did not produce sufficient collaborating information, which may have been due to the fault of the interviews.[59] This method does not appear to have been used again and future deserters and prisoners were instead given an individual general interrogation.

Five

QUAKER CHICANERY

Immediately after the Battle of Princeton, Washington believed that the British would counterattack in an act of revenge. They had to be furious over the defeats of the Hessians at Trenton in December 1776 and of the British regulars at Princeton in January 1777. Washington's army was in pitiful condition, having been chased across New Jersey, fighting two major battles, and marching from Trenton to the area of Morristown. He did not want another battle. He needed to regroup and heal the wounded.

He was on the alert for whatever the British would attempt. He ordered General Putnam to have "as many spies out as you will see proper, a number of horsemen, in the dress of the country, must be constantly kept going." They were to be doing reconnaissance but in disguise. In order to make Putnam's force seem more formidable and dissuade the British from attacking, Washington told Putnam, "You will give out your strength to be twice as great as it is."[1]

Washington in February 1777 wrote to General Putnam that

with "a retrospective view of the enemy's conduct, and comparing one piece of information with another, I am led to think, that Philadelphia must be their object." He explained what led him to this conclusion. The enemy in "New York [have] been building floats for a bridge, as is supposed, over the Delaware. Your spies therefore should be attentive, to see whether any such are brought to [Perth] Amboy." The city of Perth Amboy was under British control at the time. He also advised, "You should keep a good look out from S[outh] Amboy, as it is not unlikely, but that the reinforcement last from New York, may land there, and march from thence across." As soon as a march across New Jersey was determined to be the method of taking the British army to Philadelphia, he wanted Putnam to secure the boats in the Delaware to the Pennsylvania side to keep them from falling into British hands.[2]

Washington was cognizant that Howe wanted to capture Philadelphia and put an end to the rebellion. Capturing the enemy's capital in this period was the goal in European warfare to defeat the enemy. After the defeats at Trenton and Princeton in December 1776 and January 1777, it would be a way for Howe to redeem his reputation in the eyes of the British ministers in London.

In the April of 1777 Washington instructed General Thomas Mifflin to set up a spy system in Philadelphia. He knew that the British were making preparations to start their campaign. He did not know if they were going overland, by water, or both. He told Mifflin that "Where-ever their army lies, it will be of the greatest advantage to us, to have spies among them, on whom we may depend for intelligence; I would therefore, have you look out for proper persons for this purpose, who are to remain among them under the mask of friendship." He instructed him to have spies in Bucks County, Philadelphia, and others about Chester.[3] He believed that if the British came up the Delaware they would land near Chester. He acknowledged that Mifflin would assign this job to others and warned him to give them proper instructions. Mifflin turned to Major John Clark Jr., Colonel Elias Boudinot, and Captains Charles Craig and Allen McLane to implement the mission. Washington's instructions specifically included recruiting Quakers as spies "who have never taken an active part, would be least liable to suspicion from either party."[4] Major Clark had handled some of the secret service activities around Trenton for General Greene.[5] Having some experience in secret service operations was most likely why Mifflin assigned the development and execution of the Philadelphia operation to Clark.[6]

Clark, a lawyer from York County, Pennsylvania, was confident that he could get the Quakers, who would not fight due to religious beliefs, to be spies. He gave his opinion to General Greene:

[I]f a prudent active officer was dispatched among the Quakers near the enemy with orders to engage a few farmers as spies on this condition, that they should be excused from all military service and fines for nonattendance or not providing substitutes, it would enable his Excellency to get every information of the enemy's designs etc. and there is not one in ten of those farmers but would be happy to serve America in that situation, permit 'em to carry marketing and give them a few dollars on extraordinary occasions and I'll pawn my life, you succeed.[7]

Washington was not the only one who played a game of deception. In preparation for their move against Philadelphia, the British had fake letters, supposedly from Quakers, fall into the hands of General John Sullivan at Hanover, New Jersey. The letters indicated that the Quakers had been collecting intelligence at their yearly meeting in Spanktown, near Rahway, New Jersey, and were providing that intelligence to the British. The letters were an attempt to discredit the Quakers and make them appear to be collaborating with the British. On August 25, Sullivan sent the documents to Congress along with a letter of his own.[8]

As Washington suspected, General Howe's campaign target in 1777 was Philadelphia, the seat of the Second Continental Congress. If Howe had chosen to travel across New Jersey, he would have left the Continental Army in his rear with the possibility of having his supply route disrupted. He brought his troops to New Jersey hoping to draw Washington into a general action but Washington would not bite. Howe gave up on the plan for a major engagement and chose the safer but longer maneuver by moving his army south by water.

They landed at the Head of Elk in the northern Chesapeake Bay. As the British advanced toward Philadelphia there were several engagements that resulted in British victories pushing back the Americans. The Battle of Brandywine on September 11, 1777, had the most soldiers engaged and lasted the longest of any battle in the war. After the victory the British pushed on to the Battle of the Clouds on the 16th in East Whiteland Township, Chester County, Pennsylvania. As the combatants engaged, a horrendous rain occurred. The Americans with water-soaked cartridges were unable to fire their weapons and so moved off the field. The British artillery and wagons were bogged down in the mud and could not give chase. Four days later was the Paoli Massacre. British Major General Charles Grey led the British forces in a surprise bayonet attack on General Anthony Wayne's encampment near the Paoli Tavern. Because of the lack of musket fire, it earned Grey the nickname of "No Flint Grey."

While the British were advancing on Philadelphia in September 1777, Clark was at Elizabeth Town on September 25 overseeing the operation of spies: John Meeker and the brothers Baker and Captain John Hendricks.[9] Clark quickly returned to Philadelphia to assume his assignment of procuring intelligence there.

Clark recruited Cadwalader Jones, a Quaker farm owner from Uwchlan Township in Chester Country. He was a deserter with an $8 bounty on his head.[10] Removing the bounty was probably the motivation for Jones to become a spy. Another motivation for Quakers, who would not take up arms, to be spies was their mistreatment by the British. Colonel Tench Tilghman reported, "A good deal of Quaker property has shared the fate of the best Whig. This is a kind of proceeding that was not expected from friend Howe."[11]

Jones, the initial member of the Clark Spy Ring, submitted his first known report on the happenings in Philadelphia on October 6, 1777, to Major Clark at Red Lion (now Lionville), Uwchlan Township. Jones stated he acquired his information from Quakers who were in the city at the yearly meeting. The Philadelphia yearly meeting was held from September 29 to October 4, 1777, at the "Great Meetinghouse," which was located at the southwest corner of Second and High (now Market) Streets. They informed him of wagonloads of wounded soldiers brought into the city from the October 4 Battle of Germantown.

He said that a few days earlier a number of wagons went toward Chester to obtain provisions. He also reported that the Hessians might be planning to set up a post at Darby. Clark wrote up Jones's report and had William Dougherty take the report to General Washington at Pennypacker's Mills. Clark advised that Jones was "a person of credit" and said Washington could rely on his information. The letter gave Dougherty a pass per the orders of General Greene that read, "Permit W[illia]m Dougherty to pass all Guards to his Excellency Gen[era]l Washington Express."[12] Clark had other spies working in Philadelphia who also reported on the aftermath of the Battle of Germanton on October 4.

Washington had suggested to General John Armstrong of the Pennsylvania militia "that Newtown Square would be a good general place of rendezvous, from which [General James Potter of the Pennsylvania militia] might send out his detachments, as he should judge proper, and to which they might resort, as often as any plan or event should make it requisite."[13] Clark agreed with Washington's assessment of the practicality of using New-town Square as a base of operations, as he ran his spy ring from the William Lewis home.

On October 23, 1777, Washington acknowledged an October 22 intelligence report from Clark and told him to continue to provide intelligence. Washington, through Robert H. Harrison, one of his aides-de-camp, gave Major Clark $100 on October 23, 1777, to pay his spies and mentioned paying Dunwoody.[14]

On October 27, Clark was at Goshen, Chester County. He informed Washington that at every ferry and road leading into Philadelphia, the British had deployed Loyalist sentinels. They were doing a thorough job and were examining everyone. They were hindering Clark's spies from going into the city and getting intelligence. His spies could "now and then get by," Clark reported, but the locals watched him "as a hawk would [watch] a chicken." Because of all the attention now being given him, it necessitated his often changing lodgings to avoid being captured.[15]

Washington was not the only one who liked a good deception. Clark advised, "I counterfeited the Quaker for once. I wrote a few lines to Sir William [Howe], informing him the rebels had plundered me, and that I was determined to risqué [*sic*] my all in procuring him intelligence; that the bearer would give him my name." Clark said his spy had given Howe the name of "a noted Quaker who I [Clark] knew had assisted" Howe. Clark's "letter was concealed curiously, and the General [Howe] smiled when he saw the pains taken with it; told the bearer, if he would return and inform him of your [Washington's] movements and state of your army he would be generously rewarded."[16]

General Howe gave the spy, believed to be John Fox, a pass to travel about freely. The spy was able to walk the city, where the only soldiers he saw were guards. He saw thirty-five wagons loaded with ammunition at the Pennsylvania State House (now known as Independence Half) yard. He questioned the teamsters and was told they were headed to the lower ferry and there was to be an attack at Fort Mifflin. The enemy was stacking hay in great quantity on the commons or center square (now City Hall Square). Clark asked Washington to join in on the deception, "to make out a state of the army and your intended movements, according to Sir William's desire, or leave it to me, my spy will carry it and take a further view of their camp."[17]

Washington responded, "I . . . think you have fallen upon an exceeding good method of gaining intelligence and that too much secrecy cannot be used, both on account of the safety of your friend and the execution and continuance of your design, which may be of service to us." Washington, who had created false returns of the strength of the Continental Army to deceive the British before, did so again and drew up a bogus memorandum of his intended movements. Clark's spy carried it in to General Howe on his next trip into Philadelphia.[18]

While at White Marsh, Pennsylvania, Washington was involved in a deception at New York City. Major General Philemon Dickinson, commander of the New Jersey Militia, who was at Elizabeth Town, advised Washington that General Howe at Philadelphia had ordered reinforcements from New York to be sent to him.

Dickinson said he could get information to Loyalist Brigadier General Cortlandt Skinner in under twenty-four hours that an attack was intended on New York. He believed this would prevent the reinforcements from being sent.[19] Dickinson on November 2 advised that the British ships were loaded with reinforcements and were at the Watering Place on the northeast corner of Staten Island taking on supplies and preparing to set sail that day.[20]

Washington was pleased with Dickinson's scheme to deceive the British into believing that an attack on New York was imminent. "Your idea of counteracting the intended reinforcements for Mr. Howe's Army by a demonstration of designs upon New York I think an exceeding good one, and am very desirous that you should improve and mature it for immediate execution." He instructed, "A great show of preparatives on your side, boats collected, troops assembled, your expectation of the approach of Generals [Horatio] Gates and [Israel] Putnam intrusted as a secret to persons, who you are sure will divulge and disseminate it in New York; in a word, such measures taken for effectually striking an alarm in that city." He told Dickinson that "it is altogether unnecessary for me minutely to describe to you, I am in great hopes may effect the valuable purpose which you expect."[21]

He then let General Israel Putnam in on the plan, which was "to distract and alarm the enemy and perhaps keep a greater force at New York than they intended[.] Gen[era]l Dickinson will contrive to convey intelligence that they will look upon as authentic, that he is to make a descent upon Staten Island, you upon Long Island and Gen[era]l Gates directly upon New York. If you throw out hints of this kind before people that you think will send in the intelligence, it will serve to corroborate that given by General Dickinson."[22]

The plan did not stop the troops from going to support General Howe in Philadelphia but did cause some consternation in New York. British General Henry Clinton visited Staten Island to inspect their fortifications in anticipation of an attack from New Jersey. The British were also busy upgrading their defenses on Long Island in case the attack would come from Connecticut. An American army presence on Long Island would present a grave problem for the British in New York. With General Putnam pushing his forces south toward Kingsbridge at the northern end of York (now Manhattan) Island, the militia was called out in anticipation of an attack that never came.[23]

Washington decided to do some chicanery in Philadelphia in connection with Dickinson's, Gates's, and Putnam's efforts around New York. He instructed Major Clark to direct a letter to the British camp that would say that General Gates, "having nothing to do to the northward" because of British General Burgoyne's surrender in October, was sending "a very handsome reinforcement of Continental Troops" to Pennsylvania, but:

[W]ith the remainder of them and all the New England and York militia, is to make an immediate descent on New York, the reduction of which is confidently spoke of as it is generally supposed that a large part of Clinton's Troops are detached to the assistance of Gen[era]l Howe, and that Gen[era]l Dickinson is at the same time to attack Staten Island, for which purpose he is assembling great numbers of the [New] Jersey Militia; that the received opinion in our Camp is, that we will immediately attack Philadelphia on the arrival of the troops from the northward, and that I have prevailed upon the legislative body to order out two thirds of the Militia of this State for that purpose; that you heard great talk of the Virginia and Maryland Militia coming up, and in short that the whole Continent seems determined that we use every exertion to put an end to the War this winter; that we mention the forts as being perfectly secure, having sent ample reinforcements to their support.[24]

Washington was running a disinformation campaign. He was feeding the British multiple reports of an attack on New York coming from different sources, each lie confirming the other source's fake intelligence. By convincing the British of an imminent attack on New York, he was trying to keep as much of the British army in New York and away from Philadelphia. His army was still reeling from its series of losses and had not yet reached Valley Forge.

Not everything ran as smooth as it would appear. One of Clark's spy ring was a person who was described as "a delicate, sensible woman." While traveling toward Philadelphia she was stopped by a guard of militia under the command of Colonel

Isaac Warner of the 7th Battalion of Philadelphia militia.[25] She had taken with her a pint of chestnuts. The guard stopped her and accused her of being a smuggler who was planning to sell the chestnuts to the enemy. She told them she was going to give them away to children. A soldier she knew rode with her in her one-horse, two-wheeled carriage as he took her to see Colonel Warner. During the journey he used rude language and offered to permit her to continue her trip into Philadelphia with her chestnuts if she would agree to have sex with him. Clark was incensed over the incident and advised Washington, "Her delicacy would not permit her to tell me, but she told her husband, and 'tis from him I have it."[26] Her being delayed in traveling into Philadelphia could not have happened at a more inopportune time. The British were making preparations for an excursion. Clark reported on more problems he was having with his spies getting through the American lines. On the 3rd, the militia under Colonel Warner's command "behaved so imprudent in [detaining] my spy, Mr. Trumbul[l], yesterday; had not this happened I should have had, early this day, a complete account of the enemy's situation and design."[27]

The effort that Washington put into the Clark Spy Ring paid dividends when it brought him the advance news that the British were preparing to leave the city to go on a major expedition. The success of the Clark Spy Ring would later give impetus to restarting the Mercereau Spy Ring and starting the Culper Spy Ring in 1778. The news about the British expedition was confirmed by the Darraghs, a family of spies living on South Second Street in Philadelphia. Captain Charles Craig of the 4th Continental Dragoons when stationed at Frankford near Philadelphia was their case agent, while at other times it was their oldest son, Lieutenant Charles Darragh of the 2nd Pennsylvania Regiment of the Continental Line.[28]

On December 3, Clark reported to Washington that "the enemy are in motion." As a spy was leaving the city, biscuits were being served to the soldiers. The gossip in the city among both the people and the soldiers was that the British army was going to make a move. "Should the enemy move," Clark reported, "it will be sudden and rapid." General William Howe led 10,000 British soldiers just before midnight on December 4 on an expedition in an attempt to crush the Continental Army. Because Washington's intelligence assets had provided him with forewarning, he was prepared. In what is known as the Battle of White Marsh, which lasted from December 5 to 8, there was a series of skirmishes but the British were unable to engage in a major conflict. After three frustrating days Howe withdrew his army to Philadelphia and Washington was able to take his army to Valley Forge to await the spring campaign.

Another of Clark's operatives was stopped and the provisions the spy was using as a cover were confiscated. Washington, in order to give more force to Clark's passes and stop his complaining, included a statement in the General Orders of December 18. The first item read, "Persons having any passes from Major John Clarke [sic] are to pass all guards."[29] They were not to be delayed.

Washington understood the necessity of spies using the cover of a smuggler to protect themselves and its importance in getting intelligence. Since hard currency was always in short supply, smuggling was a way to allow the spies to reward themselves for their extremely dangerous work. Smugglers bringing provisions into Philadelphia would be a welcome sight and they were allowed to sell their merchandise at the city's markets. The city markets were a great place to discover what the army and navy were buying for their men, information that Washington needed. It was also a good place to hear the local gossip. Any foodstuffs the smugglers brought would reduce the strain on the British army trying to supply both the soldiers and the civilian population. Being a smuggler was a much safer occupation than being a spy. A smuggler who ran afoul of the law would be fined. A person caught as a spy would find themselves in jail or swinging from the gallows.

Washington informed General James Potter on December 21 that "Major Clark has wrote [sic] to me several times about some provision that a Mr. Trumbull was sending into Philadelphia by his permission as a cover to procure intelligence. This provision was seized by Colo[nel] Ranking and has been since detained by him. I desire you will give orders to have it delivered, for unless we now and then make use of such means to get admittance into the city we cannot expect to obtain intelligence."[30]

Washington sometimes had the correct intelligence but was not able to muster the forces to provide an appropriate response. The Continental Army on December 19, 1777, marched into winter quarters at Valley Forge. This would be home for the next several months until spring would usher in a new season of campaigning. The British had occupied the city of Philadelphia and had an easier time waiting for spring. Both, however, were suffering shortages of food. Clark advised that his intelligence sources were telling him, "A large body of the enemy are on their march to Darby, where they must have arrived by this time, the number uncertain but you may rely are formidable; they certainly mean to forage."[31]

Washington attempted to respond to the British raiding party scouring the countryside for food. The officers were unable to assemble a detachment to stop the British. Brigadier General James Varnum of Rhode Island explained the lack of response by the men and told Washington of his troop's condition:

> Three days successively, we have been destitute of bread. Two days we have been intirely [*sic*] without meat. It is not to be had from the commissaries. Whenever we procure beef, it is such a vile quality, as to render it a poor succeedanium for food. The men must be supplied or they can not be commanded . . . the complaints are two [*sic*] ongoing to pass unnoticed. It is with pain that I mention this distress. I know it will make your Excellency unhappy. But if you expect the exertions of virtuous principals [*sic*] while your troops are deprived of the essential necessities of life, your disappointment will be great.[32]

Washington was well aware of necessity of keeping the espionage operations known to the fewest people possible, going back to the opening days of his being commander in chief when he refused to identify who was receiving the monies for secret service activities in his account book. At the end of December, Martin Nicholls, a soldier assigned to Major Clark, deserted. How much of the operation he knew is uncertain but whatever little he knew could bring a handsome reward from British headquarters. He would have known of Clark's activities and most likely some of the American spies who visited him.

Clark assumed "he is lurking about camp in hopes of getting over [the] Schuylkill [River] and making his escape to Germantown, and from thence to Philadelphia, where his father lives." Clark asked Washington to include a notice about Martin Nicholls in a general order in the hope of preventing his getting through the lines. The notice Clark wanted sent read:

> Twenty shillings reward, exclusive of what allowed for taking deserters. Deserted from Major John Clark's quarters at Newtown Square, on the 27th instant, Martin Nicholls, a soldier, about 5 feet 2 inches high, 18 years of age, a barber by trade, wears his hair tied, is of a yellowish complexion, and much pitted with the smallpox; had on and took with him an old felt hat cocked, a blue cloth coat with metal buttons, almost new, a whiteish colored, round waistcoat, buckskin breeches, white yarn stockings, a pair of half worn shoes with yellow buckles, a good blanket coat with-out buttons, two good white linen shirts, an old knapsack with some old shirts, &c. He sometime ago waited on General Minor, and one winter on [Lieutenant] Col[onel] Clement Biddle [commissary general of forage]. 'Tis probable he may endeavor to go to Philadelphia, as his father lives there. All officers and soldiers are requested to apprehend him, and give notice to [John] Clark, Aid [sic] de Camp to Major General Greene.[33]

It is unknown what happened to Martin Nicholls.

Both armies were now settled into winter quarters. There would be little offensive activity until spring. Now was a time to heal their wounds. Clark's health was failing and he requested and received permission to go on leave.

While the Clark Spy Ring was operating, Washington assigned Captain Allen McLane and his company to operate as an independent reconnoitering force. On October 29, he gave McLane a list of intelligence he wanted him to obtain. The length and breadth of the items on the list show the depth of information Washington wanted from his intelligence networks.

1st   What number of troops supposed to be in Gen[era]l Howe's Army, and how disposed of?

2d   What works thrown up in and about the city, & what cannon in them?

3d   Have any detachments been made over to [New] Jersey, & for what purpose?

4th   How many men have they sent over there, & how many pieces of cannon?

5th   What kind of cannon, whether field pieces or larger cannon?

6th   What preparations are they making on the water, are they fitting out Ships, Gallies [*sic*], fire rafts, or floating batteries?

7th   Do they think they can stay in Philadelphia, if their shipping cannot pass the forts?

8th   Are they resolved to make any farther attempts on both the forts or either of them, and in what way, whether by storm or siege?

9th   Can you discover whether they will attempt anything against the forts and where? Observe carefully the preparations making on the river, and along the wharves, it is of great importance to know the time or near it.

10th   Is there any talk of leaving Philad[elphi]a and by what route, observe carefully what they are doing with their waggons, whether their baggage is packed up, and what directions their waggons receive?

11th Are the Tories, and friends of the British Army, under much apprehensions of their leaving town, and what preparations are they making to remove themselves, or their effects?

12th For what purpose is it understood, the bridge is thrown over the middle ferry, and what force is kept on the west side of the Schuylkill?

13th Has the bridge been injured by the late storm, or is it passable?

14th Where are the Grenadiers, Light Infantry, and Rangers, and are they making any preparations to move?

15th What number of men are sent over [by the British] to Carpenters, and Province Islands [in the Delaware River opposite the fort on Mud Island now known as Fort Mercer], and how often are they relieved?

16th In what condition are those banks since the late rain—Can waggons and carriages pass, so as to transport provisions and stores from the ships to the town.

17th In what condition are the troops for provisions, and in what articles is there the greatest scarcity?

18th How are the inhabitants situated for provisions?

19th What impression has the news of Gen[era]l Burgoyne's surrender made on the British Army?

20th Is there any conversation in the British Army, or among the Inhabitants, of Gen[era]l Howe's coming out to meet Gen[era]l Washington?

21st   What is the British Army now employed about? Note carefully the prices of every thing.

22d   Does continental money rise or fall in value, in the town?

23d   Can you learn whether there are any preparations making or any intentions to go up the Delaware, to burn the frigates & vessels there?

24th   Find out what duty the Soldiers do, and whether they are contented, how many nights in the week, are they in bed?

25th   Enquire particularly into the treatment of the prisoners, in the new gaol [jail], so that if necessary you make oath of it!

26th   Do they compel any to enlist by starving or otherwise ill treating them?

27th   Find out how far the redoubts between Delaware and Sch[u]ylkill are apart, and whether there are lines, or abattis between the redoubts.[34]

In addition to his reconnaissance mission, McLane was instructed to "send out patrols and stop the intercourse between the city and the country." He was also told to stop people from taking provisions into the city.[35] McLane requested additional troops to accomplish the tasks he was given. Timothy Pickering sent him sixty soldiers from Conway's, Maxwell's, and the Maryland brigades. They marched to Germantown where McLane took command. Pickering refreshed McLane's memory that the general's orders were that nobody was to carry provisions into the city, and also that no one from the city was to come into the country unless they planned to stay or were able to give material intelligence.[36]

One shipment of confiscated items that McLane sent to the Commissary Department totaled 115 bushels of potatoes and 600 heads of cabbage.[37] He and his men were so successful that they were given the nickname the "market stoppers." McLane wrote to Washington and enclosed an unsigned report from one of his regular spies in the city.[38]

General Nathanael Greene writing from Burlington, New Jersey, on November 28 advised that he received information from Tench Francis Jr., a Philadelphia merchant and lawyer, who had come over to Gloucester, New Jersey.[39] He said the rumor among the British officers was that General Howe had plans for an immediate attack upon the American forces unless the weather was bad.[40] The Clark Spy Ring had advised that the British were coming in force. Captain Charles Craig of the 4th Continental Dragoons, stationed at Frankford, Pennsylvania, reported to Washington on the same day. He had some inaccurate intelligence that he had received that day from inside Philadelphia. It was that the British had made a move across the Schuylkill River and were going to Wilmington. It was uncorroborated. But the information indicated that the British were under marching orders, which was true—the British knew they could not conceal this.[41] It was part of an orchestrated deception by the British to hide their destination.

Based on the intelligence Washington was receiving, he knew he needed more information. Besides operating spies in the city, McLane stopped and interrogated those persons passing into and out of Philadelphia. Washington turned to McLane on the 28th to provide some answers as to what the real British movements were. Washington told him that he was expecting an attack from the British before General Greene could return from New Jersey. He told McLane, who had taken post at Rising

Sun Tavern, I "depend upon your keeping a very good look out upon their line, and gaining every intelligence." McLane immediately responded that he had received some intelligence from a trusted old friend in Philadelphia.[42] The friend informed him, "Last night they [the British] gave out that a body [of soldiers] cross[ed the] Schu[y]lkill and to cover the deception they kept, their wagons and artillery moving through the city all night."[43] This confirmed to Washington that the British were running a deception and he needed to be prepared. British Captain Archibald Robertson of the 47th Regiment of Foot wrote in his journal for November 27, "From this day by the preparations that were made it was easily seen that a move was intended accordingly."[44]

McLane had sent in intelligence, which Washington acknowledged through Richard Kidder Meade, an aide-de-camp, on December 4.[45] The intelligence indicated that the British were on the move. It was part of a series of reports from several espionage activities that Washington had received. The attack did happen and resulted in the Battle of White Marsh, which was a series of skirmishes from December 5 through 8, 1778. British General William Howe wanted to engage the Continental Army in a major battle and crush it before the onset of winter. It would reduce the risk of attacks from the Continental Army and make their occupation of Philadelphia easier. Using the intelligence he received, Washington was prepared for the engagement and the 10,000 enemy soldiers. The British could only obtain skirmishes and after three days of frustration they retreated to Philadelphia for the winter.

The season of campaigning was over. The healing could begin. The British would enjoy the comforts and the ladies of America's largest city. The Continental Army marched into

Valley Forge on December 19, 1777. It was close enough to the British to keep their raiding and foraging parties out of the interior of Pennsylvania, yet far enough away to prevent the threat of British surprise attacks. They would have to build shelters for the winter, which were not completed till February. The soldiers were poorly clothed and undernourished. The army was ravaged by disease and illness. Congress sent a committee to Valley Forge to report on the conditions there. The twenty-six-year-old Gouverneur Morris, a New York attorney and politician, on February 1, 1778, described the status of the army at Valley Forge as the "skeleton of an army presents itself to our eyes in a naked, starving condition, out of health, out of spirits."[46] Thousands died before conditions improved.

Six

⌇

WE DANCED THE MINUET

"The necessity of procuring good Intelligence is apparent."

GEORGE WASHINGTON, 1777[1]

T he winter of 1777–1778 was spent with the British army in the warm houses of Philadelphia and the Continental Army in the cold huts of Valley Forge. With the two armies stationary until spring, there was little need for spies. For the Continental Army there were reconnaissance patrols to intercept goods smuggled into Philadelphia and to attack foraging parties from the city.

The spring of 1778 brought about changes in the playing field. The scales of power had shifted. General Howe was re-called to England and replaced by forty-eight-year-old General Henry Clinton.[2] The French entered the war on the American side by signing a Treaty of Alliance and a Treaty of Amity and Commerce, but French army would not arrive in North America until July 10, 1780, when Charles Louis d'Arsac, Chevalier de Ternay, brought 6,000 men to Newport, Rhode Island. The residents were so happy to see them, they illuminated the town on their arrival. However, it would be a long time before they would leave Newport.

The French navy became an immediate threat to the valuable British Caribbean sugar islands. The loss of the islands and slaves would be a financial blow to the British economy and particularly for the absentee plantation landowners in England.

To protect the islands, the British needed to deploy more soldiers there, so they reassigned troops from North America to protect their Caribbean possessions. These troops became available by evacuating Philadelphia and consolidating most of the North American British army south of Canada in the New York City area. To effect the evacuation, some assets, heavy baggage, cannons, stores, and invalid soldiers went by ship down the Delaware and up the New Jersey coast to New York. Because of a lack of transport ships, the remainder of the army and the civilians would march across New Jersey to New York.

Washington's intelligence was telling him the British were going to evacuate Philadelphia by land across New Jersey, which was the expected move. Washington said that a strong argument for it was based on Philemon Dickinson reporting on May 27 from Trenton on the intelligence he had just received from Perth Amboy of the preparation of flat bottom boats in Princess Bay at the southeast end of Staten Island.[3] It foretold the British moving large amounts of men and supplies from the New Jersey coast to the safety of New York. Washington told him that "our intelligence is too various to reduce their plan to an absolute certainty." One reason for the ambiguity was that the British were busy improving a redoubt in Philadelphia, thus indicating they were going to stay.[4] If they were preparing to leave, why would they be strengthening their defenses?

Lieutenant Colonel John Laurens, aide-de-camp to General Washington, sent instructions to Captain Allen McLane that "no pains should be spared to discover, if possible, the precise movement when the event is to take place and the rout[e]." They needed to know if the British forces were going to New Jersey or if they were going to march down to Chester to embark there to avoid the Cheveux de Frise in the Delaware River. Washington was concerned that the British were employing a deception. He also asked McLane to ascertain if "they may cover their real march by a pretended attempt on this army."[5]

A few days later James McHenry, secretary to General Washington, cautioned McLane, "No doubt you have properly considered how far you may trust to the intelligence of your spies, and by comparing the different accounts found out the most faithful."[6] It certainly reads like he was paraphrasing Washington about comparing spy reports to ensure that he was not deceived. McLane was now sending his reports addressed to McHenry at headquarters. He was reporting information on the British forces and the situation in the city.[7] McLane reported, "All the rum in the city was seized for the troops."[8]

On June 1 Captain McLane, who commanded a scouting party upon the enemy's lines, had been to Kensington and from there he had a full view of the harbor. He reported that very few ships remained in the city and they were mostly armed vessels.[9]

The British were giving mixed signals to keep Washington guessing as to what they were doing. They did attack three locations on June 3, at Jenk's Mill near Newtown, Chestnut Hill, and Newtown. They also attacked at Chestnut Hill on the 6th.[10]

During the Revolution the British were always short on transport ships. At this time the situation was no different. Since there were not enough transport ships, the rest of the army, the civilian population, and their baggage would have to walk or be carted across New Jersey to Sandy Hook. From there they were to be loaded onto boats and barges that were at Princess Bay for the last step of the journey to New York City. Because of a shortage of work animals, some people had to pull the carts loaded with their possessions and the elderly.

McLane's company came across a British patrol during the British evacuation of the city and captured thirty-two soldiers.[11] McLane was the first to report from within Philadelphia on June 18, 1778, to Washington that the British had evacuated the city.[12] The next day Washington ordered General Benedict Arnold to take command of Philadelphia.

The British crossed over the Delaware into New Jersey at Gloucester Point.[13] Clinton feared the Americans would attack his army as it passed through Mount Holly, New Jersey. The town of Mount Holly sat in a bowl with a high ridge to the north overlooking the town and the Rancocas Creek. The bridges that the British evacuation train would use to cross the creek were in the bottom of the bowl. It was the perfect spot for an ambush, where the Americans could cause the highest number of British and Hessian casualties. The Americans could rain fire onto Clinton's forces as they crossed. It would have been Clinton's choice for an attack had the situation been reversed. Washington shadowed Clinton across New Jersey, but to Clinton's utter amazement there was no attack at Mount Holly.

The British exodus plodded across the state with its long baggage train. An American council of war was held on June 24, 1778, at Hopewell Township, New Jersey. The enemy was moving across the state with its forces split between the Allentown and Bordentown Roads. Washington reminded the generals that the march, which was now in its seventh day, had progressed less than forty miles. Maryland-born, but Trenton resident, thirty-nine-year-old General Philemon Dickinson of the New Jersey Militia had been putting obstructions in their way, by breaking down bridges and felling trees.[14] These actions however "were insufficient to produce so great delay" and the British were scarcely hindered by the American actions. The council decided against bringing on a general action, but it did approve detaching 1,500 men to harass the left flank and rear of the British column.[15]

Washington kept his distance, shadowing the enemy looking for a good spot to engage them in battle. With the two armies on the march, spies were unable to operate, but enough reconnaissance was accomplished to keep Washington informed on the enemy's slow progress. As the British were getting close to the end of their journey through New Jersey, Washington decided he had to attack or lose the opportunity. On June 28, a day of brutal sweltering heat (reported as 96 degrees in the shade), Washington decided to attack the British at Monmouth Court House (present-day Freehold). During the battle many soldiers on both sides succumbed to heat stroke. Depending on one's interpretation, it was either a draw, as the British were able to slip away, or an American victory, as they controlled the field when the fighting ended for the day.

It was the first battle for the Continental Army after coming out of winter quarters at Valley Forge. They had entered camp lacking in most military skills. During their time at Valley Forge they tirelessly drilled under Baron Friedrich Wilhelm von Steuben with his Italian greyhound, Azor, nearby.[16] In the Battle of Monmouth the American army for the first time was able to hold their ground against a larger British force.[17] The British goal was to continue their march to New York, and under the cover of darkness they slipped away. They continued their march to Sandy Hook, leaving the Americans in command of most of New Jersey.

The British were in possession of some outposts in New Jersey and Long, Staten, and York (Manhattan) Islands. The Americans controlled most of New Jersey, most of New York north of York Island, and Connecticut. The bulk of the American forces would be encamped in northern New Jersey and the area of West Point. The actual front lines were fluid and would move depending on military expeditions. The two armies were now in relatively static positions so the use of spies on both sides returned. Spies need a fixed location to which they can return if their intelligence is to be timely.

The main front-door operation for the American secret services ran through Elizabeth Town. Both shores at this time were salt marsh with high grass making it easy for people to pass between them undetected. The distance between Elizabeth Town and Staten Island is about 600 feet. Remnants of the Mercereau Spy Ring and most other spies working for Elias Dayton crossed here.[18]

Dayton was born in and had grown up in Elizabeth, giving him local knowledge of the area and its people. It appears that he became the case agent handling the Mercereau ring in 1777. Asher Fitz Randolph, a member of the ring, continued to perform services for John Mercereau until at least February 1780 and had managed to go into and out of New York City at least eight times in 1778.[19] After Lafayette's return from France in 1780, John Mercereau coordinated the intelligence gathering for Lafayette. Marie-Joseph Paul Yves Roch Gilbert du Motier, Marquis de Lafayette, was a French aristocrat who was born September 6, 1757, in Chavaniac-Lafayette, France. His father was killed while fighting the British in the Seven Years' War (1756–1763). His mother and grandfather died when he was thirteen, leaving him a wealthy orphan. After studying in the Collège du Plessis in Paris, France, Lafayette joined the French army in 1771. Inspired by stories of the colonists' struggles against British oppression, Lafayette sailed to the United States in 1777 to join the uprising. Because of his French connections, passion, and willingness to serve for free, he was appointed a major general in the Continental Army.

Abraham Bancker began working in the ring on Staten Island in 1776. In 1780 with the arrival of Lafayette and John Mercereau's new assignment, he was relocated to New York City. There he became a clerk in a merchant's business. He was familiar with the city, as his father had a house on Wall Street and he had attended King's College (now Columbia University) but was unable to complete his studies because of the war. Bancker used the code name "Amicus Republicae" in some of his reports.

Some American spies left from Newark or the area around Hackensack or Totowa and crossed the North (Hudson) River and went to New York City pretending to be smugglers. Spies and smugglers would cross over from Monmouth County to Staten Island, the British outpost on Sandy Hook, or the British ship at anchor in Princess Bay on the southeast coast of Staten Island.

The British also recognized the ease of running an intelligence-gathering operation through Elizabeth Town. Mrs. Jane Emott Chandler of Elizabeth Town was the wife of Thomas Bradbury Chandler, a prominent Loyalist Anglican clergyman and religious author.[20] He was the rector at Saint

John's Church in Elizabeth Town, with a doctor of divinity. He fled to England in 1775.[21] She became an agent on station and coordinated information with British spies and soldiers on parole as they went back to Staten Island. No written report from her has been found, but she passed intelligence to her visitors. Perth Amboy–native and Loyalist Brigadier General Cortlandt Skinner ran the British intelligence-gathering operation on Staten Island for the duration of the war.[22] The Chandlers would most certainly have been well-known to Cortlandt Skinner, the son of William Skinner, the Anglican clergyman at St. Peter's Church in Perth Amboy.[23] It is highly likely that she was one of Skinner's agents. Another of Skinner's agents was his wife, Elizabeth Skinner, who initially sent letters to her husband through Mrs. Elizabeth Derbage, who carried the messages to General Skinner.[24] She was arrested in May 1776 by Colonel Benjamin Tupper for taking hams to a British warship. Both Mrs. Derbage and Mrs. Skinner were sent to the interior of the state to keep them from communicating with Staten Island.[25]

Prior to February 16, 1778, New Jersey governor William Livingston had permitted Mrs. Chandler to go into and return from New York because her son was reported to be at the point of death.[26] General Maxwell in a letter to Governor Livingston on April 26, 1779, had the following to say about Mrs. Chandler:

> In the way of giving intelligence to the enemy, I think her the first in the place. There is not a Tory that passes in or out of New York or any other way, that is of consequence but what waits on Mrs. Chandler, and mostly all the British officers going in and out on Parole, or Exchange, waits [sic] on her—in short she governs the whole of the Tories and many of the Whigs. I think she would

be much better in New York, and to take her baggage with her that she might have nothing to come back for.

The British had another mole living in New Jersey. Abiah Parke lived at Squan, New Jersey, in 1779.[27] He wrote on November 24, 1779, to Christopher Sower from Squan, "My friend: In pursuence [*sic*] of your recommendation I have landed Messers. Roberts, Lewis, and Garly and conducted them through the country within 20 miles of Trentown [Trenton, New Jersey]." Garly is really Patrick Garvey and Lewis is Lewis (or Louis) Lewis. Parke said he made acquaintance with a post rider for Congress, a young man who was a Loyalist and who only took the job to keep from being conscripted into military service. "From him I can procure any intelligence from the Rebel Army and expect to intercept his mail." He also mentions that he can get information from the Salt Works and signs the letter "Friend Abiah Parke."[28] Lewis Lewis had ventured from Trenton to Morristown and returned.[29]

Patrick Garvey reminded Major John André on November 8, 1779, that he had been sent to New York by a Dr. Plunkett with information. He now wanted further instructions from British headquarters. Was he to arrange for the burning of Coxestown when the supplies were collected? Was he to bring in information from that area or from Philadelphia? He was happy to do either but wanted to return to Squan with the boat when it was ready.[30] Unfortunately I was unable to find his instructions or any other information about him.

Following the success of the Clark Spy Ring in Philadelphia in the fall of 1777, the Culper Spy Ring was started in 1778 after the return of the British army from Philadelphia to New York in June of that year. It was a backdoor operation to New York City, requiring an operative in the city who would send messages by courier to Setauket, Long Island. The messages would be picked up by whaleboats coming from Connecticut and then taken by express to Washington in New Jersey. The problems with the operation were that it did not allow for depositions from the resident New York City spy and the very long travel time and multiple couriers required for information to reach Washington. It was a much slower maneuver than the front-door procedure operating out of Elizabeth Town. It also required the use of codes and invisible ink to keep its messages secret. Any liquid that dries to a clear color and is slightly acidic, such as grapefruit, lemon, or lime juice, will work. Vinegar, milk, and urine will work as well. These substances weaken the fibers of the paper. When the paper is placed near heat, the weakened fibers turn brown and the message becomes visible.

The Culper Spy Ring used sympathetic ink. Washington also offered it to Elias Boudinot for use by his spies in New York. He instructed him, "A letter upon trivial matters of business, written in common Ink, may be fitted with important intelligence which cannot be discovered without the counter part."[31] The sympathetic ink method was a two-part process. The message is written with the first chemical, which dries and becomes invisible. The application of heat will not make it visible. The application of a second liquid is necessary. This second liquid causes a chemical reaction between the two substances, which makes the writing visible. Although some believe that the sympathetic ink with its reagent to make it visible was new in the American Revolution, the oldest known printed description of sympathetic ink and reagent is from 1653, 120 years before the Revolution.[32]

Various formulas for sympathetic ink were published. One

method was to write with gall water, which was made by infus-
ing oak galls in water for a short time. If soaked for too long
the writing does not become invisible and can be seen. To bring
the message to light "you must dissolve some coppress [copperas,
or ferrous sulfate] in fair water [clear and pure water] and with
a fine caliber pencil [paintbrush] first dipt [dipped] in the coppress water, you must art[ful]ly moist[en] the inter lining of
your letter and thereby, you shall make it sufficiently legible."[33]
Another method was mixing "a little common ink with so much
water that little or nothing of the blackness appear[s] in it; with
this write your secret intentions upon clean paper. When it is
thoroughly dryed; write an ordinary epistle with another ink,
(made of gunpowder beat and mix[ed] with rain water) upon
the very letter you scribed before. The last ink will wash off with
a sponge dipt [dipped] in water boiled with [oak] galls which
will also blacken the first." Falconer, a seventeenth-century author,
wrote that the second liquid could also be the juice of unripe
white grapes, which would make the secret writing appear.[34]

At the time of the American Revolution there were three
formulas in use for sympathetic ink. The ink was made by a solution of either bismuth, gallotannic acid, or lead. The bismuth
solution was the acetate developed by ammonia water. The gallotannic acid was produced by soaking powdered nutgalls in
water and developed by an iron or ferrous sulfate solution, also
known as copperas ($FeSO_4$). By the application of ferrous sulfate as the counteragent over the area written with the diluted
gallotannic acid, the chemical reaction of the ferrous sulfate is
changed to ferrous gallotannate and makes the writing visible.
The lead ink, which was lead acetate, and also known as sugar
of lead, was developed by hydrogen sulfide. The chemical reaction changes the lead acetate to black lead sulfide (PbS).

The liquid supplied to Washington by James Jay was gallo-tannic acid.[35] Washington cautioned Tallmadge, the case agent for the Culper Spy Ring, that New York's royal governor William Tryon "has a preparation of the same kind, or something similar to it which may lead to a detection if it is ever known that a matter of this sort has passed from me."[36] William Tryon was born in Surrey, England, in 1729 and served as governor of the Province of North Carolina (1765–1771) and the Province of New York (1771–1780). When the British army and navy arrived in New York in the summer of 1776, they were placed under martial law. Tryon retained his nominal title as governor, but with little power. In early 1777, Tryon was given the rank of major-general of the provincials. A provincial soldier was armed, clothed, fed, and paid under the same discipline as a British soldier, but was only liable for service in North America. A provincial soldier served for the duration of the war.

The spies were only supplied with the writing agent and not the counterpart, which was held by their case agent. Many of the communications were written with the secret writing between the lines of an ordinary letter. In addition, the Culper ring sent some of their messages on a blank sheet of paper tucked in a ream or half ream of blank sheets.

The use of ciphers was not new, as Dr. Benjamin Church Jr.'s cipher was discovered in 1775. The Pig Pen Cipher was extremely popular and was used by the Americans, French, British, and Hessians.[37] It is a substitution cipher, which exchanges letters for symbols which are fragments of a grid. Both the sender and the receiver must agree on the placement of the letters in the grid. In the eighteenth century, people thought it looked like a pigpen and in modern times it looks like a board for tic-tac-toe. Letters in a segment of the grid are identified by the number of dots in the segment. Each letter in the message is replaced by a segment with the corresponding dots.

British Major John André was closing in on the Culpers when he was executed as a spy at noon on October 2, 1780. André had discovered the names and residences of some in the ring. A map of Setauket, Long Island, was developed and marked with key points of interest in the town. André apparently kept his findings to himself and with his execution as a spy, the intelligence was lost.

Despite what most historians claim about how operationally important the Culper Spy Ring was to the American Revolution, Washington disagreed with its effectiveness. Benjamin Tallmadge, the case agent for Samuel Culper's operation, had submitted a bill for expenditures owed to Samuel Culper. Samuel Culper Sr. was the code name for Abraham Woodhull, of Setauket. Washington responded on September 11, 1783:

I have no doubt, because I suppose S: [Samuel] C: [Culper] to be an honest Man, that the monies charged in his acc[oun]t have been expended, and therefore should be paid; but the services which were rendered by him (however well meant) was by no means adequate to these expenditures. My complaints on this head [topic], before I knew the amount of his charges, you may remember were frequent; and but for the request of Count de Rochambeau, who told me that he had put money into your hands, and would continue to furnish you with more for the purpose of obtaining intelligence through this Channel, I should have discontinued the Services of S. C.

[Samuel Culper] long before a cessation of hostilities took place, because his communications were never frequent, and always tedious in getting to hand.[38]

Washington did not have the manpower to fight a war with the British as well as secure the borders between New Jersey and New York to stop the immense amount of smuggling carried on by the public to get hard currency. As the Continental currency devalued, the temptation to engage in illicit activities grew. Abraham Woodhull, as Samuel Culper Sr., on November 23, 1778, reported, "I will note to you that much provision is brought to town (New York City) from the Jerseys privately; flour, beef, &c."[39] An intelligence report from Lewis J. Costigan, using the pseudonym "Z," to George Washington on December 7, 1778, advised as to the extent of illegal trade by the citizens of the Shrewsbury, Monmouth County, New Jersey area. The city was supplied with "not less than one thousand sheep, five hundred hogs, and eight hundred quarters or up-wards of good beef, a large parcel of cheese besides poultry."[40] This all took place despite, or even possibly with, the cooperation of Major Richard Howell of the 2nd New Jersey Regiment and a small patrol who were located at Black Point (now known as Rumson, New Jersey) just below Sandy Hook.[41] The patrol was posted there from August to October of 1778 to observe the British fleet.[42] Washington was well aware that where you find smugglers you find spies, but he could not tell how many of the smugglers were British spies. To reduce the number of British spies, he had to reduce the number of smugglers. Howell and his men were there for that purpose.

Washington was concerned about the conduct of Major Howell and his men. He wrote to Lord Stirling (General William Alexander) on October 21 that "some instances of commerce between the inhabitants and the enemy . . . may have been tolerated." Washington further instructed Stirling to investigate. He needed Stirling to find out if the men were lackadaisical in accomplishing their assignment, were taking bribes to let the contraband pass, were doing the smuggling, or were spies using smuggling as a cover. He told him, "If you discover any improper convivance [*sic*] on the part of the officers at Shrewsbury, you will take proper measures not only to prevent it in the future, but to punish it in the past."[43] Stirling was busy monitoring the number and kind of British ships inside Sandy Hook. He reported that the information he received from Major Howell did not match the number of ships reported by others at Perth Amboy who counted them and reported to him daily. He must have been reminded by Washington in the past to compare intelligence. He was quick to point out before Washington could remind him that he employed an officer of the horse as a check.[44]

The problem of smuggling and spies from New Jersey was one that never went away. General Samuel H. Parsons, on December 13, 1779, was given the job of gathering intelligence and protecting the populace between Newark and Perth Amboy. Washington instructed him, "The detestable and pernicious traffic carried on with the enemy will demand your peculiar vigilance and attention. I entreat you to pursue the most decisive measures to put a stop to it. No flags are to be sent or persons suffered to go into the enemy without a permit from The governor of the state or from head quarters."[45]

Robert Townsend writing as Samuel Culper Jr., on December 27, 1779, reported that "the Markets [in New York City] are well supply'd with fresh provisions of every kind, and will continue so while there is any cattle in Connecticut and New Jersey. A considerable number of cattle and other provisions is daily brought over from Connecticut to the East end of Long Island, and from thence conveyed to New York; and there has ever been regular supplies from [the Tory strongholds of] Shrewsbury, Middletown, and every other part of East [New] Jersey. It is almost needless to mention Kings Bridge, for it has been, and ever will be practice to get supplies that way."[46] This situation resulted in lots of contact and lots of opportunity to pass along intelligence of military importance.

While Washington was at Valley Forge after the defeat at Brandywine, the British capture of Philadelphia, and the debacle at Germantown, he still had to concern himself with espionage activities in New Jersey and New York. On the evening of January 19, 1778, just a month after the march into Valley Forge, he received a letter from Colonel Elias Dayton of the 3rd New Jersey Regiment concerning some of his spies who had been traveling from New Jersey to British-occupied Staten Island.

In the summer of 1777 Washington instructed Dayton to send spies to Staten Island.[47] Dayton had arranged for John and Baker Hendricks, and John Meeker, to go to Staten Island as spies. Baker Hendricks and Morris Hatfield had been jailed for passing counterfeit money and were recruited from the jail to become spies. They had returned from their spy mission to Staten Island by July 7. On July 26, Washington wanted Dayton's spies to go back again: "I wish you to take every possible pains in your power, by sending trusty persons to Staten Island, to obtain intelligence of the enemy's situation and numbers, What kind of troops they are [and how many] and what guards they have, their strength and where posted." He cautioned him: "General view of the whole [matter] and possessing all the circumstances, may know how to regulate [Stirling] conduct in the affair. [I need not urge] The necessity of [your] procuring good [the best] intelligence, [because the reason] is apparent and need not be further urged. All that remains for me to add is, that you keep the whole matter as secret as possible. For upon secrecy, success depends in most enterprises of the kind, and for want of it, they are generally defeated, however well planned and promising a favorable issue [or a defeat will probably depend]."[48] On August 14, Washington repeated his request to Dayton, who at this time was also responsible for the northern end of New York City in addition to northern New Jersey and Staten Island, "to keep a look out upon what may be passing about King's Bridge, in New York and on Staten Island, I wish you to take every method to collect the best intelligence you can of the situation of the enemy, their strength and motions at those several places, and communicate the same to me."[49]

Dayton's spies were running so many undercover missions and dealing in such an abundance of provisions and goods that their activities became suspicious to the local authorities. On November 20, 1777, the New Jersey Council of Safety issued warrants for the arrests of John Morse Jr., John and Baker Hendricks, and John Meeker for trading with and carrying provisions to the enemy on Staten Island. Baker Hendricks was held in the Newark jail.[50] On December 3, 1777, bonds of £300 each for John and Baker Hendricks were posted by Dayton, their case agent.[51]

Dayton wrote to Washington, on January 13, 1778, about the arrest of some of his spies. Dayton said, "[I] have already entered into bonds for their appearance at court but fear my influence will be insufficient and unless your excellency will be pleased to interfere, they will be punished for serving their country and a shameful trial for their lives conviction of having been to the enemy, condemnation in consequence, and the chance of a pardon, will be the only reward for their services, fatigues and hazard of their lives in an enemy camp, instead of thanks and a pecuniary compensation at least."[52]

Washington knew that he had to come to the protection of his spies. If the state of New Jersey made public the identity of his spies, then his chance of recruiting their replacements would be impossible. Without the intelligence of the spies, he would be operating in the dark as he would lose his eyes and ears on the British plans and movements. Washington at Valley Forge responded that he received Dayton's letter on the evening of the 19th. He immediately wrote to Governor Livingston, "I make no doubt but the prosecution will be immediately stopped upon my representation of the matter in its true light, and of my pointing out the impossibility of getting persons to undertake this kind of business in future, if they are not protected by us."[53]

He informed Livingston:

John and Baker Hendricks, and John Meeker had been apprehended upon a supposition of carrying on an illegal correspondence with the Enemy, as they had been several times upon Staten Island and that they were to be tried for their lives in consequence. In justice to these men I am bound to take this earliest opportunity of informing you that they were employed by Colo[nel] Dayton last Summer to procure intelligence of the movements of the enemy while upon Staten Island, for which purpose I granted them passports, allowing them to carry small quantities of provision, and to bring back a few goods the better to cover their real designs. Colo[nel]

Dayton acquaints me that they executed their trust faithfully; this I very well remember, that what intelligence he communicated to me and which he says, came principally thro' them, was generally confirmed by the event. Upon these considerations I hope you will put a stop to the prosecution, unless other matters appear against them. You must be well convinced, that it is indispensably necessary to make use of these means to procure intelligence. The persons employed must bear the suspicion of being thought inimical, and it is not in their powers to assert their innocence, because that would get abroad and destroy the confidence which the enemy puts in them.[54]

Washington wanted to continue using them as spies and knew if they defended themselves in court they would be useless to him.

Livingston responded to Washington's letter on the 26th explaining that John and Baker Hendricks and John Meeker were already bound in a recognizance bond to appear at the next Essex County Court of Oyer and Terminer: "As they are not committed, they are not charged with any thing in particular, but will be tried for whatever shall then appear against them." He stated "that they had carried to the enemy greater quantities of provisions than were necessary to disguise their design in going to the island."[55]

Livingston asserted that he would "interest myself in their pardon, in case they should be convicted for any thing done in consequences of the passports you mention. Upon this Sir, you may depend."

The Essex County Grand Jury informed Governor Livingston and the Council of Safety that county residents had corresponded and traded with the enemy. They blamed the Continental officers at Elizabeth Town and Newark for facilitating these contacts. They claimed that Continental and militia officers were delegating the power to grant Flags of Truce and passports, which was undermining a recent law intended to stop the illicit trade.[56]

Livingston then justified the actions of the Council of Safety in apprehending them because "the popular clamor was so loud against them, that the Council of Safety could neither in prudence nor justice refrain from causing them to be apprehended." Livingston said that he was unhappy that he could not put a stop to the proceedings because there was no *nolle prosequi* ("will not further prosecute") entry that could be put on the record in New Jersey or any power to pardon them until they had been convicted: "But what can be done, which is to interest myself in their pardon, in case they should be convicted for any thing done in consequences of the passports you mention. Upon this Sir, you may depend."[57]

Washington responded, "I am obliged to you for the interest you take in the affair of the two Hendricks and Meeker; and I have no doubt that the measures adopted, are, considering all things, best."[58] The Essex County Court of Oyer and Terminer was in session from April 16 to May 2, 1778, and the three men were never charged with a crime.[59]

Baker and John Hendricks did not leave the world of shadows. In 1780 Baker Hendricks was a captain in the New Jersey militia. John in 1780 was working as a case agent overseeing a very active American spy located in New York City.[60] Baker assisted in making payments to the spy.[61]

Baker was commissioned by Congress on September 19, 1780, to outfit two whaleboats called the *Charming Betsey* and the *Flying Squirrel* as private vessels of war. Hendricks's commission was to raid enemy shipping and outposts near Staten Island.[62]

Baker Hendricks was active in catching the enemy. On December 13, 1781, he captured five refugees on Bergen Point.[63] Just ten days later he captured eight of the enemy at Bergen.[64] On June 6, 1782, near Bergen, Captain Baker Hendricks captured seven "tatterdemalions," or people dressed in rags.[65] A week later he captured five refugees on Bergen Point.[66]

Baker Hendricks, on May 13, 1782, purchased goods that were confiscated from the enemy and sold by the Essex County justice of the peace. He then sold them to Samuel Craig, who shipped them to Pennsylvania. Officials in New Brunswick confiscated the merchandise as contraband. Craig sued and in 1783 the New Jersey Supreme Court ruled in Craig's favor. He claimed that Samuel Hayes, deputy surveyor, William Marriner, and others at New Brunswick colluded to confiscate the goods, sell them, and split the money.[67]

Governor Livingston heard rumors that Hendricks was conducting illegal business with the enemy using the protection of the commission to shield his actions.[68] On June 12, 1782, he signed a proclamation revoking the commission, publishing the proclamation in the *New Jersey Gazette* on June 19, 1782.[69]

Large quantities of provisions found their way to the British from Middletown Point (Matawan) and Shrewsbury in Monmouth County, Perth Amboy in Middlesex County, and Elizabeth Town in Essex (now Union) County.[70] Contraband from Middletown Point to Perth Amboy would have been smuggled in small boats out to the British-armed provision ship, the 112 1/2 ton brig *Ranger,* with Daniel Tinley, master,[71] stationed off the southeast end of Staten Island at Princess Bay.[72] Governor Livingston wrote that there was an almost universal uproar over the flag of trunk boats that carried supplies for the prisoners in New York. He stated that many times the complaints were not based on facts, that these boats had been carrying private merchandise in addition to their official cargos. The additional merchandise was used to trade with the enemy and bring back private goods. He suggested that Colonel Elias Boudinot, commissary general for prisoners, should have an agent stationed at New Brunswick to certify the inventory the vessels were to carry to New York and what they were allowed to bring back. He wanted the militia to intercept any smuggled items, and the seized contraband would belong to the militia. He believed that the militia would diligently enforce the measure and would put an end to the smuggling.[73] But smuggling could never be completely stopped. Spies were needed to carry on the war effort and they needed the cover of being a smuggler to execute their assignments.

American General William Maxwell, Lord Stirling, in an April 26, 1779 letter to Governor Livingston gave his opinion of the type of people who had been to Staten Island. They came back "with the addition of seven devils more than they were possessed of before, by the connections they have formed on the other side, and no doubt but some of them is [*sic*] sent over to us by the enemy."[74]

In letters to Washington, Governor Livingston indicated that the black-market trade was so brisk that the smugglers were bringing back so much British manufactured items in exchange that they were able to set up retail stores to sell the goods.[75] In New Jersey and elsewhere the smugglers were called "London traders" because of the London-made goods they brought back from New York.[76] Once inflation of the Continental currency was under way, some farmers hid their provisions and denied having any, while others who were close to the British covertly sold them for hard currency of silver and gold.[77] New Jersey passed law after law with stronger and stronger penalties trying to stop the trade, but smuggling continued to the end of the war.[78]

Lieutenant Lewis J. Costigan of the 1st New Jersey Regiment was captured in January 1777.[79] He was placed on parole in New York City, which allowed him to freely walk around the city in his Continental Army uniform. He was paroled on September 17, 1778. During his parole he was sending intelligence to the Americans.

He was later exchanged and thus was no longer bound by his parole. At the request of American Major General Lord Stirling and Colonel Matthias Ogden, Costigan did not leave New York City as he should have. He stayed and continued his usual walks in plain sight in his American military uniform, collecting information and sending his correspondence through Colonel Ogden and Lord Stirling to George Washington using the code name "Z."[80] Lord Stirling, who was at Middlebrook, New Jersey, mentioned having seen him on December 24, 1778, when it is believed he was exchanged. Costigan confirmed the news that the British army was out of bread and issuing rice in its place."[81]

If his espionage activities after his exchange were discovered, he could not be treated as a spy since he was in his 1st New Jersey Regiment uniform. He could be detained as a prisoner of war. He was warned of someone returning to New York who knew he was exchanged and so quickly left the British lines on January 17, 1779.[82]

Washington liked to play the game of deception to attempt to gain an advantage or to try and level the playing field. Washington realized that the British could also play a game of deception and always had to be on the lookout for their deceptions. It was a song to which both sides danced.

Lieutenant General John Burgoyne had arrived from England. In 1777 he was to lead a force down Lakes Champlain and George to Albany. Lieutenant Colonel Barry St. Ledger in the 34th Regiment of Foot was to come down the Mohawk River to Albany. General Howe was to come north up the Hudson from New York City. The plan was to isolate New England from the other rebelling colonies.

Lieutenant General Burgoyne wrote, while at Quebec on May 14, 1777, to General William Howe in New York that he would write letters to him that he intended to have fall into American hands. This was an attempt to have the American generals arrive at the wrong conclusions and make the wrong moves. He said such letters would be "dated at the bottom & two strokes after ye name of ye place."[83]

General Howe attempted to mislead Washington of his movements by means of a false letter. He had Lieutenant Colonel William Sheriff approach Henry Williams in the provost, which is the military jail, to be a courier to General Burgoyne in Canada with the promise that he would get a great reward if he succeeded. Williams was the son of Erasmus Williams, a member of the New York State Convention.

They knew Henry Williams would take the letter directly to the first American officer he could find. If he did not, then no harm would occur to the British. At first Williams declined the proposal of being a courier for the British. Then he decided to do a double cross and accept the mission. His plan was to deliver the dispatch to the first American officer he could locate. He was given six half Joes prior to his departure as if it were a real mission.[84] The document was dated July 20, 1777, and was written on a small piece of silk paper. It was sewed into a fold of his coat. The date of July 20 and the city of New York were placed at the bottom of the letter and they were accented by two lines as Howe stated:

New York July 20th

In this fake letter Howe tells Burgoyne that "I am now making demonstrations to the southward, which will I think have the full effect in carrying our plan in[to] execution."[85] It informed Burgoyne that Howe was sailing against Boston, with a feint toward the south.

Howe then proceeded to execute his campaign to take Philadelphia by heading south. He was hoping that Washington would think that his move toward Philadelphia was a ruse and that he was going to double back. If Washington did, then he would take the American forces to the Hudson and away from Philadelphia, which would make Howe's conquest of Philadelphia easier.

Williams left New York City on July 22. He most likely crossed at Kingsbridge since he had permission to leave and headed north into the no-man's-land between the two armies. Here he could be attacked by either side or by the bands of cowboys, predatory Loyalist troops, that robbed anyone they saw. He brought the letter to Colonel Philip Van Cortlandt of the 2nd New York Regiment in East Chester, New York.[86] After informing him of the situation, he was sent with the letter to General Putnam, who was farther north at Peekskill. Williams arrived at Peekskill on the 24th and advised Putnam that he believed the letter he was given to deliver to Burgoyne was a fake and was intended to fall into American hands. Putnam, realizing the urgency and that a ploy was in the works, quickly wrote out Williams's statements and immediately sent Williams's deposition and the letter to General Washington, who was at Ramapo, New Jersey, on the west side of the Hudson.

Washington received the documents on the 25th at Ramapo, and being circumspect, did not fall into Howe's trap. He responded the same day to General Putnam: "[A] stronger proof could not be given that the former [General Howe] is not going to the eastward, than this letter adduces. It was evidently intended to fall into our hands, the complexion of it, the circumstances attending it &ca., evinces this beyond a doubt in my mind. I therefore desire that no time be lost in sending Gen[era]ls. Sullivan and Lord Stirling with their divisions" to Philadelphia.[87]

Seven

Seven

~∾~

DOUBLE AGENTS

The British had more money than the Americans could ever scrape together. If a person's motivation for being a spy was money, then the British could buy their allegiance or get them to play a double game as Washington called it. He thought it best to keep his spies in the dark as much as possible about the Continental Army's real status: that way they could do the least amount of damage if they changed sides or were really working for the British.

He never truly trusted any double agent because of the game they needed to play to keep their credibility with the enemy. They could potentially do him more harm than good. He explained his thinking on double agents to General Alexander McDougall: "I always think it necessary to be very circumspect with double spies. Their situation in a manner obliges them to trim a good deal in order to keep well with both sides; and the less they have it in their power to do us mischief, the better; especially if we consider that the enemy can purchase their fidelity at a higher price than we can. It is best to keep them in a way of knowing as little of our true circumstances as possible; and in order that they may really deceive the enemy in their reports, to endeavor in the first place to deceive them."[1] As consequence of this view, he always tried to deceive his own double agents.

New Jersey Governor Livingston seemed to parallel Washington's reticence on double agents and those given passes to travel behind British lines. Washington hadn't the manpower to stop the unauthorized practice of smuggling but tried to control the persons traveling with official approval. Washington understood that "an officer on outpost may notwithstanding be excusable for employing a spy." He cautioned Lieutenant Colonel Henry Lee Jr. that "your pass is in reality a license to trade; and from melancholy experiences I have reason to think that those who will engage in that business are generally a pack of scoundrels who mean nothing by it but to benefit themselves by the trade which they are permitted to carry on under pretense of the better introducing themselves to the enemy and who will be of as much disservice to you by carrying intelligence to them as benefit by any they will bring from thence."[2]

Washington had to deal with spies from the enemy who tried to play a double game against him. Washington wanted to catch the British spies but wanted to treat them in a legal and humane way. He hoped it would ensure good treatment of Americans that were being held by the British.

Royal Governor William Tryon of New York sent Elijah Hunter of Bedford, New York, a letter asking him "to change his sentiments and assist the British in giving them information respecting the [American] army and state of affairs in the country."[3] He was asked "to act apparently zealous for America—not to shake the confidence of his countrymen."[4]

Elijah Hunter was the assistant commissary of forage for the

Continental Army at Bedford. As the assistant commissary for forage he would know where the American cavalry were located, what they were planning, and the supply of forage available. It was information the British could use in planning their military expeditions.

On February 27, 1779, Hunter responded to Tryon that he planned to go to Philadelphia to gather intelligence.[5] Hunter contacted Scotland-born New York City resident General Alexander McDougall, who was twenty miles distant at Peekskill, New York, on the east side of the Hudson. General McDougall, on March 21, 1779, referred Hunter, who had a plan for obtaining secret intelligence for the Americans, to John Jay, president of the Continental Congress in Philadelphia.[6] Hunter went to Philadelphia to speak to Jay about Tryon's proposal and was going to see Washington in New Jersey on his return trip back to his home. Jay recommended Hunter to be an American spy and be trusted to travel into New York City to obtain intelligence.[7] He wrote to Washington that he had known Hunter for many years: "In my opinion he is an honest man, and firmly attached to the American Cause from the commencement of the present troubles. I have seen his conduct in several instances directed by generous sentiments of honor, and a liberal pride."[8]

Washington, on March 25, told McDougall, "I have had a good deal of conversation with Mr. H—[Elijah Hunter]. He appears to be a sensible man capable of rendering important service, if he is sincerely disposed to do it. From what you say, I am led to hope he is; but nevertheless, if he is really in the confidence of the enemy, as he himself believes to be the case, it will be prudent to trust him with caution and to watch his conduct with a jealous eye."[9]

Since Washington was suspicious of all double agents, he

was concerned that Hunter might be a spy working both sides for his own personal gain. Three days later, on March 28, Washington counseled McDougall that Elijah Hunter "appears very sensible, and we should, on that account, be more than commonly guarded until he has given full proofs of his attachment."[10] To keep his identity a secret Washington used "H—" in place of Hunter's name in his correspondence.

McDougall was going to be the one receiving his reports. Hunter turned over a letter from William Tryon at Post Kingsbridge, at the northern end of York (now Manhattan) Island, to Lieutenant General Frederick Haldimand, governor of Canada, dated March 13, 1779, to Washington.[11] The letter discussed the British military situation in North America and the Caribbean but was too overly positive to be believed as genuine. After perusing the letter, Washington cautioned forty-seven-year-old McDougall that "The letter directed to Gen[era]l Haldimand was evidently intended to fall into our hands. The manner of contriving that, and some other circumstances, makes me suspicious that he [Hunter] is as much in the interest of the enemy as in ours."[12] Since the letter Hunter gave them to read was a fake to deceive them, it raised suspicion that he was in the game to provide the British with intelligence and to get their money.

Hunter, now with Washington's approval to act as a spy, wrote to the British in New York City on April 2, 1779, and stated, "[A]m happy to find it in my power to serve you. . . . I have accomplished your orders as far as I possibly could for the present and I have fixed matters upon a tolerable good plan to obtain further information which I shall convey you from time to time."[13] He provided information about increased defenses on the Delaware River and a planned attack on Detroit. He wrote, "They endeavor to keep this a profound secret. I got some hints of it from P. [Captain Jonathan Platt] afterwards I fell in company with an officer of the Maryland Line and after some discourse I drinked [*sic*] freely with him I pumped him on the subject; he told me much the same that I had heard before and confirmed it as a fact as he just came from that quarter (Tuscarora) but as we were both in the service he thought it no harm to tell me, but he enjoigned [*sic*] it upon me as a secret."[14]

Hunter turned in his first intelligence report on May 21, 1779, after traveling into New York City.[15] Another report was submitted two days later on British military plans.[16]

In August Hunter provided Washington with a note dated the 8th which had a letter enclosed from Lieutenant Colonel Banastre Tarleton. Washington read it and returned it. Washington provided Hunter with a copy of an exaggerated return of the troops fit for duty under his immediate command. Washington was still paying strict attention to detail to protect his spies. He provided Hunter with instructions to explain how he derived the numbers. He was told to say he determined them "from inquiry and your own observations of the troops when under arms upon which you formed an average estimate of the force of each regiment in the different brigades; to give your account." Wanting to help Hunter keep his cover story intact, Washington told him to say that the officers are careless in speaking of the strength of their regiments.[17]

Washington was still not totally sure of Hunter's trustfulness. The return he gave him showed the total strength of the Continental Army as 17,910, present and fit for duty, exclusive of the detachment on Sullivan's expedition. The weekly return of the Continental Army, for August 14, 1779, showed a total of rank and file and noncommissioned officers of 16,316; but when the absent, sick, and those on command were subtracted, the total fit for duty shrank to 9,532. As an added enhancement to his deception Washington told Hunter, "Boats sufficient to transport at least 5000 at a turn are now lying at the Fort [West Point], New Windsor and Fishkill Landing and can be assembled in two hours at any time." This provided the British with concerns that an attack could happen on short notice.[18]

Since Washington suspected that Hunter might really be on the British side and working against him, he decided to play the deception game. To help convince Hunter that the return of the Continental Army was genuine, he wrote to Major General Robert Howe advising him that when he spoke to Hunter to match the numbers of his corps to what Washington had provided to Hunter.[19] He again was using one lie to confirm another lie.

Hunter apparently went to Howe asking for more detail on his troops' status. Howe contacted Washington and informed him of Hunter's inquiry. Washington responded by explaining his logic:

> It appears to me that the detail he seems to desire will be rather too minute and tend to excite suspicion instead of giving him credit with the enemy. The idea of what was communicated before was to pretend that he had made general observations and inquiries in the army and had formed an average estimate of the several brigades as the result. The particular strength of each regiment would exceed this purpose, and in some measure contradict the principle. But if on his return he finds the present not satisfactory and the enemy press for what he now requires it shall not be refused. Let him in the first place make the experiment with what he has.[20]

Washington further explained to Howe, "If he can be convinced that it is more to his interest to serve us than to trust to the precarious issue of the success of the enemy in the present contest he will probably execute his business with fidelity." He told Howe that based upon the intelligence provided by Hunter and the spies he hired, he should be able to learn of the encampments and piquet at Kingsbridge. Howe was given permission to attack the enemy there.[21] One of the people Hunter hired was Mary Campbell. She delivered his reports verbally to Captain George Beckwith of the 37th Regiment of Foot, adjutant for British headquarters, and later aide-de-camp to Lieutenant General Wilhelm von Knyphausen.[22] The next day Washington again cautioned Howe about Hunter possibly being a spy for the British. If Howe thought "him as a double character, it is more than possible he would give some intimation by which the project would be ruined."[23] Howe, for whatever reason, did not attack Kingsbridge.

During an attack by the British Colonel Samuel Birch on Bedford, Hunter's house was set on fire and destroyed. Hunter, in an August 21 letter to Tryon, states that he has not lost his allegiance to the Crown:

Was I to lose all I have [I] would not alter my principal[s] [*sic*] but I must confess I have lost the main I have for since my misfortune by fire I have been plundered by the militia of all that they could carry away.[24] Since that all my rum which I had in [New] Jersey is seized and taken for the use of the army [and] my horses and other things is [*sic*] going. But all does not discourage me as I have encouragements of satisfaction at some future day and I hope my services will merit your interest in my favor . . . as you know the intelligence goes to head quarters. . . . I talk of building again this fall a small place to shelter in and if so could wish to not have it destroyed as before. I beg your advice on that subject and should always be happy to serve you on any occasion in my power.[25]

The same day he wrote to John André to get money for his losses and for information he could peddle to the Americans. He wanted to be reimbursed for the burning of his house on July 11 and the items he lost. He claimed he spent £100 hard cash being a spy for the British. The amount was most likely padded to make up for some of his recent losses. In his letter he reminded André of what he had assured him:

[T]he government at home will make me [Hunter] full satisfaction for my losses. . . . I have nothing to subsist upon but however I must wait patience and I make no doubt but you will do every thing in your power to help me in that case. You inform me that temporary subsidies shall not be with held from me that you can give me. . . . I can positively assure you that I have expended more than one hundred pounds hard cash. . . . Whether my service is of any immediate advantage you are the best judge but if it is not it would be a pity. . . . I must have cash to carry it on. Please to send me the newspapers and any other intelligence which may tend to cheer up the spirits of our friends. Please to write me how matters go abroad as we hear [little].[26]

The newspaper mentioned the arrival on Tuesday, August 20, 1779, of the *Russel*, a warship of seventy-four guns that was anchored in the North (Hudson) River. Among her cargo was £400,000 for the army.[27] Washington believed that the rest of Admiral Arbuthnot's fleet was now at Sandy Hook. Sandy Hook is a low-level barrier peninsula with seven miles of beach that stretches into Lower New York Bay. The ship channel leading into New York Bay passes close to Sandy Hook. Washington wanted to know what particular regiments came with the fleet and wanted Hunter to get that information. Also "whether there are any appearances of a speedy movement by land or water, or both from a collection of teams, boats &ca. and as far as may be the destination or object."[28] Washington told Howe that he expected Hunter to provide that intelligence.[29] There is a 1779 intelligence report of a list of warships in New York and regiments but no identity as to who the source was, as the signature was ripped off to conceal the identity.[30] It may have been provided by Hunter.

Hunter apparently reported that the enemy was on the move in the area, and, based on his intelligence, Washington cautioned Howe: "I by no means think it eligible for you to move down for the purpose of making a forage, more especially as by the intelligence of [Hunter] the enemy will be prepared to receive you."[31] Washington was fearful that Hunter had told the British something that was causing the British movement, and if he moved, Howe would be heading into a trap.

Washington told Howe, "The current of my intelligence by different hands and from different quarters bring[s] the enemy's reinforcement to about 3,000. This corresponds with your accounts and perhaps is pretty near the truth. The ignorance of the agents of — [Elijah Hunter] or the want of a proper genius for enquiry or observation may have led them to over rate their numbers, Caution however as you observe is necessary on our part. We will seem pleased with their every accounts, but believe only such of them as appears to be supported by the greatest variety of evidence."[32]

Jay wrote to Washington that Hunter had written to him in May. Hunter told Jay he had written to Washington about "a Matter of very delicate Nature" (being a spy). Hunter led Jay into believing that he would soon visit with him: "He has not however been here—nor have I received a line from him for some time past. From this circumstance I have been apprehensive of his having relinquished that business and the more so, as he intimated to me his doubts of it's [sic] being well conducted unless under your immediate direction—that the views of the gentleman with whom he first conversed on the subject, were not very extensive, and his attention to expenses too great." Jay offered to encourage Hunter to return to secret service activities if he stopped. However, "If he still perseveres, I do not wish to be informed of any other particulars."[33]

Washington came to the conclusion that secret agents who lived in the city were better able to provide meaningful intelligence than those who had to travel into the city. He believed the intelligence that those who traveled had to give the enemy to keep their cover counterbalanced the intelligence they could bring back. In September of 1779 he wrote to Jay in answer to his query if Hunter was still employed in secret service activities and explained these conclusions as follows:

With respect to the person [Elijah Hunter] you recommended last winter, he was employed in consequence;

and I have not the smallest doubt of his attachment and integrity. But he has not had it in his power, and indeed it is next to impossible that any one should circumstanced as he is, to render much essential service in the way it was intended to employ him. You will readily conceive the difficulties in such a case. The business was of too delicate a nature for him to transact it frequently himself, and the characters, he has been obliged occasionally to confide it to, have not been able to gain any thing satisfactory or material. Indeed, I believe it will seldom happen, that a person acting in this way, can render any essential advantages more than once or twice at any rate; and that what he will be compelled to do to preserve the pretended confidence of the other party, will generally counterbalance any thing he may effect. The greatest benefits are to be derived from persons who live with the other side; whose local circumstances, without subjecting them to suspicions, give them an opportunity of making observations and comparing and combining things and sentiments. It is with such I have endeavored to establish a correspondence, and on whose reports I shall most rely. From these several considerations, I am doubtful whether it will be of any advantage for the person to continue longer in the way he has acted. The points to which he must have alluded in his letter, were the movements up the North River and against Charles Town [now Charleston, South Carolina] and the expedition to Virginia. I believe the first certain information of the first of these events came from him. He has never received any thing from me. The gentleman who employed him first, had some money [200 guineas] deposited with him for confidential purposes; but I cannot tell how much he may have paid him.[34]

Hunter, on April 17, 1780, sent a report to Governor George Clinton of New York concerning Colonel James Holmes.[35] Hunter stated that while riding with Captain Jonathan Platt from his house to Horse Neck,[36] Platt told him that he believed that Holmes was now working for the British. Holmes had sent a man to get a boat ready for him at Horse Neck or Stamford, Connecticut, on Long Island Sound, in case he needed it to get across to the British territory. In the same letter he cautioned Governor Clinton that there are some untrue stories going around about his own conduct. He asked him not to believe them, that he would see him and explain what he was doing.[37] He wanted to tell him that his actions were at the instructions of Generals McDougall and Washington.

Hunter, on June 6, 1780, sent a letter to British General Henry Clinton at Verplank's Point. He used the identity "H.E." or "E.H." on documents to the British. He acknowledges he received a message containing his orders. He says he went to Fishkill the previous morning to see Governor George Clinton of New York and found him at Mr. John Naight's in the Highlands.[38] He stayed overnight to discover their plans: "I this morning set out from there and come on to General Mc Dogals [McDougall's]. Where I had some discourse with him as particular with Maj[or Richard] Platt[e] one of his A.D.C. [aide-de-camp] and at resort acts as deputy adjutant general for that department.[39] I had an opportunity of seeing the returns of the militia at the governors." Hunter provided the troop strengths and movements. "I am also afraid you will be impatient but I have spared no pains in this business"[40] and had two men with him on this trip that he depended upon.

Hunter could not be sure that his espionage work for the Americans had been kept a secret from General Benedict Arnold. In consequence when General Arnold went over to the British, Hunter stopped his secret service work. He then moved from Bedford to Pound Ridge.[41]

It appears Hunter tried to start up again in the spring of 1781. He had a meeting with Washington on April 11. That night he had a meeting with a Mr. Kenecut, who had connections within the British lines. He kept it a secret that he was upon a plan of intelligence. Previously General McDougall had approved them for a ration. This was stopped and Hunter had been providing assistance to him and his family for the last three years and now wanted the government to provide for them.[42] Hunter wrote an undated letter to Oliver De Lancey, who had replaced John André as adjutant general in 1780, and it begins with "Thursday 5 o'clock P.M." and discusses the delay of the escort of the "Flag" until the next day.[43]

On March 11, 1783, Hunter wrote to Washington about a raid from De Lancey's Corps that took cattle and nine or ten horses at the town of Bedford. He wanted to get a flag of truce to go to the British to try and get the animals returned. He reminded Washington of his having done secret service work for him in the past. He begged him to consult with General McDougall, to whom he reported about the services he provided.[44]

In the same letter Hunter wrote to Washington that because he had worked for him as a spy he was thought of being a suspicious character by his fellow citizens. As the war was winding down he wanted Washington to clear his name so he could live in peace and suggested that he contact General McDougall, who knew his conduct and character during the war.[45] Washington responded, "You obtained such intelligence, either by yourself or your correspondents, of various things which passed within the British lines, as was of considerable consequence to us." He ended the letter with, "I thought at the time and still conceive, your services were of such an interesting nature as to entitle you to the good opinion and favorable notice of your countrymen."[46] Washington, on December 1, 1783, issued him a certificate of satisfaction, which stated: "This will certify that during the late war Captain Elijah Hunter of Bedford W[est] c[hester] County, was, on the accommodation of Mr. Jno [John] Jay then President of Congress, and of Major General [Alexander] McDougall, employed on some secret services which he performed, as far as came to my knowledge, with integrity, and to my satisfaction."[47]

Seven years after the war, on February 24, 1790, Hunter wrote to Washington asking him to intercede on his behalf to obtain additional money for his secret service activities. Washington wrote back explaining that although he remembered him, he did not remember the details of his activities: "It is not possible for me, with any degree of propriety, to tread back ground I passed over seven years ago, when no application has been made to me in all that time: and when my accounts with the public closed with the resignation of my commission, especially too, as it appears by the papers handed to me, that you have been paid, agreeable to your own charge, for the services you are now desirous of bringing again to view." Washington mentioned that Hunter was employed "principally by, or thro', General McDougall, who, I well remember, had two hundred Guineas put into his hands, with which to pay those who were used as secret agents. . . . From this view of the matter you will readily see that I cannot take any other steps in it than what have been already effected."[48] Spies were always expected to make their bargain as to the monetary value of the enterprise before they went on their mission.

Ulster-born forty-four-year-old General William Maxwell's assignment during January to April of 1777 was to oversee the area from Perth Amboy to Newark along the Arthur Kill. The Arthur Kill is the narrow body of tidal water separating New Jersey from Staten Island. It is about ten miles long and extends from Raritan Bay on the south to Newark Bay on the north. Maxwell was instructed by Washington to be attentive to Loyalists who would swear allegiance to America but would be sending information to the British. His assignment was also to collect enemy intelligence. Maxwell kept a military detachment in Newark and Elizabeth for the sole purpose of obtaining information on the enemy's activities. Maxwell referred to the people who were given passes to go between New Jersey and Staten Island as "licensed spies." Some who had received passes were double agents playing both sides, and some changed sides based upon who was paying more that day.[49]

He sent a letter on April 10, 1777, from his headquarters at Westfield, New Jersey, to Major General Adam Stephen, which discussed their mutual problem of securing accurate information for Washington: "I know how you must feel as I suffered just in something the same way my self by the scoundrel that remained in and about Newark. [It] is impossible for a man to divine these things in our degenerate days and he that will go blindfolded into such matters is worse than a fool. We have a very difficult card to play [and] we have often to act by the moon or twialight [sic] and leave the world to judge of it in clear sunshine." Apparently both Generals Maxwell and Stephen were duped into believing erroneous information. Maxwell had this same problem again in August of 1778.[50] Maxwell had a reputation as a hard drinker and was brought up on charges but was unanimously acquitted.[51] His drinking may have contributed to his being deceived. Because of errors by Washington's staff and subordinates in identifying the true facts of the enemy's situation, it presented problems for Washington in sorting out what to believe. It reinforced his policy of obtaining intelligence from multiple sources to keep from being tricked or enticed into an error of judgment.

Sometimes spies were subjected to a friendly capture. Their mission was to gather intelligence from the enemy, which required them to clandestinely go behind enemy lines usually posing as a smuggler dealing in the "London Trade." Their activities would be noticed by the local Committee of Safety or the militia, and then in consequence, they would be arrested. They could not reveal their secret mission, for in doing so they would have revealed themselves to the enemy. They had to depend upon Washington to somehow extricate them out of their predicament and do it in such a way as to not uncover their secret operation.

One such case was that of John Morse. He had been arrested in New Jersey, possibly when several other members of his family were arrested for carrying provisions to the enemy on Staten Island.[52] Because of his being employed by the military as a spy, New Jersey Governor Livingston assured Washington that if Morse were convicted, he would use his office to grant him a pardon. Livingston was concerned that Morse might have been a double agent, as Morse was paying too much attention to Livingston's movements. He knew the British would have taken him prisoner if they could. He did not trust Morse and was convinced that he was a spy for the British. Washington was definitive that if it could be proven that Morse was a double agent the conviction should stand and the work he had done for the American cause should be ignored. He was not going to give a free pass for crimes committed just because someone worked as a spy. He said, "I would only mean to shield him from harm, upon a supposition that he had been no further concerned in going to the enemy than to serve us; but if he has been playing the double part and his villainy can be proved, he ought not to be screened." No evidence has been found that Morse was convicted or that Livingston pardoned him.[53]

Washington was diligent about making sure he was not deceived, but sometimes he was so overly cautious that he looked for problems where there were none. During the spring of 1778, while the British occupied Philadelphia, Jacob Bankson had come out of British-held Philadelphia and offered to be a spy for Washington. He owned property in Philadelphia County. One piece of property in 1749 was in Moyamensing, and on June 20, 1755, he bought land in Passyunk Township from Sarah Stretch.[54] His family, at the time of the British occupation of Philadelphia, was living in Princeton. Bankson operated in British-held Philadelphia with such ease that he was suspected of being a double agent working for the British. Washington asked Governor Livingston to keep an eye on him.

Alexander Hamilton, aide-de-camp to Washington, was given the job of checking him out. Washington had confidence and trust in his aides-de-camp to execute the duties of their position. Hamilton, on April 3, 1778, asked Colonel Stephen Moylan of the 4th Continental Dragoons to check out Bankson. He reported that Bankson was late of the Continental Marines. Hamilton advised Stephen Moylan of their suspicions of Jacob

Bankson being a spy for General Howe and wanted to find out his true history. He told Moylan that Bankson had left the American camp on March 24 on the pretense of visiting his family and had now returned with a renewed offer of service as an American spy: "It is doubted that whether he has not in the mean time been at Philadelphia." Hamilton advised that Washington had written to Livingston to check out Bankson. Moylan was instructed to contact the governor to discover if he learned anything and "to take cautious methods to ascertain whether Bankson has been at home, since he left camp—how long—and when he left home—in short anything that may throw light upon his designs. . . . Manage the business with caution and address."[55] Livingston had assigned a man to watch Bankson on March 29, but that same day Livingston had left Princeton for the American headquarters.[56]

Bankson's brother approached Livingston to say he was apprehensive that his brother was suspected and offered to produce a pass from Washington. Livingston told Washington, "I knew nothing of his brother nor had any reason to question his right of passing especially as he was employed by your Excellency." Livingston found that Bankson "has plenty of gold and silver. If he had no business with General Greene in his last jaunt, as he told his brother he had, it will increase the suspicion against him."[57] On April 11, 1778, Bankson was paid $100 for secret services and he would have turned in his report to someone.[58] I was unable to find out who was acting as Bankson's agent; it seems to have been General Nathanael Greene.

Livingston was concerned that Bankson knew he was suspected, so when he wrote to Washington on May 17, he wrote in Dutch because he thought Bankson was going to carry the letter. In a separate letter he told Washington that Lord Stirling could explain the letter in Dutch to him, and if he couldn't, then Livingston's sister Sarah, the wife of Lord Stirling, could. The letter, as translated by Stirling reads: "The man whom you enquire after goes with this letter to camp, he pretends to have a commission from General Washington for secret business as I am told, he goes frequently from this place to the camp, he pretends that he undertakes this journey on business with General Greene."[59] As it happened, the letter was not given to Bankson to deliver to the headquarters but was given to an express rider.

Livingston was having problems determining the person he was to be checking, as there were three brothers in the Princeton area named Bankson. He told Washington that he had recently occupied a room in a tavern and the next room was occupied by an officer named Captain John Bankson of the 2nd Pennsylvania Regiment.[60]

Livingston wrote to Washington that "he [Captain Bankson] was breaking the rules of Congress by his profane swearing, an accomplishment in which he seemed to excel the whole navy of Britain." He asked Washington for the Christian name of the person he was to check so he could do as requested.[61]

Hamilton decided the suspicions of Bankson were without merit. On June 1, 1778, Washington advised Governor Livingston that he was satisfied with Bankson and he need not trouble himself any further in the matter.

The situation gets extremely complicated when you have a whole family of spies and double agents. Who would you trust? Their apparent loyalty changed every day. The Hatfield family, sometimes spelled Hetfield, resided in Elizabeth Town, New Jersey. Some worked as double agents and others were spies for the British. One even worked at supplying the Continental Army with hides for making shoes.

Their activity started in the summer of 1776. Cornelius Hatfield Jr. managed the farm of his aged father, Cornelius Hatfield Sr. He joined the British in 1776.[62] Abner, Moses, and John Smith Hatfield were arrested for having contact with the enemy but were pardoned on the promise of good behavior.[63] They did not allow the promise to get in their way for long. In 1777, Benjamin Hatfield was sent by his brothers to Staten Island to trade with the British. He was captured on his return and offered a pardon if he agreed to serve in the American navy. It being the lesser of his punishment options, he accepted. James Hatfield was captured along with Benjamin but was sent to jail. Jacob Hatfield joined the king's army at Staten Island. He was captured with Benjamin and was discharged after taking the oath of abjuration and allegiance. The oath required the person to reject all loyalty to the king of England and swear allegiance to the state where he resided. He ignored his oath and continued to work for the British as a guide.

Washington stayed out of the Hatfield situation as long as possible, leaving the state of New Jersey to deal with them. An intercepted letter addressed to John Smith Hatfield from New York was brought to his attention. It raised the bar from smuggling a few items, which was a state problem, to a military problem involving large quantities. The letter proved that John Smith Hatfield was involved in a treasonable communication with the writer behind enemy lines and was recruiting men for the British.

Twenty-nine-year-old John Smith Hatfield had been working for Lord Stirling, who had given him a pass to go to Staten Island. No documentation about the pass has been found, but they were usually given for the person to come back with intelligence for the Americans while bringing back some items as a cover. Washington said that Hatfield was abusing the pass and "was going to the enemy with a vessel laden with flour, in which he was pressed by his correspondent to bring as many hands as he could, which is conjectured were wanted to man a privateer. I believe there is no doubt of Hatfield's guilt; though I do not know how far the evidence against him may amount to legal proof." Washington ordered Hatfield arrested and placed in jail, and he directed Lord Stirling to investigate the matter of the shipment of flour and the recruits for a privateer. He also ordered "General Maxwell without further delay to turn Hatfield over to the civil power. The vessel was also seized at the same time and is now at Middle Town Point, to be disposed of as the law shall direct."[64]

Maxwell, at Elizabeth Town, asked Stirling for any documentation, as the determination of John Smith Hatfield's innocence or guilt was now in the magistrate's hands. However, Maxwell still had custody of him. He asked that the documentation be provided to the bearer.[65] I was unable to discover what happened, but John Smith Hatfield survived the war.

Morris Hatfield was employed by the Americans as a double agent but was really an agent for the British. He had been arrested for passing counterfeit money and in July 1777 was in a New Jersey jail.[66] In exchange for a promise of leniency, he agreed to undertake and complete a spy mission for the Americans.[67] Governor Livingston did not trust him and told Washington that he thought that Morris Hatfield was "one of the most consummate villains that was ever born and engaged to watch my motions, and would be the first man to assassinate me, if he had the opportunity." American General Arthur St. Clair had written in February 1780 to Washington about Morris Hatfield that he was of very bad character and had been known to have acted as an agent for the British and he was not going to use him.

Moses Hatfield was a merchant and an ensign in the Essex County New Jersey Militia in 1776. Along with Abner and John Smith Hatfield, he had been arrested and pardoned on July 27, 1776, on the promise of good behavior. In 1779 he was selling merchandise to Washington and the Continental Army. Washington did not trust him or any other member of the Hatfield clan. General Samuel Holden Parsons received an offer from one of the Hatfields to be a spy in New York. The general told Washington that he understood that permission to conduct trade had been the inducement for a person to become involved in so risky a profession. He realized that he was not authorized to approve or even wink at such an arrangement nor had he been authorized to issue any financial offers. He asked for guidance and promised it would be "punctually complied with."[68] Washington responded negatively to the idea.[69] "From the information I have had of the character of this family of people, I am by no means satisfied that they would answer any valuable purposes, if they were employed [as spies]; and therefore I wish it to be declined, at least for the present."[70]

In January 1780 Washington sent forty-two-year-old Major General William Heathen of Roxbury, Massachusetts, an extract of a letter from the Board of War on the supposed poor performance by Mr. Moses Hatfield, commissary of hides, and an extract of a letter on the same subject from Mr. William Henry, commissary of hides at Lancaster, Pennsylvania. In response to the board's request, he ordered Heath to conduct an inquiry into Hatfield's conduct in the discharge of his duties. The principal complaint was regarding the number of hides delivered for making shoes.[71]

Washington thought Moses was a double agent and alerted his officers to be cautious in dealing with him. He advised Colonel Moses Hazen of the 2nd Canadian Regiment in January 1780, "I would recommend to you, not to repose much confidence in [Moses] Hatfield; from what I have learnt he is a suspicious character and will probably endeavor to serve the enemy more effectually than us."[72] He also advised Brigadier General William Irvine, "I would not advise you to put any great confidence in — [Moses Hatfield] he is very capable of gaining intelligence if he pleases, but I fancy he carries as much as he brings. Trade I believe is his principal object."[73] A few days later he repeated the warning with more emphasis: "The Hatfields, and those persons most likely to give you information do not fail to convey all they know to the enemy. In a word, I have good reasons to believe that H—d [Moses Hatfield] is a d[ou]ble Spy."[74]

In the spring of 1780, Moses Hatfield brought to Washington the intelligence of the strength and movements of the British army that he had seen the previous day. It was proposed that he be sent to the British at Elizabeth Town and collect more information. Washington still did not trust this family and thought he had been sent by the British to spy on the American camp. Sending him back to the British would allow him to give the British information on the American forces as to number and location. Washington expressed his apprehension to the person who introduced Moses Hatfield to him. This unknown person assured Washington that Hatfield wished the Americans well and, due to his connections, would be useful. Washington, against his better judgment, reluctantly sent Hatfield into the enemy's rear at Connecticut Farms, New Jersey, to determine the enemy's strength. Washington apparently was not satisfied with the report he received, as it was the last time Washington used him.

Eight

~

TRAITORS AND LICENSED SPIES

Since time immemorial, people have betrayed their companions and countries. They have different motives, ranging from the altruistic to the egocentric. Judas Iscariot, one of the twelve apostles, is definitely one of the most infamous traitors ever. His name is a recognized symbol of treason throughout all of Christendom. He had sold Jesus to the Sanhedrin for thirty pieces of silver. He then led them to Jesus in the garden, and betrayed him to the soldiers with a kiss. He had betrayed his friend, his mentor, and his God.

Benedict Arnold was a highly successful American field commander. He helped capture Fort Ticonderoga (May 10, 1775), delayed the British advances down Lake Champlain (the Battle of Valcour Island on October 11, 1776), and was a significant factor in winning the Battle of Saratoga (October 7, 1777). Despite these American victories, he would become America's most famous traitor.

Joseph Reed led a group of members of Congress who thought that Arnold was guilty of mismanagement of the $66,671 that was advanced to him for his 1775 expedition through the Maine wilderness to Canada. More than $55,000 was not properly documented. Arnold claimed to have given the money to officers and others for public use. Some thought Arnold had lined his own pockets with the money. Congress did not accept Arnold's answers and was withholding reimbursement to him for his expenses until the situation was resolved. Arnold was once passed over for a promotion. Congress decided to limit each state to two major generals, and because Connecticut already had two, Arnold could not be promoted. He had to watch people with lesser ability and weaker credentials be promoted ahead of him.[1] Washington was surprised that Arnold was not on the list for promotion and told him so.[2]

Arnold, on May 28, 1778, was appointed military commander of Philadelphia, a role he would assume after the British evacuated the city on June 18.[3] His instructions were to find and protect any property that belonged to the king until it could be secured by Congress and Pennsylvania.[4] Shops were closed for a week and thus could not conduct any business. On June 23, he entered into a secret written agreement with James Mease, clothier general, and his deputy clothier general, William West. Arnold arranged that goods purchased for the public use that were not wanted for the intended purpose could be sold at the price originally paid. These items could be sold immediately and did not have to wait for the shops to reopen. This gave the men a monopoly in the city, an extremely profitable arrangement for the three men. Because merchandise and food were scarce, they were sold for exorbitant prices. Arnold had requested that a brigade of government wagons with teamsters remove merchandise that belonged to Arnold, Mease, and West that was at Egg Harbor, on the east side of New Jersey, and bring it to Philadelphia where it would be sold. He claimed the merchandise was in imminent danger of falling into enemy hands and had to be moved to keep the British from taking it.

The arrangement became public knowledge. On February 15, 1779, Congress "resolved, therefore that the Commander in Chief be directed to cause the said Major General Arnold to be tried by a Court Martial for the several misdemeanors with which he so stands charged, in order that he may be brought to punishment if guilty; or if innocent, may have an opportunity of vindicating his honor."[5]

On April 20, Washington set the date for the court-martial as May 1, 1779.[6] Because of delays Washington had to postpone the trial until June or July.[7] Arnold was furious over the delay in the court-martial proceedings and the delay in the release of the money owed to him for his expenses in the Canadian expedition. Arnold decided to become a double agent for the British. It was for more than just the money, but that sure would have helped his financial problems. British General Clinton said Arnold started a correspondence with him offering his services in a manner he accepted. He gave him most important information.

Arnold maintained a correspondence from Philadelphia to British headquarters in New York City. Joseph Stansbury in Philadelphia and Rev. Jonathan Odell in New York City processed the coding and decoding of the correspondence. The documents were moved across New Jersey via the services coordinated by John Rattoon, a South Amboy tavern owner who was a British mole using the code name "Mercury."[8] However, he may have also provided a one-time intelligence report on British naval movements on May 22, 1779, to American Colonel Stephen Moylan of the 4th Continental Dragoons.[9]

General Arnold secured the command of West Point and, on July 15, 1780, offered to surrender it to the British for £20,000.[10] British Major John André came from New York by ship to meet with Arnold on the shore near Haverstraw, New York. Their meeting took place at Joshua Hett Smith's house behind the American lines. It was built in 1770 and stood grandly on a hill overlooking the King's Ferry at Stony Point.[11]

The Americans had fired on the British ship that brought André, which caused it to move downriver. He was thus unable to return to the ship that had brought him. He changed out of his uniform for the overland journey to New York City. Along the way, he was captured with plans of the defenses for West Point in his possession. Upon hearing of the capture of André, Arnold fled to the British. The news was shattering to Washington. One of his best generals had gone over to the enemy. It had been several years since Dr. Benjamin Church Jr., one of the leaders of the American Revolution, had chosen the British side. It shook the populace to have another traitor of the Blackest Dye among them. André was convicted of being a spy and was hanged on October 2, 1780, at Tappan, New York. Arnold made it safely behind the British lines. He was commissioned a brigadier general in the British army. He led British forces on raids in Virginia, and against Groton and New London, Connecticut.

Some of Washington's spies were using their passes as an excuse to trade with the enemy on Staten Island. The profit from the trade in scarce items could be considerable.

The illegal trade was a constant problem for New Jersey for

the duration of the war. Washington did not have the manpower to cover all the miles of shoreline as well as maintain the Continental Army. He was forced to leave the problem to the state. In late 1778 he wrote to Governor Livingston:

> I have already distributed largely for the security of this state, and that the safety of its inhabitants has been a particular consideration; but it is impossible to include every place. Besides the detaching to the westward there is a brigade stationed at Bergen to cover the country in that quarter. Should I venture on any further detachments from this part of the army it might very much endanger the whole. Small and unsupported cantonments might become objects with the enemy, and I should not have it in my power to give any essential service to the state at large or a serious opposition to the enemy should they show themselves in force during the winter.[12]

Even after the British surrender at Yorktown the problem did not subside. The New Jersey State Legislature was still dealing with the trade in illegal goods with the enemy and, on June 24, 1782, passed the Act for Preventing an Illicit Trade and Intercourse between the Subjects of this State and the Enemy.[13] James Madison wrote that the illegal trade threatened "a loss of all our hard currency."[14] In 1782 the British pursued a policy of avoiding military conflict but were enticing the Americans with manufactured goods to exhaust their supply of hard currency and to ruin their trade on the high seas. Madison wrote, "I have little expectation that any adequate cure can be applied, whilst our foreign trade is annihilated and the enemy in New York make it an object to keep open this illicit channel."[15] It was a variant of a cold war to get the Americans to sue for peace and for the British to obtain the best bargaining position at the peace negotiations.

Nine

~

BLACK CHAMBERS AND THE MEDICINE FACTORY

Some could argue that the national pastime of the eighteenth century was reading other people's mail. You were able to get in on all the latest gossip. In the eighteenth century there was absolutely no expectation of privacy of the mail. There was an official mail system between a few cities. If you lived out of the major cities or did not want to use the official mail system, there was another method.

Mail could be left at the local tavern. Anyone going in the direction of its destination would collect whatever mail was headed in that general direction and take it with them. They would then leave the mail at a tavern closer to its final destination. Obviously it could take a long time for a letter to get to its destination. If the couriers were nosy or bored they would read the mail they were carrying. It was their entertainment. Letters were sealed with sealing wax and an image was pressed into the wax. If the wax seal was broken or resealed with the incorrect image, the recipient would know that the contents had been read by others.

People would use pseudonyms, ciphers, or code names to hide people's identities and places. Benjamin Franklin used the pen name "Silence Dogood" to get his work published in the *New-England Courant* in 1722. Thomas Jefferson used "Devilsburg" to represent Williamsburg, Virginia. He was courting the attractive Miss Rebecca Burwell.[1] In discussing her in his letter to his friend John Page, in order to hide her identity should someone read his mail, he referred to her as "R. B., Belinda," "Adnileb," Belinda backward, and even "αδνιλεβ," Belinda spelled backward in Greek.

The earliest official effort to intercept and read the mail was established by the French. By 1590 they had set up a secret service operation to learn the contents of the mail. It was called the "Cabinet Noir" or "Black Chamber." The Black Chamber staff was to intercept incoming and outgoing diplomatic mail or the mail from persons who were suspected of being hostile to the government. A specialist on the staff in the Black Chamber would copy the seal image. The letter would then be opened and read. The specialist would make a stamp with a copy of the seal and reseal the letter so as to make it appear it had not been opened. After reading the contents the letter might be allowed to continue on its way. Sometimes the quality of the work was not always the best. William Donaldson in London wrote to Peter N. B. Livingston in New York, on September 6, 1775, that one of the pieces of mail he received on June 23 had a red wax seal over the original black wax seal. This letter had been intercepted and copied at the London Post Office.[2] In some instances dirty tricks would be used. A fake letter would be sent instead of the original or sometimes a totally factitious letter was sent with the purpose of deceiving the recipient.

The British secret service included a Black Chamber that operated within the Post Office Department. John Ernest Bode from Hanover, a constituent state of the Holy Roman Empire, was brought to England specifically to run the secret service office. He ran the office for over fifty years, from 1732 to 1784. His chief assistant was Anthony Todd beginning circa 1751, and he worked there till 1792.[3] Beginning in 1765 each secretary of state issued warrants requiring the opening and reading of *all* diplomatic mail passing through the London Post Office. Nondiplomatic mail was normally opened on suspicion or in search of certain letters. Just as the French did, the English employed specialists who restored the broken wax seals on letters.

The Continental Congress ordered a thousand copies of the portions of some intercepted letters selected by the Committee to be printed and publicly distributed.[4] Based upon intercepted mail provided to Congress from the Committee of Baltimore, the Continental Congress, on April 16, 1776, called the Council of Safety of Maryland to seize its governor, Robert Eden, and his papers.[5] He was able to embark for England before he could be arrested.

It had been a year since Concord and Lexington, and by April 1776, the practice of intercepting and opening the mail by committees and the general public to search for inimical correspondence to the United Colonies was rampant. The situation was so out of control that Congress resolved on April 16 that "no committee but the council or committee of safety in each colony, or such person as they shall, on extraordinary occasions, authorize, should stop the constitutional post, open the mail, or detain any letter."[6]

The congressional resolve reduced the number of people delaying the mail but legitimized the committee of safety in each colony to intercept, delay, open, read, and stop the mail. It confirmed the widely held belief that there was no expectation of privacy in the mail.

An instance of Washington using the intelligence derived from a mail intercept occurred in New York in the summer of 1776. The British had landed on Staten Island but had not yet pushed out the Americans from the island. When they landed, there was a gentleman's agreement that permitted the merchants' market boats to supply both the American and British forces without harassment. This permitted the merchants to get in touch with the British on Staten Island, the British on ships in New York Harbor, and the Americans in New York City, western Long Island, and New Jersey. Elias Nexsen was a New York City merchant who had a residence and a shop at buildings 18 and 20 in Burling Slip.[7]

There is a story that British General Howe on Staten Island requested Nexsen to deliver a letter to Royal Governor William Tryon, who was residing on board a ship in the harbor. Nexsen, as he was putting Howe's letter in his pocket, slipped his finger under the flap in order to loosen the sealing wafer. When he reached New York City, he went to General Washington's headquarters at Richmond Hill and provided him with the letter.[8] Washington read the letter, which told that the British were going to attack Long Island. Washington resealed the letter and had Nexsen deliver it to Tryon as requested. Nexsen abandoned New York for Second River, now Belleville, New Jersey, after the Battle of Long Island.[9] After two or three years he went into New York

City and was arrested as a spy and placed on board one of the prison ships. He was either released or more likely escaped, for when he arrived at his New Jersey residence, he had no shoes.[10]

Washington used double agents as part of his Black Chamber operation. David Gray of Hinsdale in the southwest corner of New Hampshire served in Colonel Joseph Vose's 1st Massachusetts Regiment. He showed an ability for obtaining information on Loyalist activities. During the last half of 1779 he was brought to Washington's attention, who employed him as a spy. The local Tories in Hinsdale put him in touch with a Captain Becket at Rope Ferry, Connecticut.[11] The contact made arrangements for him to cross to Long Island. He proceeded west across Long Island to Brooklyn to see a Colonel Crane, whom he knew from his hometown. Crane introduced him to fifty-eight-year-old Virginia-born Colonel Beverly Robinson of the Loyal American Regiment.[12] Robinson was also involved in British secret service activities. Robinson employed Grey as one of two couriers from New York City to Colonel Samuel Wells in Brattleboro, Vermont.[13] Colonel Wells lived in a five-bay, two-story house built circa 1773.[14] He was a resident British spy feeding information both to Canada and New York City.

Gray traveled from Long Island over the Long Island Sound to the Rope Ferry and Black Point, Connecticut, and passed through Hartford on his way to Colonel Wells. He would return to New York City through Westchester County, New York, the Rope Ferry, or Black Point.[15] However, he would detour and bring the dispatches to General Washington in the Hudson Highlands, who read the messages prior to Gray making his delivery.

On one of his trips to New York, Robinson was unavailable, so Oliver De Lancey took Gray directly to General Henry Clinton to deliver a message from Canada. General Clinton thought

Done from an Original, Drawn from the Life by Alex.ʳ Campbell of Williamsburgh in Virginia.

GEORGE WASHINGTON, Efqʳ

GENERAL and COMMANDER in CHIEF of the CONTINENTAL ARMY in AMERICA.

Published as the Act directs, Sept.ʳ 1775 by C. Shepherd.

General George Washington drawn from life by Alexander
Campbell of Williamsburg, Virginia, and published by C. Sheperd,
London, in September 1775. *(Courtesy of William L. Clements Library)*

Fishing permit issued on September 15, 1775 by British Admiral Graves for fishermen who were American spies. *(Courtesy of Library of Congress)*

British General Thomas Gage, military governor of Massachusetts 1774-1775. *(Courtesy of Library of Congress)*

Continental Army headquarters, Cambridge, Massachusetts, during the siege of Boston 1775-1776. *(Courtesy of Library of Congress)*

Letter in cipher sent by Dr. Benjamin Church, Jr., to his British contact in Boston. *(Courtesy of Library of Congress)*

Cipher key to the letter sent by Dr. Benjamin Church, Jr., to his British contact in Boston. *(Courtesy of Library of Congress)*

General William Howe, commander in chief of British forces in North America 1775-1778. *(Courtesy of Library of Congress)*

Fake letter from General Howe to General Burgoyne intended to deceive George Washington. *(Courtesy of Library of Congress)*

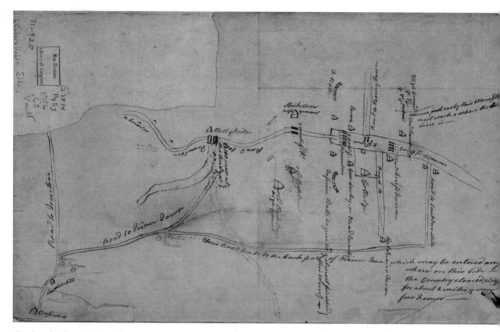

Cadwalader map of Princeton, New Jersey, based on intelligence from a spy. *(Courtesy of Library of Congress)*

Eighteenth-century French print of General John Sullivan from original by Alexander Campbell of Williamsburg, Virginia, originally published in London by Thomas Hart. *(Courtesy of William L. Clements Library)*

Washington's headquarters at Valley Forge, Pennsylvania. *(Courtesy of Library of Congress)*

Lewis House, American spy headquarters in the fall of 1777. *(Courtesy of Lisa Nagy)*

HEAD-QUARTERS, 2? ?? 1777

THE Bearer *John Fox*
has the Commander in Chief's Permiſſion to
paſs the out Poſts, without Moleſtation.
To all Concerned.

NBalfour

Aid de Camp

20

British pass at Philadelphia for American double agent John Fox. *(Courtesy of Library of Congress)*

1901 photograph of Washington's headquarters at Morristown, New Jersey. *(Courtesy of Library of Congress)*

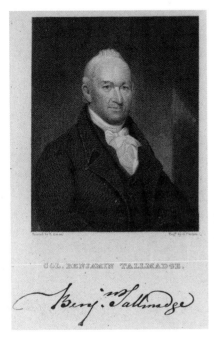

COL. BENJAMIN TALLMADGE.

Major Benjamin Tallmadge, case agent for the Culper Spy Ring. *(Courtesy of William L. Clements Library)*

Part of fake troop return in draft provided by Washington to double agent Elijah Hunter to give to the British. *(Courtesy of Library of Congress)*

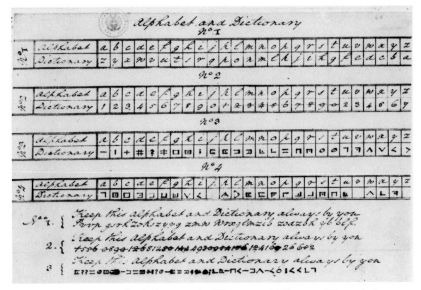

George Washington's cipher card. *(Courtesy of Library of Congress)*

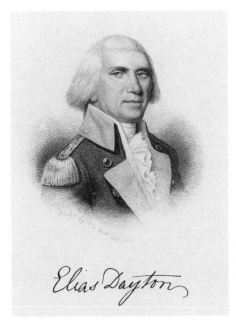

Elias Dayton was a case agent operating American spies into New York City from Elizabeth, New Jersey. *(Courtesy of New York Public Library)*

Benedict Arnold 1776 print from
Thomas Hart in London. *(Courtesy
of William L. Clements Library)*

Benedict Arnold's offer to sell West Point to the British with translation. *(Courtesy of
William L. Clements Library)*

British Major John André was hanged as a
spy in October 1780. *(Courtesy of William L.
Clements Library)*

COUNT RUMFORD.

British spy Benjamin
Thompson later known as
Count Rumford. *(Courtesy of
William L. Clements Library)*

Invisible ink letter from Benjamin Thompson to British headquarters in Boston. *(Courtesy of William L. Clements Library)*

John Jay provided Washington with invisible ink and a reagent which he received from his brother James Jay. *(Courtesy of William L. Clements Library)*

A much older George Washington.
(Courtesy of Library of Congress)

British General Henry
Clinton commander in
chief of British forces
in North America
1778-1782. *(Courtesy
of William L. Clements
Library)*

British General Charles
Cornwallis, who surrendered at
Yorktown, Virginia. *(Courtesy of
William L. Clements Library)*

The most Noble
MARQUIS CORNWALLIS, K:G:
General of His Majesty's Forces
&c. &c. &c.

Gray was trustworthy and engaged him to deliver a reply to Canada. He was given 20 guineas and promised 70 more when he returned with a response. He assisted a Lieutenant Lyman in 1781 make his escape to Connecticut. This exposed Gray as working for the Americans and ended his career as a spy. In the spring of 1782, he rejoined his former company under General William Heath at West Point.[16]

Another case of mail intercepts also involved dispatches from Canada. Mr. John Fish, from the area of Saratoga, went to see Washington at New Windsor, New York.[17] He brought with him intelligence he received from Moses Harris Jr.[18] Harris was a thirty-five-year-old cooper from Dutchess County. Gilbert Harris, his Loyalist uncle who lived at Kingsbury, talked him into serving the king by being a member of a network that transported secret dispatches from Montreal to agents in Albany. Some of the dispatches would pass through Albany to its final destination, British headquarters in New York City. Arrangements were made for Moses Harris to be the last link in the chain. He was to meet British Ensign Smith and his party coming from Canada on April 20. Smith was to turn over a number of letters and Harris was to deliver them to Albany. Harris was then to receive dispatches from Albany and deliver them to Smith.[19] Harris proposed to Mr. Fish to have Smith seized at a designated location and take the documents.

Washington sent Fish to Governor George Clinton of New York with a letter indicating a plan to have Harris take the letters to General Philip Schuyler, "who might contrive means of opening them without breaking the seals, take copies of the contents, and then let them go on. By these means we should become masters of the whole plot; whereas, were we to seize Harris upon his first tour, we should break up the chain of communication, which seems so providentially thrown into our hands."[20] Washington was having General Schuyler set up a Black Chamber operation in northern New York to intercept, read, and forward the British mail. Clinton wrote to Schuyler the next day enclosing Washington's letter and added that he did not know him but thought Mr. Fish was sensible and could keep the operation a secret. If this was a success, he promised them a reward from the state in addition to what Washington promised.[21] On April 29, Harris met at Kingsbury with Ensign Thomas Sherwood of the Corps of Loyal Rangers and John Stout. Thomas Sherwood had lived on a 150-acre farm at Kingsbury. This was one of fifteen missions he would make from Canada into New York.[22] They did not bring any dispatches as they were on a recruiting expedition.

General Schuyler responded to George Clinton that he knew Mr. Fish "for some years past as a man of good moral character and firmly attached to the cause of his country; Harris is an utter stranger to me." He was setting up a meeting with Harris on May 7.[23]

Washington responded that "I am glad to find that you . . . are entering upon the measures for intercepting the Enemy's communications. I hope you will be enabled by the assistance of the person proposed [Harris] (if he is found sufficiently faithful and intelligent) to prosecute those measures to good effect; because I think the intelligence obtained thro' that channel may be depended upon, and will eventually be of very great consequence to us."[24]

Harris delivered dispatches in Easton, New York, to Fish, who took them to Schuyler, who then altered them before returning them.[25] The dispatches were delivered to William Shepherd, a smith and cutler. While making and fixing bayonets, knives, and swords for the American cause, he was one of the British secret agents in Albany.[26]

General Schuyler sent Harris with a false letter from him to Washington to take to the British in Canada. He was to use the explanation of it being an intercepted letter for his having possession of it. The letter mentioned the destruction of Admiral George Brydges Rodney's fleet and that Schuyler was calling in Stark's brigade for an invasion of Canada.[27]

Harris identified a man coming from Canada as a deserter, but he was really a spy. His description of the man was excellent, and based on it, Higginbotham was detained. He was interrogated by General Schuyler. Because the information came from a spy, Schuyler could not say very much. He was released and he went to see a Mr. Smith at Albany.[28] Mr. Smith was most likely Dr. George Smith, whom British General Frederick Haldimand identified as his best intelligencer at Albany.[29] Higginbotham, believing he was suspected, stayed only a short time.[30] Harris was arrested by Major John McKinstrey for purchasing supplies for the enemy. He sent him under guard to the commissioners for detecting and defeating conspiracies at Albany and appeared before them on August 13, 1781. They determined he was not as dangerous as McKinstrey claimed and could be released on payment of a bond. On August 22, they determined the amount was £100 and he was released upon payment.[31] Since he was working as a spy for General Schuyler he most likely had approval to trade in goods with the enemy as his cover. If they released him, he would no longer be able to work as a spy, whereas placing him on bail actually reinforced his cover story.

Washington, in his personal library at Mount Vernon, had the Society of Gentlemen Dictionary of Arts and Sciences that contained the procedure for invisible writing. When a slightly acidic liquid is used to write a message, the writing will disappear and the fibers of the paper will weaken. When heat is applied to the paper, the treated portion that is weakened turns brown more rapidly than the untreated portion of paper. The writing again becomes visible.

The British were the first to use invisible writing during the American Revolution. Benjamin Thompson, later known as Count Rumford, was a Loyalist spy. He sent a letter dated May 6, 1775, from Woburn, Massachusetts, to an unidentified person in Boston. The document was discovered as part of British General Thomas Gage's papers.[32] The writing was made visible by using a counterpart liquid.

In December of 1776, before the Battle of Trenton, a letter sent to Philadelphia by a Loyalist with invisible writing was delivered to Washington's headquarters as being suspicious. Washington asked Lieutenant Colonel Tench Tilghman, one of his aides, to check out the letter. He held the letter near a fire to use the light to read it. When he did so, the hidden message became visible.[33]

William Smith, a Loyalist, while he lived in New York City, wrote messages with invisible writing to Dr. Thomas Smith, one of his brothers, who lived in West Haverstraw, New York. He used lime juice on scraps of paper.[34] When Dr. Smith held the scraps of paper near heat, the secret message became visible.

This first known American use of invisible writing during the American Revolution occurred in the fall of 1776. John Jay, who was at Fishkill, New York, had received a letter from Silas Deane in Paris.[35] Deane was a representative from Connecticut to the First and Second Continental Congresses. Early in 1776 Deane was sent to France to secure financial support for the

American cause. He shared the document and complained to Robert Morris in Philadelphia about it. Deane did not take care in writing the letter, as it contained many blots and, in two instances, the lines crossed.[36]

If Washington had not read the entry in his encyclopedia, he definitely learned about invisible writing by December of 1776 when Lieutenant Colonel Tench Tilghman exposed the letter that was to be forwarded to Philadelphia. The earliest known use of the practice by Washington was with the Culper Spy Ring, in 1778, which was using the practice by spring of 1779.

Washington, on May 3, 1779, informed Elias Boudinot of the method of invisible writing, which required a reagent to make it visible. It was to be used by spies working in New York reporting to Boudinot. He said he could get "a liquid which nothing but a counter liquor (rubbed over the paper afterwards) can make legible. Fire which will bring lime juice, milk and other things of this kind to light has no effect on it. A letter upon trivial matters of business, written in common ink, may be fitted with important intelligence which cannot be discovered without the counter part, or liquid here mentioned."[37] None of the original spy reports using invisible ink to Boudinot have survived nor has mention which of the original copies of the reports used the invisible ink. The agent and reagent were also used by the Culper Spy Ring.[38] A letter in the Benedict Arnold treason correspondence was written in invisible ink.[39]

James Jay provided Washington with an initial supply of invisible ink that used an agent and its reagent. George Washington's supply of agent and reagent was running out. On April 9, 1780, he wrote, "The liquid with which you were so obliging as to furnish me for the purpose of private correspondence is exhausted; and as I have found it very useful, I take the liberty to request you will favor me with a further supply. I have still a sufficiency of the materials for the counterparts on hand. Should you not have by you the necessary ingredients, if they are to be procured at any of the hospitals within your reach, I would wish you to apply for them in my name."[40]

On April 13, Jay sent Washington a supply of "medicine" (invisible ink and reagent) in a little box. He apologized for the small quantity, explaining that it was the last of what he had brought back from Europe. Jay reported:

> I have now the principal ingredients for the composition by me, and the rest may be procured: but the misfortune is, that I have no place where a little apparatus may be erected for preparing it. The composition requires some assistance from chemistry; an out house is so small, and so well inhabited, that there is not a corner left where a little brick furnace, which a mason could build in two hours time, can be placed. A log hut for the purpose might be soon run up, but it is also out of my power to effect this, neither bricks, boards nor lime are to be purchased here, nor a carpenter nor mason to be had without great difficulty, if at all. I beg you will not infer from hence that I would rather decline the undertaking. So far from that being the case, if you shall think it worth while, and will only direct [Lieutenant] Colonel [Udny] Hay to furnish the workman, and other requisites, I shall soon have the satisfaction of sending you such a supply that you may not only use it freely yourself, but even spare a little to a friend, if necessary, without the apprehension of future want.[41]

Washington instructed Deputy Quartermaster General Lieutenant Colonel Udny Hay at Fishkill, "Sir James Jay has requested the assistance of a few artificers for a day or two to erect a small elaboratory [sic]. As he purposes making some experiments which maybe of public utility and has already furnished me with some chymical [sic] preparations, from which I have derived considerable advantages I think it proper to gratify him. You will therefore be pleased to furnish him with the necessary hands. And should a few boards or such matters be wanting to compleat [sic] the building which is to be of logs, you will also procure them, if it be in your power."[42]

We know that Jay had his laboratory constructed because in a September 19 letter from Fishkill, he apologizes to Washington for not getting the "medicine" to him sooner.[43]

Ten

PETITE GUERRE

In the eight years of the American Revolution, between the Battles of Concord and Lexington in 1775 and the British evacuation of New York in 1783, there were more periods of no or minor activity than major battles. The two opposing armies would be inactive but were still a threat to make a sudden attack. The armies would send out foraging expeditions to obtain what was needed. Both sides had to be on guard of any movement by the enemy. It was a time of small war, or Petite Guerre.

Such a situation occurred after the Continental Army arrived in Morristown, New Jersey, in January 1777. The two armies were at rest and not much was happening. There was also a decreased amount of espionage activities during a Petite Guerre because there was little to report. For the Americans the reduced spy activity also had its roots in fiscal concerns. Hard currency to pay spies was always a problem and Washington was frugal in spending it. He knew that armies rest, heal, and resupply during winter and the new season of campaigning would come with spring. This happened with each winter of the war.

At the end of February he was concerned "that this Petit [*sic*] Guerre will be continued long, I think matters will be transacted upon a larger scale. The troops at [New] Brunswick have been considerably reinforced of late, and Gen[era]l Howe and Piercy are said to have come over, their number there and the dependent posts, must be from 10[,000] to 12,000; from these circumstances, It is highly probable, nay almost certain, they mean to make a push; their object is a secret, only known to them, tho' I have my conjectures."[1] He did not have to wait long before the British advanced into New Jersey. General Howe's goal was to take Philadelphia, but he could not leave a refreshed and healthy Continental Army in his rear as he went across New Jersey to Philadelphia. Frustrated at being unable to draw Washington into a major battle, he retraced his steps to Perth Amboy and then evacuated his main army back to Staten Island. He took his army to the Chesapeake and began his successful campaign to capture Philadelphia. The British held the city from September 1777 until June 1778, when they returned to New York.

In December 1779, General Clinton left New York, taking the war to South Carolina. He left Hessian General Wilhelm von Knyphausen in charge of the British forces at New York. With the main fighting having moved to the south, there was nonetheless still a war to be waged in the north—a Petite Guerre. There would be few large-scale military offensives. When there was a Petite Guerre, Washington had definite plans for the troops: "I would recommend keeping your force as much collected and as compact as the nature of the service will admit, doing duty by corps, instead of detachments, whenever it is practicable; and above all exerting yourself most strenuously and assiduously, while the troops are in a camp of repose, to make them perfect in their exercise and maneuvres [*sic*], and to establish the most perfect system of discipline and duty; the good of the service, and emulation of corps, will I am perswaded [*sic*], prompt the officers and men to devote their whole time and attention to the pleasing and honorable task of becoming masters of their profession."[2] Washington was astonished while reading a newspaper provided by Major Barber through Lord Stirling. He said, "It is surprising the enemy have such intelligence with respect to our movements." It made him realize how good the enemy's intelligence-gathering network of spies was.[3]

Washington had discussed with Lafayette the idea of a proclamation to the Canadians. "If it is not already done, I think it ought not to be delayed." It should be:

> dwelling on the happy opportunity it will afford them to renew their ancient friendships with France, by joining the allied arms and assisting to make Canada a part of the American confederation with all the privileges and advantages enjoyed by the other members; cautioning them by no means to aid the enemy in their preparations for defending the Province . . . you should hold yourself up as a French and American officer charged both by the King of France and by Congress with a commission to address them upon the occasion. . . . The more mystery in this business the better. It will get out and it ought to seem to be against our intention [for it to be known].[4]

It was another deception being played.

Washington had decided to give the British something to worry about. On June 4, 1780, he sent Benedict Arnold in Philadelphia a draft of a proclamation in French addressed to the

French-speaking inhabitants of Canada. It was a call for them to join with the French forces destined for Canada in the cause of the United States. This was intended only to deceive Clinton in New York into thinking that the attack would be made in Canada and not New York.

Arnold at this time had already been secretly in a traitorous communication and negotiations with John André at British headquarters for a year about going to the British. Arnold was to provide the copy to a trustworthy printer to make a proof sheet and send the proof to Washington for corrections. Once approved he wanted 500 copies. The printer was not to keep a copy or allow any out of his possession.[5] As soon as Arnold received the draft, which was a day after Washington sent it, he tried to find a printer who understood French and that could be trusted but did not have any success. He arranged with Mr. David Claypoole on Second Street to do the printing, but Claypoole did not understand French and did not have type for some of the letters of the French alphabet.[6] The first attempt was filled with errors and had to be done a second time. This is what Arnold sent to him. He was departing Philadelphia and left the original draft and a proof sheet with Mrs. Arnold. He advised Washington that she would deliver them as he ordered.[7]

Arnold sent a letter on the 7th to George Beckwith at British headquarters in New York, informing him that he received the proclamation from Washington. He left a copy with Joseph Stansbury, who handled his correspondence with the British. He was to forward it to British headquarters.

Arnold continued that the French minister that day told him that 8,000 French troops were to go to Canada. He provided his itinerary in order to give a British agent a chance to confer with him. "If meet a person in my mensuration [of something like my rank] who has the token [a ring] agreed on, you may expect every intelligence in my power which will probably be of consequence. When fully authorized by Sir Henry Clinton to treat I wish to have a conference with one of your officers in whom we can place a mutual confidence."[8]

Stansbury that day ciphered the proclamation and sent it off addressed to "G. B. Ring, executor to the late John Anderson, Esq., in care of James Osborne." G. B. Ring was George Beckwith, who had kept one of the rings agreed on as a token to prove the message was authentic. Beckwith had temporarily taken the place of John Anderson (John André) and was to be reached through James Osborne (Rev. Jonathan Odell). Stansbury wrote that the proclamation "must be a profound secret."[9] The documents traveled safely across New Jersey and arrived at British headquarters. General Henry Clinton sent on August 31 a translation to Lord George Germain in London.[10]

While the war raged in the south there was one major battle in the north, the Battle of Springfield, New Jersey, on June 23, 1780. There were 6,000 British and Hessian troops under the command of General Knyphausen involved in the fighting. They attacked and were repulsed by 1,500 Continental troops plus 500 New Jersey Militia under the command of General Nathanael Greene. British General Clinton had General Alexander Leslie with 6,000 men proceed to the general area to attack Washington should he come out of Morristown to attack Knyphausen's flank. General James Robertson remained in reserve in Elizabeth Town with five regiments (1,865 men). The British had 13,865 involved in this operation.

Greene, as instructed by Washington, was trying to get the best intelligence on the British movements and plans. Thomas Pool was a double agent who was working directly for Washington and the American headquarters. Alexander Hamilton, aide-de-camp to Washington, knew of Pool's secret service activities and most likely was his control agent.[11] Pool returned on June 22 at 5 p.m. "from Elizabeth Town, he says that General Clinton with the whole British Army will be in motion this evening. He further says that three thousand are to embark for Kings Ferry, if the wind and tide favor their designs. The residue of the Army are to March towards Kings Ferry by Newark and Slauter dam (a little above Acquackanunk) [Acquackanonk included present-day Clifton and Passaic]. Their object is to cut off your Excellency from the mouth of the Clove, and prevent your getting into West Point." The gentleman was to meet the British at the West Farms this evening a little back of Newark directly on the back route to Acquackanunck.[12] Greene had not been advised how trustworthy Thomas Pool was. He was beginning to doubt the intelligence he provided. At 10 p.m. Greene wrote to Washington, "I have been impatiently waiting in consequence of the intelligence received this afternoon from Mr. P—l [Thomas Pool] to hear of the enemy's beginning their march. . . . I do not know what kind of credit is to be given to this Mr. P— [Pool] but he says he is employed by your Excellency and that he is willing to forfeit his life if every thing he tells is not strictly true as far as he can determine from the appearance of things. May not the enemy be apprised of his being a double spy and indeavor [sic] to ploy him off accordingly, in order to mislead our attention[?] I told him of the consequence of deceiving us, would be nothing less than a forfeiture of his life. He really appear[e]d to be sincere but I begin to doubt his intelligence."[13] After the battle the British would no longer need to have Pool continue to scout out the American forces. Pool continued to operate as a double agent for Washington but was eventually discovered and sent to a British prison for the duration of the war.

Before the Battle of Springfield the British had their spies in the field trying to get intelligence of the American situation. One such spy was Daniel Martin. He used the code letters "MD" when he wrote from Chatham, New Jersey, on June 17, 1780, to General Knyphausen that "Young Tennifly is killed and Claussen[,] Hutchinson[, and] Lacy who were with him are taken and I suppose be hanged."[14] A court-martial of the line was planned to be held on the 17th at 9 a.m. at the old house near the forks of the road between the first and second lines of the army. However, it was delayed until June 18. Lieutenant Colonel Return Jonathan Meigs of the 6th Connecticut Regiment was president of the general court-martial proceedings held at Bryant's Tavern.[15] John Clawson, Ludwick Larick, and William Hutchinson were tried on the charge of "coming from the enemy with arms and found lurking as spies in the vicinity of the army of the United States" and by more than a two-thirds margin sentenced to death. Washington confirmed the sentence and ordered that they be hanged the following morning at guard mounting.[16]

Martin, in his June 17 letter, also wrote, "[T]he rebels put me immediately under guard as soon as I got to Newark and from there to Colonel Courtney's quarters and from thence to headquarters. Thank fortune I had a proper flag of truce and a certificate of my exchange and likewise my old parole." The document is docketed "to be depended upon" by Captain George Beckwith, of the 37th Regiment of Foot, who was at this time an assistant to Oliver De Lancey on military intelligence.[17] On July 3, 1780, from Paramus, Daniel Martin, this time using the code letters "DM," wrote to General Henry Clinton. He wrote that he was supposed to meet the British army at the west farm but instead found Lee's Light Horse and the Militia, which "I found made it impossible to get down with out being taken up as a spy as I was stopped twice that night." He mentioned that he came out by way of Elizabeth Town: "I at last made out to get my trunk with what few things I had in it by entering as a Volunteer in the Mr. Washington's Army . . . should be glad that you would send out a note by the bearer what you wish me to do next."[18] He was finally able to make his escape and returned to New York on March 18, 1781.[19]

There was a change in the sand dunes that made up a portion of the New Jersey coastline early in 1778. It opened the Shrewsbury River to the sea and the inlet remained open until 1800.[20] This changed Sandy Hook from a promontory into an island that was controlled by the British army. At times the British navy had a warship stationed at the Hook. Sandy Hook was even called "Refugee's Town," where Tories could receive protection from the British military stationed there.[21] This would have made it possible for a small boat from Shrewsbury to go out of the inlet and head north to drop off merchandise either to the sloop *Eagle* at Princess Bay, to refugees, or to the military encampment at Sandy Hook.[22] Governor Livingston stated that the illegal trade had depleted Bergen County by August of 1778 and had shifted its focus to Shrewsbury and that the state was unable to stop it.[23]

Lieutenant Enos Reeves of the Pennsylvania Line wrote that "there has been an amazing trade carried on from [New] Jersey shore to the city of New York, but we hope to put a stop to it."[24] It was wishful thinking, as they could not raise enough men to guard the entire coastline. Washington left the enforcement of the illegal trade to the state. He had Brigadier General David Forman of the New Jersey Militia station observers in the

Raritan Bay area to keep a watchful eye on British shipping. Colonel John Stillwell watched from his house atop Garrett's Hill.[25] He used a spyglass provided by General Forman.[26] His reports on the movement of ships in Raritan Bay and Sandy Hook were in the form of a diary and were given to David Forman, who then provided them to Washington.[27] Martha Tallman Seabrook, who lived at Shoal Harbor, worked as an agent in sending reports of observations.[28] Captain Thomas Lyell, who lived in Perth Amboy on the hill overlooking Raritan Bay and Staten Island, kept a lookout for Washington.[29] It is said the Tories gave Brigadier General David Forman the nickname of "Devil Dave."[30]

During the Petite Guerre, Washington did not have major battles to fight but did have little incidents that required his attention to limit the damage. The enemy was trying to use Americans who decided to pledge allegiance to the Crown. Not every traitor was a general such as Benedict Arnold or a key administrator such as Dr. Benjamin Church Jr., who was director of the Continental Army's Hospital Department; there were others of lesser rank.

William Bernard Gifford enlisted as a second lieutenant in Captain Bloomfield's Company of the 3rd New Jersey Regiment on February 7, 1776.[31] He rose quickly through the ranks. He was promoted to first lieutenant on August 10, 1776, and to captain on November 20, 1776.[32] He was wounded at the Battle of Monmouth on June 28, 1778. He, Andrew McFarland, Major John Eccleston, commander of the outpost, and Major Mathias Williamson, deputy quartermaster general in New Jersey, were taken prisoner at Elizabeth Town on January 25, 1780, by a British expedition for the 1st and 4th Battalions of the New Jersey Volunteers under the command of Abraham Van

Buskirk and guided by Captain Cornelius Hatfield Jr., New Jersey Loyalists.

Buskirk wrote to Colonel Sir Thomas Stirling concerning the surprise raid on Elizabeth Town. He praised Hatfield for leading his men through deep snow to a "beaten road" where the traffic had compacted the snow, which took him directly into the town. Once there they surprised the American garrison, taking fifty-two men prisoner.[33] Rev. James Caldwell blamed the people the Americans used as spies for leading the enemy in a raid on Elizabeth.[34]

Gifford's confinement during his captivity was liberal to such an extent that he was able to court and marry Ann Voorhies at New Utrecht, Long Island, on April 1, 1780.[35] For a prisoner to earn money to support his new wife was extremely difficult. Gifford, at New Utrecht, Kings County, Long Island, was in a financial bind. On November 10 he tried to raise the money by offering to work for British Major Oliver De Lancey as a spy. He would go back into the American lines to settle his exchange and to provide military intelligence. De Lancey had suggested that Gifford take an officer with him to support his cover and Gifford suggested Captain Bateman Lloyd, who belonged to Gifford's regiment: "I think it will be in my power, if it should be the Com[mander] In chief[']s desire, to send or bring in such intelligence as may be of service . . . if you sir will point out what the Commander in chief, wou[l]d wish me to do, I'll endeavour to execute it with the greatest pleasure." Gifford's encouragement to go on this mission was because he was in financial trouble. He was a newly married man who was a prisoner. It was not a situation where he could support his wife. He explains it best when he is asking for a loan: "[T]he sooner I go out the better, you know sir my situation as to cash, if you can procure me a little, I shall esteem it a most particular favour, and will pay you when I return."[36]

Gifford was sent to New Jersey on his mission. He prepared his report on November 28 and said, "I have been at Trenton dined and spent the evening with G. L. [Governor Livingston] and several of the council and assembly. They say they will make this new money pass as specie, they have noted their quota of troops to be raised." Gifford then gave his opinion that they would not be able to accomplish the raising of the new troops and getting people to accept the new issue of paper money: "The Legislature are fearful you mean to establish a post at [Perth] Amboy. They say if you do it will greatly distress them, if you were to establish a post there commanded by an active and enterprising officer, it would answer many valuable purposes. I shall set off for W. P. [West Point] to morrow."[37]

Gifford was looking to find a way to get his report into British headquarters in New York City. He learned that British Lieutenant Thomas Hughes of the 53rd Regiment of Foot was being exchanged and had just arrived in Elizabeth Town, having left Lancaster on November 22. Hughes and a Lieutenant Brown were awaiting for transportation across the Arthur Kill.[38] They stayed at a tavern in Elizabeth Town owned by a physician who had plenty of books. Hughes says that he met Gifford on November 30 and agreed to take his report to the British adjutant general in New York City. Hughes and Brown were taken across to Staten Island in a fisherman's canoe on December 2. It took Hughes till December 4 to arrange transportation across the harbor to New York City. Upon his arrival he delivered Gifford's message to the adjutant general at headquarters.[39]

Gifford's next letter, dated December 7, 1780, to De Lancey, reported that he tried to get to West Point but "met the Brigade near Kings Ferry on their way to Pompton. I cou[l]d not then with no pretense proceed any further. I am now exchanged and can't possibly return to New York which much vexes and disappoints me." This change in status presented him with problems. He was anxious, as he could not get to his wife nor collect his pay:

> I mean in a few days to go to the Rgt [Colonel Dayton's 3rd New Jersey Regiment] and resign [as captain], after that I shall return as soon as possible to N[ew] York, and will abide by the British Army if they shou[l]d go to the utmost ends of the earth, if you wish to write to me, send it by Mr. Vernon to be left at Mrs. Vergereau's where it will be safe. I must by the favor of you Sir, to pay a little attention to my W [wife's?] estate, I am fearful that the wood will be cut, and the buildings injur[e]d, as I have no other friend but yourself, a word from you will be sufficient.[40]

Colonel Francis Barber, a native of Princeton and an officer in the 3rd New Jersey Regiment, suspected that Gifford wanted to go to the British and advised Washington on December 11 of his concerns.[41] Barber said when Gifford came out of New York, he was exchanged. Gifford then met up with the brigade on its way from West Point to Pompton about December 1. Gifford informed him that he was not exchanged but was soon expected to be and was out on a parole. His parole was until December 14 and then he was required to return to Long Island.

Washington advised Barber, knowing that he needed more proof before he could do anything and told him:

If there are good reasons for suspecting Capt[ain] Gifford's fidelity, I would by no means give him a discharge
from the army, because he might then go off to the
enemy, and we should not have it in our power to treat
him as a deserter should he fall into our hands again. I
would at any rate bring him to a trial on his arrest; something may, in the course of it, turn up, which may give
sufficient grounds for securing him afterwards, if the
sentence of the court should not find him guilty in a military point of light. Should he be cashiered, and then
go off, the enemy will not have much to boast of, from
the acquisition of such a character.[42]

Gifford's statements made Barber extremely suspicious. He
decided to interview some gentlemen who had lately been exchanged and get their opinions. They were also suspicious of
Gifford's motives. Barber informed Gifford that he was under
his orders to remain at Elizabeth Town due to crimes committed before his capture, particularly disobedience of orders in
leaving the regiment a day or two before his capture.

A few days after Gifford arrived at Elizabeth Town he tried to
resign and forwarded his captain's commission to Colonel Barber. Barber acknowledged to Washington that he did not have
proof of his suspicions, otherwise he would have arrested him.[43]

On January 18, Gifford prepared a report for De Lancey on
a situation in the New Jersey Line: "The detachment at Chatham
is much dissatisfied, also the rest of them at Pompton, Parson
[James] Caldwell is now paying twenty dollars of this new trash
[money] to each officer and five to each private. This is a present from the state."[44]

Barber told Washington of Gifford's request to resign and

his suspicions of his motives. Washington informed Barber on January 21, "Having considered the affair of Capt[ain] Gifford since I saw you, I am upon the whole of opinion, as we have no testimony against him that we are at liberty to make use of, it will not be advisable to molest him. It would have an arbitrary appearance, to commit him to or keep him long in confinement without a prosecution. I would however advise that you take measures to have him closely watched, and if possible drawn into some snare that will unfold his practices. His resignation must be accepted without further delay."[45] He was just too dangerous to have around the army, which was reeling from the Pennsylvania Line Mutiny and its repercussions. It resulted in the discharge of 1,250 infantry and 67 artillery men, and 1,150 men were given furloughs. Washington's statement—"we have no testimony against him that we are at liberty to make use of"— implies that he had intelligence from one of his spies concerning Gifford. If he used that intelligence, he would be putting that spy in extreme danger, as the British could easily learn the source. This was not the first time Washington could not use what he knew without endangering one of his spies. He learned he had to protect his sources or lose another Higday.

While at Elizabeth Town, Gifford prepared a report to De Lancey that Pennsylvania governor Joseph Reed offered the Pennsylvania Line mutineers 100 guineas for the two spies they captured. They turned down the money but instead voted to turn over the two spies.[46]

Once Barber informed Gifford that his resignation was accepted, Gifford did not waste any time and departed for British territory. Oliver De Lancey said that Gifford, "who I had corresponded with came over to us;" that is he came into New York on the 21st.[47] Lieutenant Thomas Hughes saw Gifford in New

York City on January 22, 1781.[48] Royal chief justice William
Smith wrote in his memoirs that Gifford came into New York
City on the 21st. Gifford had thrice tried to see General Clinton
without success. Smith told Samuel Mabbot, a banished Quaker,
to tell him to come see him.[49]

That evening there was a great wind and a snowstorm. The
next morning (Tuesday the 23rd) Nicholas Hoffman trudged
through three inches of snow to get to Smith's residence. Upon
arrival he told him that Gifford was going to try one more attempt to see General Clinton.[50] Hoffman had told Smith about
Gifford's capture nine months ago and his discharge from his
parole seven weeks ago: "He intimated when he went out [to
New Jersey] that he should quit the rebels as he now has." What
he wanted to tell Clinton was not in his reports. He claimed that
the mutineers were waiting for the British army to come into
New Jersey. If there was a descent into New Jersey they were prepared to join them. Smith then wrote up this account and sent
it to General Tryon.

The next day Smith complained to Scotland-born Andrew
Elliot, lieutenant governor of the province of New York, of the
lack of success Gifford had in seeing General Clinton. He promised to find out why. Gifford had provided printed copies of
correspondence between Joseph Reed and the Pennsylvania
mutineers.[51] Hoffman revealed they had gotten word of the New
Jersey Line Mutiny, which would be put down by force. Gifford
never did get to see General Clinton but did see Oliver De
Lancey, "who charged him to say nothing to any man."[52]

Colonel Elias Dayton, in December 1780, had discussed with
Washington a plan of having a former deserter work for him as
a spy. The spy in question was former Lieutenant William Mc-
Michael of the 3rd New Jersey Regiment, who had deserted to

the British on August 14, 1776.[53] Loyalist Captain Thomas Ward had sent him under a flag of truce in the American line. Colonel Dayton, on April 6, had him arrested as a deserter from his regiment:

> [F]or which I have a precedent, tho I would wish to have your Excellency's opinion upon the propriety of the measure, which will be very necessary if for any reason your Excellency should not approve of my intentions with respect to McMichael. He seems to agree very heartily to engage in our service and assures me that he has it greatly in his power to serve us; how far he is sincere, a trial only can evince. He has intrigue, firmness, understanding and ev[e]ry other requisite to answer every expectation. I have proposed to suffer him to make his escape, which I shall do as soon as I receive your Excellency's approbation.

He wanted to make sure that he had Washington's concurrence of employing him as a spy before allowing his escape. He also wanted to know what could be offered to McMichael in payment for his service and any advice as to method of communication.[54]

Ward, commanding at Bergen Point, complained of the treatment of his flag of truce under the command of Lieutenant McMichael. He claimed it was "entirely unprecedented, contrary to the Laws of Nations and the Rules of War, and as my Flags have always been received and treated with the Respect due to them; Must request that Lieut. McMichael be immediately delivered or a certain time for his return fixed, if not within the immediate reach of this flag, or that you would assign your reasons in writing, why he is detained by return of this conveyance."[55]

Washington agreed to try McMichael as a spy. He preferred allowing him to escape because returning him "would imply that we think we have no right to seize upon a deserter in all cases whatever and wherever we can find him, a point which I would always insist upon, more especially as it may one day be brought in question where a gentleman of high rank, who formerly belonged to us, may be the object."[56]

Washington wanted the information but did not want to be the case agent handling McMichael. How far McMichael "may be depended upon or how used, I leave it with you to determine." He assigned Dayton to the job but as per his usual practice he provided detailed instructions on what Dayton was expected to provide:

> The material informations will be—previous notice of any movements—and an exact account from time to time of the numbers and positions of the enemy—and of the strength and destinations of detachments when any are made, specifying the corps if possible—I think it must be an easy matter to ascertain the corps now remaining in and about New York—noting their stations— This I would wish done as soon as possible. As to fixing any certain reward I cannot do it. It ought always to depend upon the importance of the service performed or intelligence communicated, and in that proportion I am willing to promise compensation. Be pleased to make enquiry whether there is any talk or appearance of another embarkation, and if there should be, what is said to be the destination.[57]

Dayton received Washington's letter on the evening of April 13 and in his April 14 response he said, "I believe without a doubt that another embarkation is in great forwardness and that in every point it will be more respectable than that of the last." He enclosed a letter from Captain John Scudder, commanding at Elizabeth Town, which was in a great measure confirmed by his private intelligence from the city. Dayton was perplexed at the number of soldiers leaving New York: "How they can spare such a number of men from New York consistently with their own safety is to me very mysterious and what I cannot reconcile with my idea of their strength and numbers."[58]

Shortly after, he heard from McMichael, who gave him information that "Colonel [John] Con[n]olly with his corps [was] to proceed to Quebec as soon as possible, to be joined in Canada by Sir John Johnson with a number of Tories and Indians said to amount to three thousand.[59] His rout[e] to be by Buck Island, Lake Ontario, and Venango and his object is Fort Pitt and all the adjacent posts. Con[n]olly takes with him a number of commissions for persons now residing at Pittsburg[h] and several hundred men at that place have agreed to join to make prisoners of Colonel Broadhead and all friends to America. His great influence in that country will, it is said, enable him to prevail upon the Indians and inhabitants to assist the British in any measure."[60]

Connolly had submitted another plan on November 25, 1780, to General Clinton for an attack on the western Pennsylvania frontier. On April 20, 1781, Connolly sent a letter to General Clinton advising him that "in my secret negotiations with the inhabitants of Northumberland County and with all the other Loyalists upon the East side of the Allegheny Mountains Plan to raise troops at Pittsburgh."[61] Clinton sent a letter of introduction of Dr. Connolly and his plan to Cornwallis in Virginia dated June 9, 1781.[62] Clinton gave tacit approval to Cornwallis's assisting him, but the attack would be from the south.

Washington was at New Windsor, New York, and needed to know what the enemy status was in New York. In three weeks he would meet with French General Jean-Baptiste Donatien de Vimeur, Comte de Rochambeau, commander in charge of the French forces in North America. Washington wanted to take back New York and hoped he and Rochambeau would agree on a plan for an attack. On May 1, he wrote to Colonel Elias Dayton, commander of the 3rd New Jersey Regiment, "The knowledge of the present state of the enemy in New York and its dependencies with regard to the total strength, and the particular disposition of the corps, is of so great and interesting importance, that I must request you will have the goodness to turn your earliest and strictest attention, to obtain and communicate the information of these things, with the greatest certainty and precision."[63] He also wanted explicit detail: "Should the Detachment, which has been so long in preparation, sail from New York; I should wish to be informed as expeditiously as possible of the moment of its departure[,] the particular corps it consists of, their strength, and the destination; as also of the number of the regular force (including all the established corps) still remaining on Staten Island, in New York and at King[']s Bridge, specifying the Reg[imen]ts by name, and noting the distribution at each post with as much accuracy as possible."[64] Washington wanted Dayton to establish a correspondence with New York by way of Elizabeth Town for the purpose of obtaining intelligence of the enemy's movements and designs. He wrote in his diary "that by a comparison of Acc[oun]ts proper and just conclusions may be drawn."[65] He was very clear that he wanted to compare intelligence so that he would not make a mistake.

Dayton's report of May 8 cannot be found and may no longer exist. He had told of the sailing of the fleet. Washington asked him to confirm or contradict the information he provided. He wanted this accomplished "as speedily as possible and with as much precision as you can, as to the number of ships of war, troops and destination. The number of ships of the line mentioned by your informant must be false except [if] the enemy have received a reinforcement."[66]

Dayton responded from Chatham, New Jersey, on May 9 that he "shall do every thing in my power to comply fully with the requisition contained in it, altho[ugh] I have of late experienced much greater difficulty in gaining good intelligence from the other side than formerly. I am in daily expectation of having an interview with the person mentioned lately, when I have effected which, I hope to be able to communicate many interesting and important matters."[67]

Dayton's report was received on the 11th. He indicated "10 ships of the line, and 3 or 4000 troops had sailed from New York."[68] Washington hurriedly sent off a letter to General Rochambeau at Rhode Island: "[H]ave this instant received a Letter from Col[onel] Dayton (an Officer of intelligence in the American Army near Elizabeth Town) which contains the inclosed Paragraph,

> His information must I conceive, have magnified the enemy's force, both in ships of the line, and in the strength of the detachment. Nor do I conceive the fleet could have sailed on the 8th as he mentions, on account of the wind

and weather; still less am I disposed to believe that New Port [Newport, Rhode Island] is the object of this armament; but as intelligence thro' another channel pointed to that epoch for the sailing of the fleet; I have not delayed a moment in giving the information as I received it, and shall thank your Excellency for handing it to the Admiral [Charles René Dominique Gochet, Chevalier Destouches, who was temporarily commanding the French fleet at Newport].[69]

Washington also sent an extract of the letter to Congress. He informed them:

As this is the first Information, I thought proper to communicate it, altho[ugh], from the circumstances of the wind and weather at the time the fleet is said to have sailed, as well as from the number of ships of the line (of which there were not so many at New York) and strength of the detachment, it does not carry the strongest marks of credibility; if founded on fact, it will undoubtedly be soon confirmed, thro[ugh] other channels, of which I shall not fail to advise Congress.[70]

Washington wrote in his diary on May 12 that the information on the sailing of troops provided by Colonel Dayton was correct. He received the same intelligence "from two sensible deserters from King[']s Bridge which place they left yesterday morning at two o[']clock."[71] On the 15th he received a letter from Samuel Culper Sr. dated May 1 about the sailing of a fleet from New York that was to depart on the 2nd. If all the troops scheduled to depart had left, then the balance of soldiers remaining in New York would be about 4,000.[72] The time frame of two weeks for transporting the letter is an indication of how stale some of their intelligence was.

On the 16th, Dayton had informed him:

[T]he British fleet had sailed the 8th Inst[ant]. I have since discovered that the mistake took its' [*sic*] rise from the circumstance of a great part of it having fallen down below the watering place on that day.[73] I would now acquaint your Excellency that the fleet really sailed on Sunday, convoyed by six ships of the line. Their delay thus long has I imagine been occasioned by one of their largest ships striking upon the shoals near the west bank which was got off with great difficulty. The transports which sailed amounted to about twenty—the number of troops does not exceed 2000 nor do I think it much less—All reports appear to confine their destination to Virginia and then Delaware.[74]

One ship of the line with three or four frigates only are left in York harbor—twenty five transports set for sea and entirely empty are at anchor in the North River stream. I am told, there are not 300 men in the city and those principally Highlanders.[75]

The number reported is an obvious error and adding a missing zero would only bring the total in the city before the departure to 5,000 (3,000 who stayed plus 2,000 that left), which would still be significantly lower than what would have been expected. Dayton ended the report saying that he has not been able to get "the desired interview" with his spy.[76]

With the agreed-upon goal of this year's campaign being to

attack New York, Washington needed to clarify what was really happening there in order to plan the attack. On May 28, he wrote to Dayton, "The late accounts from New York are mysterious and perplexing. . . . As I am very anxious to learn what they are really doing in New York, you will oblige me by obtaining and sending me an accurate intelligence as possible."[77]

Washington acknowledged the receipt of a June 2 letter (letter not found) from Dayton. He tells Dayton to check into his sources because he appears to be getting bad intelligence. He was concerned that bad intelligence and a deception of some sort was being played on Dayton. He specifically told Dayton:

> It is very unaccountable that so many indications of an evacuation of New York should be reported to you and that they should come from no other quarter—I have a very good channel of intelligence by the way of Long Island [the Culper Spy Ring] and no movement is mentioned but that of a fleet bound to Europe—I cannot help suspecting that there may be some design in propagating the report of an evacuation, while they have some other purpose in view. You cannot oblige me more than endeavoring to ascertain whether any thing extraordinary, and what, is passing among them.[78]

Based on recent intelligence, Dayton advised, "The present appearances in New York seem rather to indicate a defense [rather] than an evacuation. I have received nothing very particular or material from there, since my last letter to your Excellency.[79]

After Yorktown the major battles were over and the armies in the north were in stand-pat mode. The use of spies slowed, as not much was happening around New York.

When the British were evacuating New York in 1783, many American officers were trying to get to the city to purchase goods and property at bargain prices from the departing Loyalists. Washington tried to keep the fraternizing of the two armies to a minimum. He informed Major General Alexander McDougall, "I have ever been averse to officers going to New York as every slight pretext. I was always ready to grant my permission when real business required their presence."[80]

Eleven

❧

DECEPTION BATTLE PLAN: THE OBJECTIVE

At the beginning of 1781 the war was not going well for the Americans. In the south, Charles Town (now known as Charleston), South Carolina, was unconditionally surrendered on May 12, 1780, by General Benjamin Lincoln to British General Henry Clinton. Georgia had been in the possession of the British since December 1778. The war at this time in the south definitely was in the British favor, while the war in the north had been a stalemate since the Battle of Springfield, New Jersey, on June 23, 1780. The Continental Army had experienced the Pennsylvania Line Mutiny on January 1, 1781, the largest mutiny in United States Army history. The soldiers believed their period of service expired and wanted to leave, among other concerns such as fraudulent enlistment documents. During the mutiny several soldiers and officers were killed and wounded. The mutineers with four cannons in tow marched out of Morristown headed to

Princeton and Congress in Philadelphia. Washington wisely realized he needed to stay in the Hudson Highlands to ensure the safety of West Point. It was too important of a military chess piece to allow it to fall into enemy hands. The president of Pennsylvania, Joseph Reed, negotiated the settlement of the mutiny. It resulted in the reduction of 2,467 men from the Pennsylvania Line of the Continental Army.[1]

There were strong grumblings by men from other states. The Massachusetts soldiers threatened to mutiny on January 17. It looked like the Continental Army was about to unravel. The Pennsylvania mutiny was followed by the New Jersey Line Mutiny. When Washington at New Windsor heard the news at about 10 p.m. from Colonel Israel Shreve of New Jersey, he knew he had to move quickly and decisively. He had to determine the outcome and not leave it to politicians or he would lose more men. Within an hour, he ordered General William Heath at West Point to put together a detachment of 500 or 600 of the most robust and best-clothed men, properly officered. It was thought they would be the men least sympathetic to the mutineers. Washington emphatically told Heath that he was determined "at all hazards to put a stop to the proceedings, which must otherwise prove the inevitable dissolution of the army."[2] By 11 p.m. orders were sent to Major Benjamin Troop at Ringwood, New Jersey, who was there with 100 Connecticut soldiers to cancel his previous orders to come to West Point. He was to hold the men there and be ready to march if needed. Other letters on the situation went to Colonel Fredrick Frelinghuysen, Colonel Israel Shreve, and former General John Sullivan, who was now a Continental congressman.

The next morning Washington hurried south to West Point.

Once there he ordered Major General Robert Howe of North Carolina to take command of the men General Heath assembled. Washington gave him very specific orders:

> You are to take the command of the detachment, which has been ordered to march from this post against the mutineers of the [New] Jersey line. You will rendezvous the whole of your command at Ringwood or Pompton as you find best from circumstances. The object of your detachment is to compel the mutineers to unconditional submission, and I am to desire you will grant no terms while they are with arms in their hands in a state of resistance. The manner of executing this I leave to your discretion according to circumstances. If you succeed in compelling the revolted troops to a surrender you will instantly execute a few of the most active and most incendiary leaders.[3]

The quick executions were a demonstration to convince the soldiers that mutinies would not be tolerated and would be severely punished with a quick death.

At daylight about 6:43 a.m. on January 27, General Howe's forces surrounded the huts of the New Jersey Line mutineers.[4] He ordered his men to present their loaded field pieces. He then ordered the mutineers to parade in front of the huts. He arrested the ringleaders, gave them a speedy drumhead field court-martial at which they were convicted and sentenced to death. He selected six of the mutineers to fare the firing squad. They executed Sergeant David Gilmore and John Tuttle.[5]

On April 9, 1781, Washington did an analysis of his army's

situation. His opinion was "we are at the end of our tether, and that now or never our deliverance must come."[6] He wanted and needed a victory to keep the army together. The bigger the victory the better.

It was at this time that General Washington and French Lieutenant General Rochambeau learned that Admiral de Grasse was bringing a French fleet from France to the Caribbean.[7] Rochambeau and Washington agreed to a strategy meeting in Wethersfield, Connecticut. The Wethersfield Conference was held in the three-and-a-half-story frame Webb House.[8] Rochambeau informed Washington they would be able to count on the arrival of de Grasse's fleet in American waters later in the summer. The main question to be resolved was the objective for the summer campaign. Rochambeau said Virginia offered the best hope for a successful campaign. Washington pushed for an attack on the British in New York. He was driven for a reprisal against the British for their capture of New York.

They agreed to attack New York as the primary objective for 1781 but acknowledged that Virginia was an alternative. Washington wrote in his diary on May 22:

> Fixed with Count de Rochambeau upon a plan of campaign—in substance as follows. That the French land force (except 200 men) should march so soon as the squadron could sail for Boston—to the North [Hudson] River & there, in conjunction with the American, to commence an operation against New York (which in the present reduced state of the garrison it was thought would fall, unless relieved; the doing which w[oul]d enfeeble their Southern operations, and in either case be

productive of capital advantages) or to extend our views to the southward as circumstances and a naval superiority might render more necessary & eligible.[9]

Washington on May 31 wrote to General Lafayette in Virginia, "Upon a full consideration of our affairs in every point of view, an attempt upon New York with its present garrison . . . was deemed preferable to a Southern operation as we had not the command of the water."[10] The British with a superior navy could force their way to General Cornwallis at Yorktown and evacuate his army from Virginia.

The plan for the 1781 campaign season was a coordinated American and French attack on New York. For the plan to succeed it required the assistance of the French fleet to come to New York to bottle up the British fleet and take command of the waters around York (Manhattan) Island. With the French navy in command of the water surrounding the island, the American and French forces could safely cross over to the island as well as retreat if necessary.

As long as the British controlled the waterways around New York, the British army there was virtually indestructible. British General Clinton could not work with Admiral Arbuthnot and had threatened to resign unless Arbuthnot was replaced. He was called home and Admiral Robert Digby was sent to replace him. Admiral Thomas Graves would command in Arbuthnot's place until Digby's arrival. The situation did not improve under Graves. Clinton requested Admiral George Rodney to come north from the Caribbean to attack French Admiral de Barras in Newport and protect New York.[11] Rodney had departed for England two days before Clinton's request arrived in the Caribbean. Frustrated at being unable to coordinate plans with the

British navy, Clinton's policies became ever more conservative. William Smith, who pictured himself as Clinton's consultant, became more frustrated at Clinton's inactivity. He ranted in his memoirs on July 4, "He is incapable of business. He consults No Body. All about him are idlers and ignorants."[12] Another observer at headquarters denounced Clinton's indecisiveness saying that he, "[l]ike the hungry ass between bundles of hay, for want of preference starves."[13] While Cornwallis was campaigning over large swaths of territory in the south and becoming the favorite of the ministry in London, stationary Clinton in New York was losing favor.[14]

British spy James Moody, a former Sussex County, New Jersey, farmer, left New York City on May 18 and traversed over to New Jersey. He crossed the Hackensack River by using a canoe that he kept concealed there. He waded through the water at Saddle River. However, the country now was aware he was in the area, which caused Washington to change the route of the express rider carrying the mail by way of Pompton. Moody had someone whose person and voice most resembled him to impersonate him in the country away from his real position and raise an alarm. The militia was sent in search of the false Moody.[15]

The real Moody sat in wait for five days for the mail courier. On June 3 he intercepted a mail carrier who was carrying thirteen pieces of Washington's mail.[16] Moody made his way back to New York. He arrived at Clinton's headquarters on June 4 with the captured mail. When Clinton received the intercepted letters, he was euphoric and gave Moody a reward of 200 guineas.[17] Frederick Mackenzie, deputy adjutant general, wrote, "The capture of this mail is extremely consequential, and gives the Commander in Chief the most perfect knowledge of the designs

of the enemy."[18] Clinton was described as "elated" when informing William Smith, New York chief justice, of the capture of
Washington's mail.[19] Clinton later said this mail led him to adopt
a "policy of avoiding all risks as much as possible, because it was
now manifest that, if we could only persevere in escaping af-
front, time alone would soon bring about every success we
could wish."[20]

The reason the letters, which identified an attack on New
York, were believed was because of the intercepted letter of
May 29 from Washington to Dr. John Baker, his Philadelphia
dentist. Washington requested "a pair of pincers to fasten the
wire of my teeth." He also requested "scrapers as my teeth stand
in need of a cleaning and I have little prospect of being in Philadelphia soon."[21] If Washington was going to Virginia, he would
make a stop to visit his dentist in Philadelphia to fix his teeth
and would not need to request the scrapers be sent to him.

Clinton estimated Washington had at least 5,000 men with
him. He based this estimate on a report from Stewart, an American commissary, which stated he gave out 8,000 rations. Clinton believed the ministers in England were always ready to
accept the lowest estimate of Washington's forces.[22] Washington
always took amusement in preparing false troop strength reports for the eyes of the British spies.

Clinton feared an attack on New York City coming from
Long Island just as the British did when they first landed in
1776. Should the combined American and French fleet command the waters around York Island and the combined armies
have possession of Long Island and the Bronx, his army could
be starved into submission.

On June 8, Washington and Rochambeau learned that de
Grasse had arrived in the Caribbean. Admiral de Grasse's mes-

sage to Rochambeau arrived on June 15 and said that he would be bringing the main French fleet to American waters as early as July 15. The focus of the American and French military campaign at this date was to attack New York.

On June 18, General Rochambeau, commander in chief of the French Expeditionary Force, led the French army out of Providence, Rhode Island. The first unit was Le Régiment Bourbonnais dressed in white with black facings. On the 19th was the Régiment Royal Deux-Ponts, whose coats were made of deep sky-blue wool with citron, the distinguishing color. The lapels and cuffs were citron and the horizontal pocket flaps were piped in citron. Régiment Soissonnais, in white with red facings, followed on the 20th, and the Régiment de Saintonge, which wore a white regimental with green wool facings and sleeve cuffs, arrived on the 21st.[23]

After spending a year in Rhode Island they were on the move across Connecticut to Westchester County, New York.[24] Ezra Birch raised a company of teams to move the baggage of the French army from New Town, Connecticut, to White Plains, New York.[25] Upon arrival, Rochambeau took over the widow Sarah Bates's house as his headquarters, turning the farmhouse into the French military nerve center.[26]

When the French army reached the Continental Army at White Plains, the destitute appearance of the soldiers in rags and the large number of armed blacks shocked the French. Upon arrival Rochambeau changed his opinion of the possible success of the campaign as planned and did not think they could take New York City.

For the French navy to reach New York City, it had two options to come through Long Island Sound, but getting past Hell Gate was too risky and they would have to proceed one ship at a time. The other option was to enter Lower New York Bay via the ship channel at Sandy Hook, which required crossing a sandbar. It would leave their ships open to raking fire from both the British ships positioned in Princess and Raritan Bays and a British battery on Sandy Hook.

General Clinton firmly believed that the French navy was going to connect with its army. He had advised Admiral Sir George Brydges Rodney, on June 28, 1781, that "De Grasse [has the] intention of coming here during hurricane months, and that this post [New York City] will be his first object."[27]

On August 14, a ship arrived in New York City from the Chesapeake Bay and brought news that Cornwallis had bivouacked at Yorktown, Virginia. It was on this very day that Rochambeau and Washington also learned of Admiral de Grasse's change of plan and that he was now going to the Chesapeake Bay with his fleet.

There was another mutiny on May 20 at York, Pennsylvania, showing that mutiny could rise again.[28] Because of it and these recent developments of August 14, Washington wrote in his diary, "Matters having now come to a crisis a decisive plan to be determined."[29] He knew that his dream of recovering New York City was not going to happen and a new goal for the campaign had to be developed. He would use all he learned going all the way back to his experiences in the French and Indian War in deception and espionage to achieve his objective. He had to, as he needed a victory to keep his army together.

Lieutenant Général des Armées Navales François-Joseph Paul, Marquis de Grasse Tilly, Comte de Grasse, brought his fleet to the coast of Virginia and would support any action in that region. With Rochambeau unsure of success and the French navy in Virginia, the plan for an attack on New York was shelved.

Washington and Rochambeau conferred and agreed upon an action against Cornwallis, who was occupying Yorktown, Virginia. If de Grasse was not coming to Rochambeau and Washington in New York, then they and their armies would go to de Grasse in Virginia. The new plan required moving much of both the Continental Army and the French forces to Virginia. They needed to get there as fast as possible before Cornwallis headed back to North Carolina or was rescued by the British navy.

The goal of the new campaign would require that half of the American army stay in the Hudson Highlands to protect West Point and keep pressure on British General Clinton in New York City. The other half and the French army would move about 400 miles to Yorktown and lay siege to Cornwallis's army. The maneuver was difficult. The new plan had de Barras and his fleet stay at Newport until needed, then sail from Newport, Rhode Island, to the Chesapeake Bay to join up with de Grasse's fleet. Together they would close the avenue of escape by sea for General Cornwallis while the combined armies would attack by land.

On August 17, Washington and Rochambeau, needing to coordinate activities, jointly wrote to de Grasse:

> In consequence of the dispatches received from your Excellency by the frigate *La Concorde* it has been judged expedient to give up for the present the enterprise against New York and to turn our attention towards the South, with a view, if we should not be able to attempt Charles town itself, to recover and secure the States of Virginia, North Carolina and the Country of South Carolina and Georgia. We may add a further inducement for giving up the first mentioned enterprise, which is the

arrival of a reinforcement of near 3000 Hessian Recruits. For this purpose we have determined to remove the whole of the French Army and as large a detachment of the American as can be spared, to [the] Chesapeake.[30]

Because of the change in objectives for the campaign, Washington decided to use what in modern terms is called a Deception Battle Plan. The opening phase in running a successful Deception Battle Plan is to have a clear objective of what you are going to accomplish and what you want your enemy to do. The second is to know the enemy's assumptions. The third element is the method selection or the operational options you are going to use. The fourth is the execution of the plan, while the fifth is to exploit your advantage.

British Lieutenant General Frederick E. Morgan, a World War I veteran, in the spring of 1943 became chief of staff to the Supreme Allied Commander. When General Dwight Eisenhower became Supreme Allied Commander, Morgan became deputy chief of staff. Morgan was responsible for planning Operation Overlord, which was the code name for the Allied invasion of northwestern Europe in World War II.

The objective was to make a landing in German-occupied France and establish a beachhead. Once established, they would then break out into the French countryside. The most obvious choice was the Pas-de-Calais opposite Dover, England. It was the shortest distance across the English Channel, twenty-one miles, and it exposed the invading force to enemy fire for the shortest amount of time. It was the location the German military would have chosen. Morgan, however, selected Normandy because of its distance from the obvious choice, because it was one of the two best landing spots, and was still within range of Allied air cover. Morgan wanted the Germans to concentrate their efforts at the wrong beach, the Pas-de-Calais.

Operation Desert Storm (August 2, 1990–February 28, 1991) was the United States' and allied national response to Iraq's invasion of neighboring Kuwait by dictator Saddam Hussein on August 2, 1990. During Operation Desert Storm, American General H. Norman Schwarzkopf Jr. used a Deception Battle Plan in liberating Kuwait from seven months of occupation. The objective was to move Iraq's best-trained troops, the Republican Guard, so that Schwarzkopf could turn their flank and attack across the lightly defended desert. Schwarzkopf wanted them to be defending the two obvious choices of the Shatt al-Arab waterway (Arvand River) or a direct assault north from Saudi Arabia into Kuwait.

George Washington's new objective in 1781 was to quickly take the combined American and French armies across New Jersey by stealth. He desperately wanted to avoid being delayed by having to fight the British and Hessians during their march through New Jersey. If he could get his forces across the Delaware River and into Pennsylvania, they would be out of reach and the British forces in New York would be unable to hinder them from going to Virginia. Once in Virginia they would combine with Lafayette's troops and soldiers from the French fleet for an assault on General Cornwallis at Yorktown while the French fleet of warships controlled the entrance of the Chesapeake Bay.

Twelve

~

DECEPTION BATTLE PLAN: ENEMY ASSUMPTIONS

The first part of the Deception Battle Plan was Washington's objective; that is, what he wanted to accomplish. The second part was to know what the enemy's assumptions were. What did the enemy, the British, already think, want to think, or most likely believe? By knowing what the enemy wants to believe, it is easier to convince them that that is what is going to happen. They are predisposed to the event.

Resident British spies in Albany and Swiss-born British General Frederick Haldimand at Quebec had been reporting to British General Henry Clinton in New York City that American and French armies would attack New York or Canada as their objective for 1781. Haldimand, governor of the province of Quebec, based on new intelligence from Albany, advised Clinton that there was not going to be an attack on Canada that year but that New York City was the objective of the American campaign.[1] The American mail that was captured in early June by James Moody confirmed Haldimand's message that the objective was a combined attack on New York. British spies operating in New Jersey and the Hudson River area of New York were also telling British headquarters the same story, that New York City was the campaign objective.

Washington, in order to strengthen the British belief of an attack on New York City, had the American and French forces engage the British. American and French troops on July 15 exchanged fire with British ships in the Hudson River. The Americans had one killed and one wounded. On July 19, American artillery at Dobbs Ferry fired on British ships in the Hudson. It did not produce any casualties but got the attention of the British. On July 22, the American and French forces attacked the British line at Kingsbridge and ships in the Hudson. Three or four British were killed and eight or ten were captured.[2] On the night of July 28, based on information probably obtained by a spy, the British had sounded an alarm that the American and French forces were marching on New York.

The plan Washington designed was to let British General Clinton to continue to believe what he already believed, which was that New York City was the objective for the campaign by the combined American and French armies and navy. Clinton did not know where or when but was sure it would materialize. Washington now had to make the deception fit what Clinton believed. As long as Clinton believed New York would be attacked, he would not bring his army into New Jersey to attack the combined American and French forces. He would continue to hold his troops in readiness in New York, waiting for an attack on the city that would never come. Clinton's forces were hectically preparing to defend New York City, Long Island, and Staten Island. After the war Clinton stated that "had they [the combined American and French forces] intended New York an attempt upon Staten Island was probable and if it succeeded we should have been in a scrape."[3]

Clinton had the Hessian Grenadiers busy at work fixing "the fort at Hell Gate for the defense of that passage from the [Long Island] Sound." Hell Gate is a narrow tidal strait in the East River with rocks and strong converging tides from the Harlem River Strait, Long Island Sound, the Upper Bay of New York Harbor, and lesser channels, making navigation hazardous. As dangerous a passage as it was, Clinton was leaving nothing to chance in case the Americans or French would venture to attack coming through the passage.

The Continental Army had experienced three mutinies in 1781. Clinton had to wonder if Washington was desperate enough for a victory to hold the army together that he would risk attacking through Hell Gate. He had taken bold moves before. After his army retreated across New Jersey into Pennsylvania in December of 1776 and recruitments were about to expire, he tempted fate. He crossed the ice-strewn Delaware River in the dark and made a desperate attack on Trenton, New Jersey. The victory at Trenton against the Hessians, and a few days later at Princeton against British regulars, had the effect of holding the Continental Army together.

A person by the name of Hamilton came from the Clove into New York City on August 28 and told of seeing on Saturday the 25th both Rochambeau and Washington with their armies at Paramus, New Jersey. They were there with more than 6,000 men. He said the men talked of an attack on Staten Island but he believed they were going southward. This may have been another piece of false information that Washington leaked to a spy. An unattributed report came into New York on Friday night that American and French armies were in motion but it did not say where they were going.

Captain George Beckwith reported information from an unidentified person from Hackensack, New Jersey. The informant, on August 20, was in the company of American Major John Mauritius Goetschius of the Bergen County, New Jersey, Militia. The American troops were reported to be on their way to Baltimore, Maryland.[4] Captain Beckwith advised that if they were going to Delaware, they would go by way of the Newark Mountains (now known as the Oranges) and "if their goal was [to attack] Staten Island then they will go to Elizabeth and Gen[era]l [Cortlandt] Skinner will of course have it in his power to clear up this matter this night."[5] The gossip running rampant among the Hessians was that the combined American and French forces "have gone for Rhode Island [and] others think they are both crossed the North River."[6] If they had gone to Rhode Island they could be planning to attack eastern Long Island. In other words, no one had any knowledge of what was happening but all had an opinion.

Clinton, always cautious, was anxious to consolidate his forces into a defensive position in New York. He moved regiments around like pieces on a chess board. Lieutenant John Charles Philip von Kraft said "all these changes led us to anticipate, a few days hence, some as yet unknown expedition"[7] was in the planning. With all the movement everyone was anticipating a major incident. On the 23rd, Kraft wrote in his journal that the Hessian troops knew that the American and French armies were somewhere in New Jersey and they would not be making an expedition into New Jersey.[8] The question circulating among the men was: What were the Americans and the French going to do?

The British were always sending out spies to try and determine Washington's course of action. Just as important as when the attack would occur was where and how. The American forces had made thirty-three incursions from New Jersey to Staten Island up to this point in the war. The British were waiting for number thirty-four.

The British had sent out Jacob Brower of Essex County; William Sproule of Captain Joseph Crowell's Company, 1st Battalion New Jersey Volunteers, commanded by Lieutenant Colonel Joseph Barton; and Ezekiel Yeomans, an experienced spy and a resident of Kakiat, Orange, now Rockland County, New York, to determine what was happening.[9] Their answers would determine the course of action for the British defense. They reported that the greatest part of Washington's army had passed to the west side of the Hudson and was currently between the Clove and Paramus. The rumor was that they were going to Philadelphia. These reports only partially met the preconceived ideas at British headquarters. It was believed that if Staten Island was the target, the American and French armies would move south as if headed to Philadelphia and then quickly turn or come back to make a surprise assault. On August 18, Clinton in order to bolster his defenses in the city moved the 54th Regiment of Foot from Paulus Hook, New Jersey, to New York City, and they encamped with the 38th Regiment of Foot. Naturally the residents in New York City were in a state of panic over the prospect of an attack from the combined American and French forces. The consensus among the city's residents was that General Clinton and the British army were unprepared should there be an attack in force.

In World War II, the Germans knew there was going to be a landing in France by the Allied forces at either the Pas-de-Calais or Normandy. They believed that it would be at the Pas-de-Calais. It would have been the location they would have chosen. The German military operations up to this point in the war had been blitzkrieg, bold, quick-moving strokes, and the Pas-de-Calais fit that modus operandi. The British and American armies could cross the English Channel the fastest by landing at the Pas-de-Calais. The Allies needed to help convince the Germans that their assumption was correct.

In Desert Storm, the Iraqis had recently completed an eight-year war (September 22, 1980–August 20, 1988) with Iran over the important Shatt al-Arab, a river formed by the confluence of the Euphrates and Tigris Rivers that was historically the border between the two countries. The Iraqis thought this would be the main target, just as in the previous war. It was an important channel for oil exports for both Iran and Iraq. To them an attack across the desert in the west was the least likely possibility. The Iraqis concentrated their forces where they thought they would engage the enemy. This positioning of the Republican Guard, their best unit, allowed American General Norman Schwarzkopf to run what he called his "Hail Mary," a reference to a last-second long-distance play in American football. General Schwarzkopf wanted to move his army across the desert and assault the Republican Guard from their lightly defended rear.[10]

Thirteen

~

DECEPTION BATTLE PLAN: METHOD

Washington, having completed the first and second parts of the Deception Battle Plan, was now able to go on to the third part, the method selection. In other words, what options were available and selecting what would be used.

In World War II the objective of the plan was to lead the Germans to believe that the invasion of northwest Europe would come later than was planned and to expect attacks elsewhere. FUSAG, a fictional First United States Army Group headquartered in Dover, England, was poised for a landing at the Pas-de-Calais directly across the English Channel. The operation was called Fortitude South. The fake army was equipped with insignia, rubber balloon tanks, a small detachment of real soldiers, constant radio traffic, and blow-up landing craft. German prisoners of war who were being released through the Swedish Red Cross were accidentally on purpose allowed to see some of the staged activities of FUSAG, which they then reported back to German command. The clincher was assigning American General George S. Patton Jr. to command FUSAG rather than any other general. The Germans believed that Patton was the most aggressive of the Allied generals and he would have been their choice to lead the major landing in Europe. He was the general they feared the most and they had to prepare for him.

In order to conduct a massive invasion of Europe from England, military planners had to stage units all over the United Kingdom. The units that would land first would be assigned to a position nearest to the embarkation point. Because FUSAG with Patton as commander had been placed in the southeast of England at Dover, the closest point to France, German intelligence deduced that it was the focal point of the invasion force because it was opposite Pas-de-Calais and, therefore, the likely landing point.

In Scotland another army was practicing for winter mountain warfare. It was called Fortitude North and its purpose was to indicate a possible assault across the North Sea to German-occupied Norway. Because of the threat to Norway, German reinforcements that could have been sent to France had to stay and defend Norway.

In the Mediterranean there was the threat of an Allied attack on the Balkans called Operation Zeppelin. This was a British-run operation designed to keep more possible reinforcements from the future scene of the action. Vendetta was a planned landing of the United States Seventh Army on the southern coast of France.

The Allies were able to convert a group of German spies into double agents. The double agents in England sent back to Germany information about the plans for a landing at Pas-de-Calais, which is what the Germans expected to hear. Double agent Juan

Pujol García provided information to the Germans that the landing would be at the Pas-de-Calais. It confirmed not only what they wanted to believe but what they were getting from other sources.

During Desert Storm, Marines were practicing amphibious landings while American naval vessels thoroughly searched the water for mines in preparation for the amphibious landing. As in World War II, false high-volume radio traffic, in this case to the east, was used to reinforce the Iraqi military's preconceived ideas of where the Allied forces were and what they were planning to do. During Desert Storm, a new possibility was available. General Schwarzkopf manipulated the information that was provided to the television news reporters. It was used to further convince the Iraqis that their concept of the Allied plan was correct.

During the American Revolution the deceptions were on a smaller scale, but Washington had options available to him in running his deception. Writing after the war, Washington outlined his deceptions: "Much trouble was taken and finesse used to misguide and bewilder [General] Sir Henry Clinton in regard to the real object, by fictitious communications [letters], as well as by making a deceptive provision of ovens, forage and boats in his neighborhood, is certain."[1] In addition, Washington intentionally deceived his own troops as to what the objective was and where they were going. If his men did not know what the destination was, it could not be either accidentally or intentionally leaked to British spies. He had been betrayed in the past by Dr. Benjamin Church Jr. and General Benedict Arnold, who were trusted members of his military family. The enemy would be left in the dark as to what was transpiring until the secret could no longer be kept.

"Nor were less pains taken to deceive our own army; for I had always conceived, when the imposition did not completely take place at home, it could never sufficiently succeed abroad,"[2] Dr. James Thacher wrote in his journal. "Our destination has been for some time matter of perplexing doubt and uncertainty; bets have run high on one side, that we were to occupy the ground marked out on the Jersey shore, to aid in the siege of New York, and on the other, that we are stealing a march on the enemy, and are actually destined to Virginia, in pursuit of the army under Lord Cornwallis."[3] Washington had previously made marches under the cover of darkness to make an escape from a dangerous situation. After the Battle of Long Island, he moved the army across the East River at night in August 1776 to avoid annihilation by General Howe. On January 2, 1777, he slipped away at night from Trenton and General Cornwallis and proceeded to engage the enemy at Princeton the next day.

Washington had to make things feed Clinton's assumptions but they could not be obvious or Clinton would realize it was a deception. It was a fine line. If Clinton realized that a deception was in play, he could then run a counter-deception and set a trap for Washington and the American and French forces.

The British army had used a pontoon bridge connected with some floats three times during the war. On December 10, 1777, it was used to span the Schuylkill River, which was 434 feet across. It was used at Spuyten Duyvil Creek (also known as Spiking Devil and Spijt den Duyvil), a distance of 160 feet. General Clinton could refloat the pontoon bridge, as was done the third time. In June 1780 it was used to bring their soldiers quickly across from Staten Island to New Jersey to make an attack on the American stronghold at Morristown.[4] It resulted in the Battle of Springfield on June 23, 1780. Washington did not want his troops to enter a battle and get bogged down in fighting their way across New Jersey. He wanted to get them to Virginia as fast as possible. Washington had precious little time to implement his plan.

Washington used fictitious communications during this deception. There is a story of false mail. A blacksmith and sometime courier by the name of Benjamin Montayne carried some dispatches that were intended to fall into the enemy's hands. The mail indicated the plan of attack was New York City. Washington as usual provided specific details to ensure the outcome he wanted. Montayne was at Fishkill and Washington told him to cross over to the west side of the Hudson. He was to travel by the way of Haverstraw and Ramapo Pass, also known as the Clove, to Morristown. The Clove was an area infested by Loyalists. There was a high probability that the correspondence the thirty-six-year-old carried would be taken from him while traveling this route. He was indeed intercepted and relieved of the mail. However, instead of just taking the mail, he was taken prisoner and was incarcerated in the sugar house jail in New York City.[5]

Well-crafted misinformation could keep your enemy from leaving their fortifications because of a fear of being attacked by a phantom army in the open field. Washington wanted Clinton to fear an attack by the combined American and French armies and a soon-to-arrive French fleet.

Washington, in a March 1781 meeting with General Philip Schuyler, advised him that the best help he could give the war in the south was a strong presence toward New York City. They met again on June 25 at Poughkeepsie. After this meeting Washington and Schuyler attempted to provide a diversion on July 15, 1781, by sending a false letter dated at Albany to Washington that Schuyler had arranged to be carried to the British. The letter indicated that the two units of the French fleet would join off Boston and attack British General Frederick Haldimand at Quebec. The letter also stated that Schuyler agreed with Washington that they should fake an attack on New York City.[6] The letter did reach its destination with General Haldimand in Canada.

Washington noted in his diary on August 19, "French bakery to veil our real movements and create apprehensions for Staten Island."[7] In the French army, bread was a significant part of their diet. Building large bake ovens for the French indicated that they planned to be in the area for an extended period of time, as if they were going to conduct a siege. The ovens were built at Chatham along the Passaic River. They supplied the French army when it passed through on the way to Virginia. As part of the deception strategy, preparations for ovens also to be made for the army near Sandy Hook were drawn up but no record of them being constructed has been found. Washington wrote in his diary, "Contracts are made for forage to be delivered immediately to the French Army upon their arrival" at the place near Sandy Hook.[8] British spies would hear about the forage contracts for the French near Sandy Hook and report the news to British headquarters. Since the French were not going to Sandy Hook, Washington could contract for large quantities of forage for the French because the contracts would become active. It would provide confusion at British headquarters as to what was happening.

As early as August 15 it was planned for a detachment to collect bricks at Perth Amboy for building the ovens at Chatham. The British had an artillery post at the seventeenth-century two-story manor house made of native fieldstone, known as the

Billopp House on Staten Island, opposite to the city of Perth
Amboy. It is also known as the Conference House for the September 11, 1776, conference between British Lord Admiral
Richard Howe and Benjamin Franklin, John Adams, and Edward Rutledge. The British and Hessian soldiers stationed there
were to observe the activities in the city. By collecting the bricks
at Perth Amboy down at the water's edge it ensured that it
would be seen by the British and Hessian artillerists at the Billopp House, who would send the information to British headquarters.[9] British General Clinton believed that the enemy
forces taking position at Chatham threatened Staten Island.[10]

As part of the deception Washington instructed Colonel
Elias Dayton on August 19 to take the New Jersey Continental
Line and Moses Hazen's 2nd Canadian Regiment under his
command. They were to take post on the heights between Chatham and Springfield, New Jersey, for the ostensible purpose of
protecting the French bakery.[11]

As part of his deception strategy Washington wanted thirty
boats that were built along the North (Hudson) River, mounted
on carriages, and taken in the line of march. Intelligence had
been received at British headquarters in New York City that
carriages were being built on the Hudson River north of New
York. This intelligence reported that the carriages were "100
yards from the dock at Kings Ferry and 600 [yards] from the
block house at Honey [Stony?] Point, and a string of them close
to each other of 300 yards."[12] This fed Clinton's idea of a water
assault on either York or Staten Island. In his diary Washington
mentioned that the thirty boats were part of the deception but
he also saw them as useful to him when they reached Virginia.[13]

The British military usually had two armed boats patrolling
the North River. However, in the middle of June the American

spy boats were able every night to come down the river as far south as Fort Lee to observe the activities and defenses.[14] William Smith urged Generals Benedict Arnold and Clinton to take action against the boats. Smith in a draft letter to Tryon indicated that he had no other answer as to why the Americans had built boats and wagons other than to transport them over land.[15]

The Americans were collecting boats between Newark and Perth Amboy for a planned landing on Staten Island. Another way to get boats was to steal them. Colonel Elias Dayton, on August 5, met with two of his people, Anthony Hollingshead and Nicholas Stag. They had devised a plan to capture a gunboat and whaleboat in Newark Bay and also attack the post at Bergen. Jabez Sayers, a resident of Newark, had discovered the plot. At first he was unable to get across the river to New York but the next day was able to get to the fort at Bergen. The only one he knew there who would keep his cover was Captain Thomas Ward but he was in New York. He returned to Newark and sent a letter to Isaac Ogden but it was never delivered. Isaac Ogden was an attorney from Elizabeth Town and had been a member of the New Jersey Provincial Congress from May to August of 1775, when he resigned. He was employed by Brigadier General Cortlandt Skinner to provide intelligence.[16] Alexander Hamilton called him "the most barefaced, impudent fellows that ever came under my observation. He openly acknowledged himself a subject to the King of Great Britain and flatly refused to give any satisfaction to some questions that were put to him."[17] Sayers was finally able to get in to New York City on the night of the 15th. He contacted Ogden during the day. Stag had set up a plan to deliver the post at Bergen to the Americans. Since Stag had been captured, his plan could not be executed. Sayers reported that 200 of Colonel Dayton's men were three miles west of Newark and claimed to be foraging, but he believed that they were preparing for an attack on the fort at Bergen.[18] No attack was made.

Another piece of the plan was repairing the road leading to the crossing of the Spuyten Duyvil at Kingsbridge. The repair made the road serviceable for use by wagons and artillery mounted on carriages. It indicated to the British that an attack was imminent at the northern end of Manhattan.[19] General Clinton had the local militia busy working on improving the defenses at Kingsbridge in preparation for the expected attack. William Smith was losing his patience with General Clinton. He wrote in his memoirs, "We enterprise nothing."[20]

∿

Fourteen

DECEPTION BATTLE PLAN: THE STING—EXECUTING THE PLAN

In this phase of the Deception Battle Plan, the planning was over and everything was in play and the game was live. Washington would now find out if all his efforts at deception had worked. The big risk was that the British saw through the deception and were running their own counter-deception. If so, Washington and the Continental and French armies would be heading into a trap.

In executing the Normandy invasion during World War II, planes dropped chaff over the English Channel, which on radar simulated a large fleet of ships approaching the Pas-de-Calais. This helped the Germans to continue to believe that the main landing was going to be at the Pas-de-Calais. The Allies also dropped both real and dummy parachutists, which resulted in the German army spending their time and manpower tracking down soldiers that did not exist, as they were unable to tell at a distance which parachutists were real and which were not. Numerous other operations projected landings from the Mediterranean, the Balkans, and northern Norway. The deception plan worked as hoped: the Germans kept forces at these possible landing sites and away from Normandy. They also held some of their forces in reserve waiting for an attack at the Pas-de-Calais that never happened. The Allied army landed at Normandy with stiff opposition but was able to establish a beachhead. Once the landing was secured they moved inland before the Germans realized there would be no landing at the Pas-de-Calais. It was the beginning of the operation to liberate Paris.

In Operation Desert Storm, in addition to defending the Shatt al-Arab, the Iraqis were waiting for a northern amphibious landing from the sea that never took place. Meanwhile General Schwarzkopf was able to execute his Hail Mary play. The army advanced through the desert and the lightly defended Iraqi rear. The strategy was so successful that the army advanced 100 miles in 100 hours and liberated Kuwait City.

During the American Revolution, Washington was getting his troops prepared for the long arduous march to Virginia. On August 5, 1781, he tightened security at the Continental Army's encampment. He directed that "[n]o person excepting those belonging to the army is to come into camp from the country above or northward of the camp but by" three specific entrances. A commissioned officer was posted at each of the places who was to give a specific short ticket to such persons as he permitted to pass into camp. Washington ordered that "[a]ny person found in camp not belonging to the army without such a ticket is to be taken up as a spy and conducted to the general of the day."[1] To build up the stamina of the soldiers who would be marching to Virginia, he ordered on August 12 that "[n]on commissioned officers and soldiers to be served with a gill of rum per man this afternoon."[2] On August 15, he issued a General Order that said, "Army will hold itself in the most perfect readiness to move at the shortest notice."[3] The combined American and French armies had difficulty getting started. The general lack of horses and bad condition of the horses in the French army were part of the reason for the delay in the departure until August 19.[4] British spies were very active and intelligence of the French army's preparations and movements reached the British headquarters in New York City on the 20th.[5]

Because of the deception plan, all of Washington's discussions about the destination were focused on an attack at Staten Island and a placement of troops at Sandy Hook to assist the French fleet in getting over the sandbar. By keeping the real destination a secret even from most of the officers and all of the enlisted men, Washington believed it would reduce the chance of an accidental leak or intentional divulging of the real objective to British spies who were always about. In keeping the men from discovering what was happening, he did not issue General Orders between August 20 and 27 except for baggage concerns on the 22nd and a position assignment on the 24th.[6]

Jonathan Trumbull Jr., one of George Washington's aides-de-camp, noted in his journal on August 21, "French ovens are building at Chatham in [New] Jersey. Others [ovens] were ordered to be prepared at a place near the Hook [Sandy Hook, New Jersey]. Contracts are made for forage to be delivered immediately to the army on their arrival at the last mentioned place [Sandy Hook]. Here it is supposed that batteries are to be erected for the security and aid of the [French] fleet, which is hourly expected. By these maneuvers and the corresponding march of the troops, our own army no less than the enemy are completely deceived."[7] Rochambeau wrote that the ovens were built to supply the French army on the march.[8] They also supplied the French army on its return from Virginia. These schemes were to lead the British to think that the French would be stationed to the south and west of Staten Island. The only possible explanation for such maneuvers would be an assault on Staten Island.

On August 21, Washington instructed Colonel Sylvanus Seely of the Morris County New Jersey Militia to proceed to the town of Connecticut Farms and wait until General Benjamin Lincoln's troops marched for Springfield before beginning his movement. Once there, Seely was to stay and keep constant patrols on the Arthur Kill "as far as [Perth] Amboy till the French Army has passed Princeton and then act under the orders he may receive from [New Jersey] Governor [William] Livingston."[9] Seely was also to keep a vigilant lookout both by land and water toward York (Manhattan) Island (New York City) and provide reports of any enemy movement by express to Washington.[10] Washington wanted to be certain he was not headed into a trap. He wrote to Colonel Dayton and instructed him "to use your best endeavors to obtain intelligence from York and Staten Islands, that we may know what effect our late movements have produced; ascertain the strength of the enemy on Staten Island; and whether any troops have arrived from Virginia."[11] Dayton had overseen spies operating out of Elizabeth Town. Washington wanted him to call upon whatever secret service assets were available to see if his deception strategy was working. He wanted to know: "What boats could, on an emergency, be procured between New Ark [Newark] and [Perth] Amboy for transporting troops if they should be required."[12] As always, Washington provided specific instructions to ensure that the exact intelligence he wanted would be provided.

When the plan of the campaign was to attack against New York, Washington and General Schuyler met on Sunday, June 17. During their discussion Schuyler offered to construct at Albany bateaux for the assault on New York. On Tuesday, Washington accepted his offer.[13] On July 21, Schuyler advised that eighty-four bateaux were completed as to carpenter work, and forty or forty-one were ready to be delivered.[14]

On July 29, the 2nd New York Regiment brought the completed boats south. The light infantry company brought down the next batch, the remainder of the regiment the balance.[15] Washington wrote in his diary on August 1 that all 100 boats were completed at Albany, the same number at Wappinger Creek by the quartermaster general, and old ones repaired.[16]

He also started calling out troops in Delaware, Maryland, and Pennsylvania.[17] On August 24, he instructed Brigadier General David Forman of the Monmouth County militia to observe the British fleet at Sandy Hook.[18] He needed to know when the British left for Virginia to support or extract Lord Cornwallis and his army. This was a race to Virginia, and Washington needed to win.

Colonel Sylvanus Seely of the New Jersey Militia got the orders to begin his march on the 27th from Dobbs Ferry.[19] Colonel John Lamb with his 2nd Continental Artillery Regiment and the Rhode Island Regiment went by way of Pompton to Chatham. The design of the combined American and French armies' movements started to circulate among some of the French officers on the 27th.[20]

Washington tried to time the sequence of events to produce the effects he wanted. As with every operation on such a grand scale, not everything worked as planned. In order to enhance the deception as a preparation for an amphibious assault on Staten Island, the thirty boats were to be moved to a staging area at Springfield, New Jersey. They needed to be mounted on carriages for the trip.

It was an important piece of the plan to keep Clinton convinced there was going to be an attack on Staten Island and for him to keep his forces prepared to defend it. There was a delay in getting the boats moving. Washington complained to Major General Alexander McDougall on August 18 about the delay in moving the thirty boats from Wappinger Creek to Kings Ferry to begin the journey with the troops. McDougall at West Point replied that he rounded up the boats as fast as possible.[21] Washington ordered 150 men to bring thirty of the aforesaid boats to Kings Ferry, from whence the men were to return immediately to West Point.[22] Washington wrote in his diary as the French army was traveling, he had thirty flatboats "(able to carry about 40 men each) upon carriages—as well with a design to deceive the enemy as to our real movement, as to be useful to me in Virginia when I get there."[23]

Washington must have asked Quartermaster General Timothy Pickering to check on the condition of the roads the army was going to use to ensure there would be no unforeseen problems or delays because on August 21 at Kings Ferry, Pickering wrote to Washington that he had sent someone to examine the roads: "I have sent an express to go with him [the inspector] as far as Ogden's Iron Works [near Boonton, New Jersey] . . . to bring back his report whether that route be practicable for carriages." He also had the inspector of the roads continue on to Dods Tavern and then return.[24]

Washington on the 24th instructed General Lincoln on

his line of march for each day and the progress he was expected to make.[25] On the 25th, Colonel Philip Van Cortlandt was instructed to take command of the clothing, the boats, and entrenching tools and take them to Springfield, and upon arrival to report to General Lincoln. His assignment was to catch up to the army, which was already on the move. He was to travel by the way of Suffern, Pompton, Two Bridges (an unincorporated community in present-day Wayne Township), and Chatham.[26]

It was determined that the road passing by Samuel Ogden's Iron Works along the Rockaway River, near Boonton, would be difficult for the carriages carrying the boats.[27] Washington was concerned that his boats would not reach Springfield in time for British spies to see them and report back to their minders. He had Tench Tilghman write travel instructions to Philip Van Cortlandt on the 27th. He wanted him to keep upon the road from Pompton to Morristown until he came to the place known by the name of Dods Tavern. There he was to turn to the left and proceed to the fork of Passaic River. From thence he was to take the same road upon which the artillery moved to Chatham.[28]

Van Cortlandt on the 28th had only gotten as far as Pompton and was still over twenty miles from Chatham. He was having a difficult time corralling the boats, as some were lagging three miles behind the main fleet. He said it would be two more days before they all got to their destination.[29]

On August 27, Washington advised Colonel Samuel Miles, deputy quartermaster general at Philadelphia, to get watercraft together at Trenton: "I have delayed having these preparations made until this moment, because I wished to deceive the enemy with regard to our real object as long as possible, our movements have been calculated for that purpose and I am still anxious the deception should be kept up a few days longer, until our intentions are announced by the army's filing off towards the Delaware."[30]

In New York the men of the Hesse-Cassel Jaeger Corps believed "Washington plans to attack New York"—except Colonel Ludwig von Wurmb. The colonel had been given the authority to employ spies, and they reported to him that "the [American] commissary had ordered forage and bread as far as Trenton and along the Delaware River and an American woman, mistress of a distinguished French officer, was sent to Trenton, where she is to await the arrival of the army."[31] The woman was the mistress of Donatien Marie Joseph de Vimeur, Vicomte de Rochambeau, son and aide-de-camp of Jean-Baptiste Donatien de Vimeur, Comte de Rochambeau.[32] She had followed the French troops when they left Rhode Island.

When a deception strategy is used, there is always the possibility of a counter-deception. Washington's intelligence was that the British "have been throwing troops upon Staten Island." He had to wonder if the British discovered his deception and were preparing to attack his troops while on the march, or had they bought his deception strategy and were preparing to defend Staten Island? Only time would tell. As it turned out, General Clinton was indeed running a deception of his own. He had a sham deserter deliver a fake letter from François Jean, Marquis de Chastellux, negatively reflecting on Rochambeau and his command.[33] The messenger was to claim to be a friend to Rochambeau and was to collect intelligence while at the French camp. Rochambeau sent him back to the British camp to try and obtain more information.[34]

When the French troops reached Pompton on the 26th, Rochambeau sent Jacques Pierre Orillard de Villemanzy, the French commissary of war, orders to work on establishing the bakers' ovens and to bring up supplies for the ovens. "He was let into the secret and told that it was our intention to nourish the army from that bakery in its march to Philadelphia."[35] Villemanzy was instructed that they needed to convince the enemy that the design was for an attack on Staten Island. "He did so well with this that he caused himself to be fired upon by the English batteries [on Staten Island] in trying to collect the bricks which were at the mouth of the Raritan [Perth Amboy]."[36]

Washington wrote in his diary for August 29, 1781, "The whole [army] halted as well for the purpose of bringing up our rear as because we had heard not of the arrival of Count de Grasse and was unwilling to disclose our real object to the enemy."[37] He wrote the next day, "[A]s our intentions could be concealed one march more. [Because of the] idea of marching to Sandy Hook to facilitate the entrance of the French fleet within the bay."[38] Although the entrance to Lower New York Bay is wide, it is not very deep. To get the French warships into the bay, some of the cannons would have needed to be removed to allow the ships to get over the sandbar. Washington allowed the rumor to circulate that they were going to help the French fleet get over the bar. He had already put out the rumor of building batteries at the Highlands for that purpose.[39] Washington fell back on his old practice of using one lie to support another lie.

British headquarters was concerned with what Washington was doing. Oliver De Lancey, adjutant general to the British army at New York, had heard that a body of troops were moving to Newark and ordered Major Thomas Ward, commanding the Loyal Refugee Volunteers at Bergen Neck, New Jersey, to send out as many people as he could to find out what was happening.[40] Ward sent two men, David Demaree and Green, to the Clove and two others to Newark. The men going to Newark were having a difficult time getting there. On the 23rd Ward sent out John Moore to see what he could discover. He reported to Oliver De Lancey that Moore was able to pass among the American troops.[41] Isaac Ogden received an intelligence report from New Jersey. The spy reported on a conversation with Bill Livingston, the son of New Jersey Governor William Livingston.[42]

Washington arrived in Philadelphia on August 30 or 31.[43] Robert Morris offered his house to him. He and Rochambeau were "received by crowds of people with shouts and acclamations."[44] He left the city on September 5 and had traveled three miles below Chester, Pennsylvania, when he received word of the safe arrival of de Grasse and his fleet in the Chesapeake Bay.

Rochambeau traveled from Philadelphia to Chester by boat. As he approached the shore he later wrote, "We discerned in the distance General Washington was standing on the shore and waving his hat and a white handkerchief joyfully . . . MM. de Rochambeau and Washington embraced warmly on the shore."[45] At this point Washington knew his successful deception strategy had given them the chance to capture Cornwallis and his army in Yorktown.

Fifteen

~

DECEPTION BATTLE PLAN: EXPLOITATION

The fifth element of the Deception Battle Plan was to exploit your advantage. It was about achieving the objective—and more—if possible. Washington's objective was to get the Continental and French armies across New Jersey without being attacked by the British. After clearing New Jersey, Washington now had the chance to get the armies quickly to Virginia. And once there, he could coordinate the American army and the French navy to force British General Cornwallis's surrender.

During World War II, the Allies had multiple deceptions as to landings in Europe that caused the Germans to divide their forces. They had so convinced the Germans that the landing at Normandy was a deception that while it was happening, the Germans were still waiting for the landing at the Pas-de-Calais. The panzer tank corps was held in reserve waiting for General Patton and the First United States Army Group (FUSAG) to land. Meanwhile the Allies exploited their deception and started moving out into the countryside from their beachhead in Normandy.

General Norman Schwarzkopf's deception had the Iraqis looking for an amphibious landing from the Persian Gulf or a northerly thrust from Saudi Arabia. The coalition forces attacked through the desert from the west on February 24, and the ground war began. They were able to continue the destruction of the Iraqi army while the Iraqis were still waiting for an amphibious landing in the east. Although the bombing lasted for weeks, American ground troops declared Kuwait liberated just 100 hours after the ground attack was initiated. Once the remnants of the Iraqi army were out of Kuwait, the mission was completed.

In the American Revolution, British General Clinton had written to Cornwallis on August 27 that Washington's movement might be to take a defensive position at Morristown "from whence he may detach to the southward."[1] Clinton still believed that while some of the forces might be going south, the bulk of the American and French troops were going to take up position in New Jersey west of Elizabeth Town preparing for an attack on Staten Island. As long as de Grasse's destination was uncertain, Clinton believed that the allies would probably not move their entire force to the south. It was not until September 6 when Clinton received Cornwallis's letter of September 4 and Sir Edmund Affleck's letter of September 5 announcing de Grasse's arrival off the Virginia Capes, that "Mr. Washington's design in marching to the southward remained no longer an object of doubt."[2]

British headquarters was hoping to intercept American or French dispatches to determine what Washington and Rochambeau were doing just as James Moody had in June. The British had sent spies into the country to gather whatever intelligence they could. They were actively trying to intercept the mail. British spy Moody thought the usual route for the express riders carrying the American mail was through Pompton, New Jersey.[3] General William Heath, who was at Peekskill, New York, reported to Washington, who was already at the Head of Elk (Elkton, Maryland), that the southern post rider was stopped on September 3 at Pumpton (Pompton, New Jersey) and relieved of the mail.[4]

The British had sent spies into New Jersey but needed to send someone into Connecticut to intercept the express riders between the troops still in Rhode Island and the forces along the Hudson. There was a chance that they could ascertain what was happening through those dispatches. They assigned Nehemiah Marks, the son of a Derby, Connecticut, merchant, to intercept the dragoon that carried the dispatches in Connecticut. He was the leader of a group of armed men based on British Long Island that operated in Connecticut. They used whaleboats to cross the Long Island Sound to Stamford and other coastal Connecticut towns to spy and be couriers to British spies based in Connecticut. On September 4, Marks told Oliver De Lancey that he needed three men to man his boat in order to put two volunteers, John Marks Smith and Millington Lockwood of Greenwich, into Connecticut, where they would hide in the woods waiting to intercept the express rider.[5] Marks, upon his return to Long Island, wrote a report about his trip while he was at Fort Franklin in Lloyd Neck, Long Island. The only person he saw was a black slave. The slave told him that 1,000 foot soldiers and some light horse would approach near to Kingsbridge.

The slave's master "bid him tell me that meant to stop our troops going to the southward by their pretending to attack up at King['s] Bridge."[6]

George Knox of the 9th Pennsylvania Regiment resigned his commission on April 20, 1780, and resided at Newark, New Jersey. He was breveted captain by Congress, on July 26, 1779, for leading the first unit known as the Forlorn Hope at the storming of Stony Point and for his heroism in "braving danger and death."[7] The Forlorn Hope was the first wave of soldiers to attack a fortification. It had an extremely high mortality rate. Knox went to the Refugee Post at Bergen Neck "to offer his services to government in the military line." He said Washington was below Philadelphia but only had 600 to 900 men with him and the New Englanders were with General Heath in the Hudson Highlands. It appears that British intelligence knew Washington had a much larger force with him. The British arrested Knox as a spy.[8]

Washington's deception was run so effectively that the British were trying to sort out who was still in the northern New Jersey and New York area. They did have some help from the Philadelphia newspapers of September 5 that were circulating in New York City on the 14th.[9] The papers reported that Washington's troops passed Philadelphia on the 3rd and the French troops on the 4th and 5th. The regiment of Soisonnois was to be reviewed in Philadelphia on the 5th.

Captain Ludwig August Marquard, who was an aide-de-camp to Lieutenant General von Knyphausen, had been running a secret service operation out of the Morris House since February 1781.[10] He reported to Oliver De Lancey that the reports of Sheldon's Dragoons, also known as the 2nd Regiment of Continental Light Dragoons, having crossed to the west side of the

Hudson River were not true. His information was that 1,000 soldiers were coming from North Castle to attack Kingsbridge.[11] Only about twenty of Sheldon's men went with Washington to Virginia. The rest stayed in Westchester County. Marquand followed this report two days later with another report, on the troops on the east side of the Hudson River.[12]

General Clinton blamed the tardiness of the British navy in repairing their ships for the delay in taking his army to Virginia to evacuate General Cornwallis and his army.[13] British headquarters was busy trying to get intelligence to keep track of American and French troop movements.

Washington was concerned about protecting West Point and what might transpire while he was in Virginia. Before Washington had left the Hudson Highlands, he sent instructions to General William Heath that he was to take command of the troops being left behind. His instructions cautioned him but left open the use of aggressive action if positive results could be achieved. He wrote, "The Security of West Point and the posts in the Highlands is to be considered as the first object of your attention." Washington gave him the latitude of "striking a blow at the enemy's posts or detachments, should a fair opportunity present itself." He added an aside: "(render it advisable to keep the enemy at New York in check to prevent their detaching to reinforce their Southern Army)."[14]

An intelligence report on the movements of Major General William Heath came from South Amboy (John Rattoon) on September 24, 1781, to Sir George Beckwith. Rattoon advised, "If an army of yours would come into the Country it would alter the face of things."[15] Mr. R. (John Rattoon) from New Jersey gave information that he obtained from a gentleman in Jersey, which had been written by Major Elias Dayton to his friends. Captain George Beckwith reported that two spies sent out to Maryland and Pennsylvania on September 10 to obtain intelligence had returned on September 27 and advised that the French and New York troops had marched by land to Baltimore. They were going to proceed to Annapolis and then join up with the combined American and French armies in Virginia.

To keep the British guessing about what troops were where and create a diversion, Jacob Van Wagoner was sent to Fort De Lancey at Bergen Point on October 6. He went into the fort to find out the military weakness of the fort. He questioned the men cutting wood as to the ammunition and weapons at the fort and if they were in working order. He left at sundown.

At dawn Fort De Lancey was attacked. The Americans were repulsed and were followed during their retreat along the bay road. The attack was a success, as its purpose was to set the other British posts on alert. At about two in the afternoon, Loyalist Captain Ward saw two men in a canoe crossing the bay. He hid until the boat landed and Van Wagoner and Garret Frealin disembarked. During questioning they claimed to have seen no one and to have only gone as far as the ferry house. Captain Ward later received reliable information that the two had been in Newark and had met with rebel officers. Ward then had Van Wagoner apprehended and ordered on October 8 that he be confined on board the *Clinton*, a galley. Van Wagoner remained confined there until David Mathews, mayor of New York, became security for his release.[16]

General Clinton had managed to keep in contact with General Lord Cornwallis by means of ciphered letters sent with messengers who made the trip from New York City to Yorktown in small boats. One of the couriers was driven ashore near Little Egg Harbor on the New Jersey coast. The courier, after giving a promise of a pardon, turned over the document he was transporting. James Lovell, a member of the Continental Congress and an expert in cryptography, quickly decoded it, as Clinton and Cornwallis were still using the cipher already known to Lovell.

Lovell had sent the cipher solution on September 21 to General Washington at Yorktown. He suggested that Washington have his secretary make a copy of it in case the same cipher was still being used between Cornwallis and Clinton.[17] On September 8, Cornwallis sent a ciphered letter to Clinton. The brig *Sea Nymph* of Philadelphia intercepted the dispatch boat off Cape Charles, Virginia, on the 10th.[18] The letter was delivered on the evening of September 23 to General Mordecai Gist at Baltimore. He then sent it during the day to Washington.[19] Washington, on October 6, advised Lovell that the cipher worked on the intercepted letter between Cornwallis and Clinton, as his secretary was able to decipher a paragraph of the letter.[20] The letter provided him with information on the conditions inside the British encampment at Yorktown. Washington assured Lovell that a copy of the ciphers was forwarded to General Greene.[21] Lovell, on October 14, confirmed to Washington that British officers were all using the same cipher.[22]

The cipher used between British Generals Clinton and Cornwallis was good for the first page of the document. Any number 30 and above was a null or had no value. A change in the numbers occurred after a series of four to seven nulls were used. The letters "I" and "J" were interchangeable.[23] The following is their cipher chart:

Line	A	B	C	D	E	F	G	H	I/J	K	L	M
1	19	9	17	13	16	7	12	8	14	15	26	4
10	23	22	6	19	9	17	13	16	7	12	8	14
14	5	24	29	1	25	23	22	6	19	9	17	13

Line	N	O	P	Q	R	S	T	U	V	W	X	Y	Z
1	18	21	3	2	11	5	24	29	1	25	26	22	6
10	15	26	4	18	21	3	2	11	5	24	29	1	25
14	16	7	12	8	14	15	26	4	18	21	3	2	11

Lovell also reported that the British were using Entick's Dictionary of 1777, which was printed in London by Charles Dilly. A notation of 115.1.4 represented page 115, first column, fourth word from the top of the page.[24]

Sometimes things come your way from where you least expect them. Another attempt at operational assistance used in exploiting the advantage came from Richard Peters and James Rivington, the publisher of the semiweekly *Royal Gazette* in New York City.

Richard Peters, secretary of the Board of War, told Washington that he had procured access to a person at Rivington's printing office[25] and that the person was "ready to furnish any important papers as intelligence." He advised that this person would only trust the person Peters had used before in contacting him and "he in N[ew] York will trust no other. I mention this to your Excellency that if you can think of any material use to be made of this you will please to take advantage of it thro' me as it is confined to my knowledge only. . . . I some time ago procured a copy of the British signals for their fleet & gave them to the minister of France [Anne-César de La Luzerne] to transmit to Compte de Grasse.[26]

"I had again sent in the person employed on the former occasion & he has brought out some addition[al] signals & among
them those for the troops now embarked on boa[rd] the fleet
on their present enterprise to the Chesapeake." The person who
went to get the signals the second time on Long Island was Allen McLane and he reported that he received them from James
Rivington. He wrote, "I returned [from the cruise on the *Congress*] in the fall [and] was employed by the board of war to repair to Long Island to watch the motion of the British fleet and
if possible obtain their signals which I did threw [*sic*] the assistance of the noted Rivington. Joined the fleet under the Count
d Grass [*sic*]."[27] Peters had stated this was the second meeting
where Rivington provided the British navy signal codes to his
courier who was McLane.[28] In the McLane Papers at the New-
York Historical Society a manuscript states, "On his return he
was stationed by the Board of War near Sandy Hook to corre-
spond with R[ivington] of New York [and] received the signals
for the British fleet out of New York [and] delivered them to
Count de Grass [*sic*]."[29] He had traveled by barge from Shrewsbury, New Jersey, to Long Island.[30]

Peters said that McLane was charged with taking the second
set of codes to Comte de Grasse and if necessary to Washington.[31] Washington wrote that McLane "was entrusted by the
Board of War [Peters] with the delivery of dispatches of importance to his Excellency the Count de Grasse, which commission
he executed with great ability."[32]

Peters had told Washington that his contact at Rivington's
printing office, which was Rivington himself, was ready to furnish any important papers, meaning documents, as intelligence.
Rivington, as the royal printer, would have access to anything
the British wanted secretly printed. He supplied two printed

versions of the British naval signals to McLane on his two errands. Peters mentioned that the two versions of "the signals have been reprinted with no alterations but the change of the name of Arbuthnot for Graves.[33] The written part was copied from the original given to be reprinted."[34]

The signals would have provided the French navy with a quicker read on the planned movements of the British navy. The benefit of knowing the enemy's signals allows the opposing navy to know the commands as soon as they are displayed. Knowing what the signals meant, the French would not have to wait to see what formation the British navy was creating and then respond. They could respond to the signals as soon as they were given. This knowledge is not going to win you a battle, as you still have to fight the fight.

Rivington in New York City communicated to Peters in Philadelphia by ads placed in his newspaper. In the issue of July 11, 1781, on page 3, column 3, appeared this notice: "[T]he person to whom Mr. Lemuel Jones Nelme [appears to be a pseudonym used for Peters] wrote a letter dated from Fish-Kill [behind the American lines] April 27[, 1781,] which did not come to his hand till yesterday the 10th of July 1781." The notice said, "[C]ome to New York where he will receive information of matters momentous and interesting." It goes on: "[E]njoy the happiness of meeting his parents, proper information; and directions are left with the printer, to whom Mr. Nelme will be pleased to repair." In other words, see the printer, James Rivington, to get your intelligence. Londoner Lemuel Dole Nelme in 1772 wrote *An Essay Towards an Investigation of the Origin and Elements of Language,* a speculative book on the origin of languages and alphabet symbolism. Nelme says that letters are symbols of things. Alphabetic symbols are used to construct ciphers. Rivington being a printer would have known of the book.

Two notices were in the September 29, 1781, issue of the *Royal Gazette.* When put together Rivington requested a meeting at his paper mill on Long Island.

On page 2, column 3, the ad read: "The person to whom Nimrod wrote the two letters, begs leave to inform him that he received them this morning, and acknowledges himself much obliged to him, but earnestly wishes to have an immediate interview at anyplace Nimrod may by letter appoint. Nimrod may depend upon the honor of the author of this advertisement, in every respect." The Nimrod of the Old Testament was a great hunter. The ad was requesting a meeting but did not provide a location.

An ad on page 3, column 3, was marked off with a finger pointing to it to ensure that it was not missed: "The printer feels much concern at being obliged to make use of paper on which this gazette is printed, its quality so very mean and disgraceful, is entirely owing to a want of supply from the [paper] mill on Long Island, which he hopes will be early enough for the next publication." He indicated that he was going to be at his paper mill until his next newspaper was published.

James Rivington as the royal printer would have had no difficulty traveling to his paper mill on Long Island to accomplish the government's business. Allen McLane crossed from Shrewsbury near Sandy Hook to Long Island for their meeting. McLane returned to Shrewsbury and then left by a small boat to see Peters in Philadelphia. Peters in Philadelphia then sent McLane to deliver the signals to de Grasse, taking his letter of October 19. McLane delivered the signals to de Grasse, who then sent him to Washington with a copy of the signals.

Washington wrote to Peters, at the Continental Congress War Board, on October 27 that he received his letter of the 19th, which was brought by Captain McLane. He also thanked him "for the intelligence you have communicated; the *particular mode* [Peters to McLane to Rivington] you have adopted to obtain information, I think may be very usefully employed, and is a fortunate expedient; the necessity of its use to our present operations is happily at an end, if continued, it may be of importance to some future designs."[35] Washington, having explained that the latest information arrived too late to be used by the French navy in Virginia, said it still might be of use elsewhere. Washington then wrote on the 29th to the Chevalier de La Luzerne that the "Count de Grasse having been so good as to submit the inclosed signals to my sight and improvement; agreeable to his desire, I take this first opportunity to return them to your Excellency by a safe conveyance, and hope they may be of signal advantage to the commanders of his Most Christian Majesty's Naval Armies."[36] It is unknown when the first set of British naval signals that Peters had given to Luzerne was delivered to the Comte de Grasse. It is possible that he had the first set in time for the Battle of the Capes on September 5, 1781.

Washington on his arrival in Virginia used the secret service assets that General Lafayette had established. In order to keep track of Cornwallis's movements, Lafayette developed an intelligence operation. Because Colonel James Innes was a 1771 graduate of the College of William and Mary and was acquainted with the residents of Williamsburg, Virginia, and its surrounding area, he was ordered to set up a spy network that sent people into the British camps at Yorktown and Gloucester. Innes, on February 11, 1782, explained to Governor Benjamin Harrison that he was authorized by General Lafayette to pay 10 guineas to those who could prove that they had been in the British camp and more for significant information, and that "provisions [were] furnished to those persons whom I sent to Williamsburg, under the pretext of carrying supplies to market" but were actually sent there to gather intelligence. He set up a network on both the north and south sides of the York River.[37]

On July 13, Washington was still obsessed with attacking New York and told Lafayette to prepare for the possibility that Cornwallis might take a strong post at Portsmouth or Williamsburg and send a detachment of troops to New York or South Carolina.[38] Washington at the time was still concerned over actions in the south and on July 30 told Lafayette that "above all things I recommend an augmentation of your cavalry to as great a height as possible. It may happen that the enemy may be drove to the necessity of forcing their way thro' North Carolina to avoid a greater misfortune. A superiority of Horse upon our side would be fatal to them in such a case."[39] He wanted Lafayette to be able to harass Cornwallis and keep Cornwallis where he was.

Charles Morgan was a farmer from Monmouth County and a member of the New Jersey Brigade. He was sent on a mission to enter Cornwallis's camp as a deserter. It was hoped that he could convince Cornwallis that he could not make a successful dash to North Carolina. He told Cornwallis he was agreeable to fighting under Washington but not under Lafayette, a Frenchman. Once there he was to convince the British that Lafayette had enough boats that he could move all his troops across the James River in three hours. It persuaded Cornwallis that he could not escape to North Carolina before Lafayette could attack.[40]

James Armistead was a twenty-one-year-old slave of William Armistead of New Kent County, Virginia; with his master's permission he enlisted with Major General Lafayette sometime after Lafayette's arrival in mid-March 1781. Lafayette had sent James to Portsmouth, Virginia, on a number of occasions to deliver messages to other American spies and to pick up information from British Brigadier General Benedict Arnold's camp. Arnold conducted a series of raids in Virginia, capturing the city of Richmond and destroying supply houses, foundries, and mills.

James Armistead had been a successful operative for Lafayette at Portsmouth so Lafayette sent James on a similar mission into Cornwallis's camp at Yorktown. Lafayette wrote to General Washington, on July 31, 1781, that he had a correspondent who was working as a servant of Lord Cornwallis. James went to Cornwallis's camp claiming to be an escaped slave. He delivered to the British a copy of Lafayette's fabricated orders for military units that did not exist. On August 25, Lafayette wrote to Washington that "I have got some intelligence by way of this servant I have once mentioned . . . they [British] were fortifying Yorktown."[41] According to some accounts James was hired by the British to spy for them.

The British fleet under the command of Admiral Thomas Graves did not leave Sandy Hook until October 19 and arrived off Cape Charles, Virginia, on the 24th. General Clinton, immediately on arrival, sent Lieutenant Blanchard instructions to take a whaleboat to contact John Dennis, the resident British contact, at Smith's Island and collect his information on the position and strength of the French fleet and see if any information had arrived from Lord Cornwallis. Cornwallis had surrendered to the combined American and French forces on October 19, 1781.

General Clinton sent a report to Lord George Germain from the ninety-gun second-rate ship of the line *London* off the Chesapeake Bay on October 29, the day the fleet went back to

New York.[42] Clinton said that he received the information that Cornwallis had proposed terms of capitulation on the 17th from the pilot of the HMS *Charon*, a forty-four-gun fifth-rate ship, and from some people they had picked up offshore.[43]

Clinton clearly placed the blame on the British navy for Cornwallis's surrender at Yorktown. In his report he claimed the surrender could "have possibly been prevented could the fleet have been able to sail at or within a few days of the time we first expected. At least I am persuaded we should have saved to His Majesty's Service great part of that gallant army together with its respectable chief whose loss it will be now impossible I fear to repair." Obviously Clinton was not going to mention how Washington tricked him into staying in New York while the combined American and French armies marched across New Jersey. Washington's objective was a quick and unmolested march from New York through New Jersey to Virginia right in front of him. Washington, like Generals Frederick Morgan and Norman Schwarzkopf, used a Deception Battle Plan to achieve his military objectives. Washington had pulled together all he learned in espionage to make victory possible. As one defeated British intelligence officer, Major George Beckwith, is often quoted as saying, "Washington did not really outfight the British. He simply out-spied us."[44]

Sixteen

CONCLUSION

Washington started adult life as a Virginia plantation owner, which is a nicer way of saying a farmer. He had served in the Virginia militia during the French and Indian War. The experience he garnered in espionage and military tactics during that war was overlooked by the British leaders of his day and by most historians. His experiences while an emissary to Saint-Pierre, commandant of Fort Le Boeuf, and under British General Edward Braddock were the cornerstone to developing the American spymaster of the American Revolution.

That Washington out-spied the British is a commonly held notion, and for many it means he had more spies than the British. The opposite is true. The British had more money in hard currency to pay for intelligence and thus had more spies. Washington, though, was better at the military application of the intelligence his spies brought him. By comparing intelligence from several spies, he was able to determine what information was true and what was false. He was able to identify the deceptions the British sent to him. When needed, his spies helped deliver false information to the enemy.

The common belief that when Washington became commander in chief of the Continental Army at Cambridge, Massachusetts, he had no military skills in the field of espionage is absolutely false.

Washington as a young man in the French and Indian War first learned how useful and necessary espionage and deception were. On his expeditions to what is now western Pennsylvania, the French had deceived him several times. They tried to lure his Indian allies from him. They sent spies into his camp to gain an advantage. If he was going to protect the men under him, he had to know what the French were doing in their fort. He had sent George Croghan as a spy to the French fort at the Forks of the Ohio.

He quickly developed an understanding and competency with operating independent spies and deceptions during the French and Indian War. His experiences on the western Pennsylvania frontier showed he was quick in understanding the situation, then determining a course of action, and implementing the objective. He discovered the enemy at the time, the French, had sent spies to determine what he was doing. He sent those same spies back with false information. He seemed to take delight in playing the game of deception and reversing events. In order to motivate his Indian allies he told them the falsehood that the French wanted to kill their chief, Half King. While at Fort Le Boeuf, he played the role of a spy and collected intelligence on the fort. As an aide-de-camp to General Braddock he would have had knowledge of Braddock's cipher. It is unknown if he actually used it.

One of the best pieces of advice given to Washington came in 1755 from Landon Carter. He told him, "[I] recommend to you the utmost caution never to depend on a fancied security nor trust too far to the information of those who may be benefitted by deception."[1]

There are two goals for every general: to defeat the enemy and to avoid defeat. Lieutenant General David Richard Palmer said, "A skilled strategist derives his primary purpose from an analysis of the situation at any given moment and the integration of that analysis with long-range or national goals. In the Revolutionary War, some seasons demanded victory, others the avoidance of defeat. The watchword on some days was audacity, on others it was caution. Washington seemed always to know which was appropriate."[2] He knew to protect the identities of his spies and thus did not identify them by name in his expense register.

Washington had both failures and successes in the field of espionage. Also some of the activities were well-planned-out events and others were the result of luck. Reality demolishes Parson Weems's story of Washington as the boy who could not tell a lie. To the contrary, Washington seemed to enjoy the details of playing tricks on the British. He would use one lie to verify another lie and have the lies come to the enemy from different sources. He used fake mail and reports that accidentally on purpose fell into the enemy hands. The British were so used to his inflated troop returns that when they intercepted a genuine troop report at the Battle of the Brandywine they did not believe it.

He realized if deception worked for him that he had to be diligently on the lookout for deceptions from the enemy. He usually verified one spy's intelligence with that of another or several others to keep from being deceived. However, there were occasionally times when he had to use his instincts and trust a single spy's information. In such cases he would assess the situation and take decisive action even though he lacked the amount of data he normally wanted.

Along with deception there was the game of double agents, which both sides played well. Some played the double game for the money while others did it for patriotism. There are double agents from the American Revolution who were so good at their craft that to this day it is impossible to determine their true feelings and for whose side they worked.

Intelligence gathering was not only finding out how many men and cannons the enemy had. Washington routinely asked his spies to find out precisely the kind of food, forage, and other particulars that the British and Hessians were providing to their men. If the men were being given rations that were already cooked, it meant they would be moving very soon. If they were provided food that had to be cooked they were most likely not going anywhere that day. The quantity of rations would give an idea as to the length of the expedition. If they were given winter coats or summer attire, it would indicate if they were going north or south from New York. The type of forage provided to the horses would tell the distance.

He also employed Black Chambers to carefully open and read enemy mail and then carefully reseal the letters and send them to their recipient. This provided the opportunity to replace the letters with contents more favorable to the American cause. Washington embraced technology in the form of codes, ciphers, and invisible inks to transmit intelligence from within enemy lines. When the supply of sympathetic ink stain was running out, he ordered the construction of a laboratory to manufacture it. He ensured that the spies who depended upon it had it. To keep anyone from finding out that they were using invisible ink, they called it "medicine" in their correspondence.

There were four phases to the American Revolution according to Lieutenant General Palmer. The initial phase was the beginning of the war at Boston. Washington took command at Cambridge, Massachusetts, of what was barely an army. It was more of a dysfunctional mob. For him it was a "run all risks" to win. The rebels had little to lose and all to gain. Lieutenant General Palmer said, "Washington attacked at every turn taking the strategic offensive to the full extent of his limited power."[3] He used existing assets like the ferrymen to continue gathering intelligence. His early attempts at espionage produced few results. Someone devised the idea of using fishermen as cover to get a spy into and out of the city. The three fishermen obtained a permit from the British admiral on September 15, 1775. His first spy ring was discovered by the British most likely through the treachery of the traitor Dr. Benjamin Church Jr.

The second phase was entirely different from the first. It started with the rebels in control of all thirteen rebelling colonies. There was a functioning Continental Congress giving guidance. The Congress declared the former colonies a new nation independent from Great Britain. It now had territory to defend and control. The British arrived at New York with overwhelming manpower of their own, Hessian mercenaries, and a powerful navy.

Washington started the campaign by defending territory, New York and Long Island. After a series of crushing defeats and losing New York and most of New Jersey, his army was chased to Pennsylvania; they slid back to the first phase of win-at-all-costs. He launched a surprise attack at Trenton and defeated the Hessians encamped there. A few days later at Trenton his army was about to be overrun by Cornwallis and for the only time in the war in order to escape, he ran the risk of taking his army between the British and the ocean. For the entire war he always kept the possibility of taking his army to the interior of the continent. His army then engaged the British regulars at Princeton and defeated them. This defeat of British regulars by these rustic Americans was hard for the British to swallow. They could accept the defeat of the Hessians, the hired help, at Trenton. The loss by British regulars was unfathomable.

Washington took his army to the safety of the Watchung Mountains of northern New Jersey. The location was at least a day's march from the water. Should the British land and attempt to assault the encampment, the Americans would have time to respond or withdraw.

When the British arrived on Staten Island, the Mercereau Spy Ring provided intelligence from Staten Island. It helped to clandestinely deliver fliers to Hessian soldiers on Staten Island. It accomplished what it was asked to do. Once the armies were moving, there was not enough time to run an effective espionage network. Spies operate best between stationary targets. When the fox chase across New Jersey ended, Washington was once again able to make effective use of spies. At Philadelphia, he had the successful Clark Spy Ring as well as other agents working solo.

The third stage began with the signing of the alliance with France on February 6, 1778. Later Spain and Holland joined the conflict. What began as a civil war on the North American continent had grown to engulf much of the world. The British on October 19, 1778, captured the French colony of Pondicherry on the Indian subcontinent after a siege of nearly eighty days.

The British sent a fleet to attack the Dutch settlement at the Cape of Good Hope on the southwestern tip of Africa. The entire globe, including the sugar islands of the Caribbean, became a battlefield. British assets could no longer concentrate solely on the thirteen rebelling colonies. They had to protect their colonies as well as Great Britain itself from attack. It was after the British evacuated Philadelphia and returned to New York that the Culper Spy Ring was started and the Mercereau Spy Ring was restarted. Elias Dayton's group and many individual spies were given assignments. Washington coordinated activities with the French in deceiving British General Clinton in New York, leading to the surrender by Cornwallis at Yorktown, Virginia.

The final phase of the war saw the fighting occur outside North America. It also involved the negotiations for the peace. For Washington the objective was still an offensive one but he could not afford a defeat. He also had to keep the army together, as many thought the war was over and wanted to go home. There was the risk of the army dissolving. Washington turned away from the Culper Spy Ring, as it did not produce timely intelligence. Spies were still used but they operated independently with their case officers.

When the news of Cornwallis's surrender reached Benjamin Franklin in Paris, he was ecstatic. He described to John Adams his astonishment at the masterful coordination of the American and French forces and especially Washington who organized it:

Most heartily do I congratulate you on the glorious News! The Infant Hercules in his cradle has now strangled his second serpent, and gives hopes that his future history will be answerable. I inclose a pacquet [*sic*] which I have

just received from General Washington; and which I suppose contains the Articles of Capitulation. It is a rare
circumstance, and scarce to be met with in history, that
in one war two armies should be taken Prisoners completely [*sic*], not a man in either escaping. It is another
singular circumstance, that an expedition so complex,
form[e]d of armies of different nations & of land &
sea-forces, should with such perfect concord be assembled from different places by land & water, form their
junction punctually, without the least retard by cross ac-
cidents of wind or weather, or interruption from the
enemy; and that the army which was their object should
in the mean time have the goodness to quit a situation
from whence it might have escaped, and place itself in
another from whence an escape was impossible.[4]

For the duration of the American Revolution, Washington
was fixed on one goal, independence from British rule. He never
wavered from this objective. He used deception and his spies to
reach the final victory. The apex of his development was the
Deception Battle Plan, where he coordinated many activities in
sequence. In 1781 he had to move the American and French
armies across New Jersey without being attacked and drawn
into a battle. He needed to get the combined armies to Yorktown
to conduct a siege of General Cornwallis. He used everything
from his bag of tricks. He used fake letters, deceptions of an
amphibious assault on Staten Island, preparations for a planned
attack at Kingsbridge.

In the highlands near Sandy Hook, for an army that was not
going there, he used the preparations for bake ovens, artillery
emplacements, and forage contracts that would never be used.

He collected bricks at Perth Amboy where it would be observed by the enemy, while real bake ovens were built at Chatham. Washington employed the collection of boats between Perth Amboy and Elizabeth; and the movement of thirty boats on carriages from New York to Springfield, New Jersey, to indicate an amphibious landing on Staten Island. He also was busy gathering intelligence to ensure the British were not running a counter-deception and preparing a trap for him as well as to determine if his plan was working.

The success of the operation led to the eventual surrender of General Cornwallis at Yorktown and an end to the major fighting of the American Revolution and the ultimate victory over the most powerful military of its day. Washington had grown from a Virginia farmer to the eighteenth century's greatest spymaster.

ACKNOWLEDGMENTS

No historian ever does all the research by himself. One needs to know when he needs help and whom to ask to get the best answer. Networking is the key to answering questions and finding that elusive nugget of information to solve a conundrum. The following are the people who were kind enough to answer some of my questions or point me in the right direction when I had wandered off course.

I am appreciative of the information provided by Douglas Bradburn, director; Mark Santangelo; Sarah Myers; and the rest of the staff at the Fred W. Smith National Library for the Study of George Washington, Mount Vernon, Virginia. I would like to thank Edward G. Lengel, editor in chief; Benjamin L. Huggins; and William M. Ferraro at the Papers of George Washington at the University of Virginia, Charlottesville, Virginia.

I also want to thank John C. Dann, former director; J. Kevin Graffagnino, director; and the staff at the William L. Clements Library at the University of Michigan at Ann Arbor, Michigan. The staff have been assisting and encouraging me with my research on espionage since 1992. Another who has helped is Thomas Lannon, Acting Charles J. Liebman Curator of Manuscripts at the New York Public Library.

I need to thank Katherine Ludwig and Paul Davis of the David Library of the American Revolution in Washington Crossing, Pennsylvania. They have expended much effort to help me discover the answers to some of the more unusual research topics and they have responded quickly to my inquiries.

There are some I have consulted to assist in researching individuals identified in the book: John L. Bell on all things Boston; Todd W. Braisted on Loyalists; Robert A. Selig on Allen McLane's movements; and Salvatore F. Tarantino on Sheldon's Horse, the 2nd Continental Light Dragoons. Also Don N. Hagist, Nancy Webster, and Philip D. Weaver have provided answers to my inquiries. I want to thank Scott Martin of the Shapiro Science Library at the University of Michigan, Ann Arbor, for help with some chemical concerns. My appreciation to the Mount Laurel Library, Mount Laurel, New Jersey, for arranging interlibrary loans for me.

I also want to thank my literary agent, Donald Fehr with Trident Media Group, New York; my editor; Marc Resnick, executive editor at St. Martin's Press; Jaime Coyne, assistant editor; and Fred Chase, copy editor.

Many thanks to my daughters, Jennifer Ann Nagy and Lisa Marie Nagy, for their encouragement and help. I want to especially thank Ida Marie Nagy, my wife, for having such enormous patience, understanding, and encouragement while I wrote this book.

APPENDIX

Major General Edward Braddock's Cipher*

* William L. Clements Library, University of Michigan.

NOTES

Abbreviations Used in Notes

CP   Henry Clinton Papers, William L. Clements Library, University of Michigan, Ann Arbor, Michigan.

DGW   Donald Jackson and Dorothy Twohig, eds. *The Diaries of George Washington.* Vol. 1, 1748–1765; Vol. 3, 1771–1775, 1780–1781. Charlottesville: University of Virginia Press, 1976, 1978.

GWP   George Washington Papers, Library of Congress, Washington, DC.

JCC   *Journals of the Continental Congress, 1774–1789.* Washington, DC: United States Government Printing Office, 1904–1937.

PCC   Papers of the Continental Congress, 1774–1789. Microfilm. National Archives and Records Administration, General Services Administration, Washington, DC.

Introduction

1. George Washington to Robert Hunter Morris, Governor of Pennsylvania, January 1, 1756, Series 2, Letterbook 3: 16–17, George Washington Papers, Library of Congress, Washington, DC. Hereinafter GWP.

2. George Washington to Benjamin Tallmadge, June 27, 1779, Varick Transcripts, Letterbook 9: 128–30; GWP; George Washington to Benjamin Tallmadge, July 5, 1779, Varick Transcripts, Letterbook 9: 163–64, GWP.

3. The spelling and capitalization of the letter had to be corrected to make it readable. George Higday to Henry Clinton, July 13, 1779, Henry Clinton Papers, William L. Clements Library, University of Michigan, Ann Arbor, Michigan, 63:9. Hereafter CP.

4. Provost report for New York City, August 28, 1780, CP 119:14.

5. Mason Locke Weems, more commonly known as Parson Weems, *The Life of Washington the Great* (Augusta, Georgia: George P. Randolph, 1806), 8–9.

1. French Lessons

1. His eyesight problem is also known as "lazy eye." He would weigh between 210 and 220 during the American Revolution. Ron Chernow, *Washington: A Life* (New York: Penguin, 2010), 29–30.
2. Robert Dinwiddie was the son of Robert and Sarah (Cumming) Dinwiddie and was born in Glasgow, Scotland, on October 2, 1692. He died at Gloucestershire, England, on July 27, 1770. He was a British colonial administrator who served as a customs official in Bermuda (1727–1738) and lieutenant governor of the colony of Virginia from 1751 to 1758. Since the governor of the colony at that time was mostly an absentee position, he was the de facto head of the colony.
3. Lawrence Washington (1718–1752).
4. Mary Ball Washington (1708–1789).
5. George would inherit the 260-acre farm that would later be called Ferry Farm and ten slaves. Until he turned twenty-one his mother managed the farm.
6. The Fairfax Land Grant was made by exiled English King Charles II in 1649. http://www.lva.virginia.gov/public/guides/opac /lonnabout.htm.
7. Thomas Fairfax, 6th Lord Fairfax of Cameron (October 22, 1693–December 9, 1781), was the son of Thomas Fairfax, 5th Lord Fairfax of Cameron, and of Catherine, daughter of Thomas Culpeper, 2nd Baron Culpeper of Thoresway.
8. George William Fairfax (February 26, 1729–April 3, 1787) when he was twenty-four years old married eighteen-year-old Sarah Cary, later known as Sally Fairfax. He was seven years older than George Washington.
9. The Blue Ridge Mountains have a bluish color when seen from a distance. The area is rich in biodiversity with many chestnut, hemlock, oak, and pine trees. The chestnut trees were decimated by the chestnut blight in the 1900s.
10. Captain Isaac Pennington (son of Abraham Pennington and Catherine) was born May 16, 1715, in Albemarle County, Virginia, and died September 17, 1760, in Enoree, Berkeley County, South Carolina. He married Mary Williams on December 8, 1733, in Cecil County, Maryland.

11. William Nelson at York, Virginia, to George Washington, February 22, 1753. General Correspondence, GWP.

12. James Thomas Flexner, *George Washington* (Boston: Little, Brown, 1968), 1:55.

13. British National Archives, Kew, Richmond, Surrey, United Kingdom, Colonial Office Papers, C.O. 5/1328, ff. 45–46.

14. Jacobus Van Braam was born in Bergen op Zoom in the Netherlands on April 1, 1729, and died on August 1, 1792, in Charleville, France.

15. Christopher Gist was born in Baltimore in 1706 and died in 1759.

16. John Fraser (1721, Scotland—April 16, 1773). His name appears as Frazer, Frazier, and Fraser.

17. Chief Shingas (1715–1788) was also known as Shingas the Terrible for his activities in the French and Indian War. http://oxfordindex.oup.com/view/10.1093/anb/9780198606697.article.2000936.

18. Half King was Tanacharison or Tanaghrisson (c. 1700–October 4, 1754). Iroquois who had migrated to the Ohio Country were generally known as "Mingoes," and Tanacharison emerged as their leader at Logstown.

19. Chernow, *Washington*, 34.

20. Philippe Thomas Chabert de Joncaire was called Nitachinon by the Iroquois. He was a trader, officer in the colonial regular troops, Indian agent, and interpreter. He was baptized on January 9, 1707, in Montreal; son of Louis-Thomas Chabert de Joncaire and Marie-Madeleine Le Gay de Beaulieu. He married Madeleine Renaud Dubuisson on July 23, 1731, and died circa 1766.

21. Sunset for Erie, Pennsylvania, on December 1, 1753, was 4:52:31 p.m.

22. Jacques Legardeur de Saint-Pierre was an officer in the colonial regular French troops, explorer, and interpreter. He was born October 24, 1701, at Montreal, son of Jean-Paul Legardeur de Saint-Pierre and Marie-Josette Leneuf de La Vallière. He was killed in the Battle of Lac Saint-Sacrement (Lake George) in 1755.

23. Flexner, *George Washington*, 1:68.

24. Donald Jackson and Dorothy Twohig, eds., *The Diaries of George Washington*, vol. 1, 1748–1765 (Charlottesville: University of Virginia Press, 1976), 148. Hereinafter *DGW*.

25. Washington's description of the fort was: "4 Houses compose the Sides; the Bastions are made of Piles drove into the Ground, &

about 12 Feet above sharpe at Top, with Port Holes cut for Cannon & Small Arms to fire through; there are Eight 6 lb. Pieces Mounted, two in each Bastion, & one of 4 lb. before the Gate: In the Bastions are a Guard House, Chapel, Doctor's Lodgings, & the Commander's private Store, round which is laid Platforms for the Cannon & Men to stand on: there is several Barracks without the Fort for the Soldiers dwelling, cover'd some with Bark, & some with Boards, & made chiefly of Logs, there is also several other Houses such as Stables, Smiths Shop &ca: all of which I have laid down exactly as they stand, & shall refer to the Plan for Explanation. I cou'd get no certain Account of the Number of Men here; but according to the best Judgement I cou'd form, there is an Hundred exclusive of Officers, which are pretty many. I also gave Orders to the People that were with me, to take an exact Account of the Canoes that were haled up, to convey their Forces down in the spring, which they did, and told 50 of Birch Bark, & 170 of Pine; besides many others that were block'd out, in Readiness to make." Ibid., 149.

26. Ibid., 69.
27. "Journey to the French Commandant: Narrative," Founders Online, National Archives, http://founders.archives.gov/documents /Washington/01-01-02-0003-0002.
28. William Trent (1715–1787) was a native of Lancaster, Pennsylvania. He was appointed captain of one of the four companies raised in Pennsylvania in 1746 for the campaign against Canada as part of King George's War (1744–1748). In the 1740s he had built up a considerable Indian trade and formed a partnership with George Croghan. He was an agent for the Ohio Company in the construction of storehouses and a fort. Dinwiddie to Trent, January 27, 1754, Robert Dinwiddie, *Official Records of Robert Dinwiddie, Lieutenant Governor of the Colony of Virginia, 1751–1758* (Richmond: Virginia Historical Society, 1883), 1:55–56.
29. Marquis Ange Duquesne de Menneville was born circa 1700 at Toulon, France, and died September 17, 1778, at Antony, France. He was governor general of New France from 1752 to 1755. Duquesne was instructed to secure the Ohio Valley, where French sovereignty was being threatened by English traders, and to this end in 1753–1754 he sent an expedition south under Paul Marin de La Malgue (also La Marque) to establish a series of forts. A second expedition in 1754 completed the occupation of the area with the building of Fort Duquesne.
30. *DGW*, 1:163.

31. Joshua Fry was born in Somersetshire, England, around 1700. He immigrated to Essex County, Virginia. He started a boys' grammar school attached to the College of William and Mary and later chaired the college's Mathematics Department. He married Mary Micou Hill, the widow of a wealthy plantation owner from Spotsylvania County. He served as a member of the House of Burgesses, and as a justice of the peace for Essex County. When Albemarle County was founded, Fry was named chief surveyor. After he fell from his horse, he died from his injuries on May 31, 1754.

32. Edward G. Lengel, *General George Washington: A Military Life* (New York: Random House, 2005), 31.

33. George Washington to Robert Dinwiddie, March 9, 1754, *DGW*, 1:174, footnote 19.

34. Peter Hog (1703–1782) was a native of Edinburgh and about 1745 settled in Augusta County, Virginia. He signed his name Hog not Hogg.

35. Adam Stephen was born in Scotland circa 1718 and died in 1791. He studied medicine at the University of Edinburgh. He briefly had a career in the British navy. He immigrated to Virginia and started a medical practice. In September 1776 he was given the rank of brigadier general in the Continental Army. He was promoted to major general on February 19, 1777. In October 1777 he was charged with "Acting unlike an officer" at Germantown and was dismissed from service in November 1777.

36. Claude-Pierre Pécaudy, Sieur de Contrecoeur (1706–1775), began his career in the French army with the rank of ensign in 1729. He advanced to the rank of captain in 1748, and in 1754 was ordered to construct a fort at the Forks of the Ohio and was put in command of French forces in the Ohio Country. He retired from the army in 1759, and in 1774 he was appointed to the legislative council of the province of Quebec. Fernand Grenier, "PÉCAUDY DE CONTRECŒUR, CLAUDE-PIERRE," in *Dictionary of Canadian Biography*, vol. 4, University of Toronto/Université Laval, 2003–, http://www.biographi.ca/en/bio/pecaudy_de_contrecoeur_claude_pierre_4E.html.

37. Ward's name sometimes appears as Wart. For Ward's deposition on his surrender, see William J. Darlington, ed., *Christopher Gist's Journals with Historical, Geographical and Ethnological Biographies of His Contemporaries* (Pittsburgh: J. R. Weldin, 1893), 275–78.

38. *DGW*, 1:177–78.

39. Gist's residence was roughly forty-eight miles south of Fort Pitt.

Christopher Gist was born in 1706 in Baltimore, Maryland. The date and location of his death are uncertain.

40. *DGW,* 1:185–87.
41. Ibid., 1:185.
42. Ibid., 1:182.
43. Ibid., 1:184.
44. Ibid., 1:177–78, 188.
45. Half King, written by John Davison, interpreter, to George Washington, May 24, 1754, ibid., 1:191.
46. Ibid., 1:192.
47. Great Meadow is near Laurel Hill approximately eleven miles southeast of present-day Uniontown, Pennsylvania. Ibid., 1:191–92, and footnote 51–52.
48. The new moon occurred on May 22, 1754, and the first quarter was not till May 29, 1754. U.S. Naval Observatory, Astronomical Applications Department. http://aa.usno.navy.mil/cgi-bin/aa _phases.pl?year=1754&month=5&day=20&nump=50&format =p.
49. Dawn calculated at NOAA Solar Calculator at http://www.esrl .noaa.gov/gmd/grad/solcalc/; ibid., 193, footnote 55.
50. Mingoes are an Iroquoian-speaking group made up of peoples who migrated west to the Ohio Country in the mid-eighteenth century, primarily Seneca and Cayuga. *DGW,* 1:194.
51. The site of the French camp is present-day Jumonville's Rocks, three miles north of Summit, Pennsylvania.
52. *DGW,* 1:195.
53. George Washington in the camp at Great Meadow to Augustine Washington, May 31, 1754, Founders Online, National Archives, http://founders.archives.gov/documents/Washington/02-01-02 -0058.
54. Pierre Jacques Drouillon de Macé was born in 1725. He had been commissioned in 1750 and had served in constructing forts in the Ohio Country.
55. Horace Walpole, *Memoirs of the Reign of King George the Second,* 3 vols. (London: H. Colburn, 1847), 1:400.
56. *DGW,* 1:195, footnote 59.
57. Ibid., 1:197–98.
58. Ibid., 1:198.
59. Ibid., 1:199.
60. Construction started on May 30, 1754. Ibid., 1:100.
61. Joshua Fry was born on May 31, 1700, at Crewkerne, Somerset, England, and died on May 31, 1754. He was buried in Rose Hill

Cemetery, Cumberland, Maryland. On June 4, Dinwiddie wrote to Washington appointing him to the command of the Virginia Regiment. Dinwiddie, *Official Records of Robert Dinwiddie*, 1:193–94; *DGW*, 1:200.

62. No copy of the letter has been located.

63. *DGW*, 1:209.

64. Kaquehuston might be Kekeuscung, who later became a Delaware chief.

65. George Croghan was born circa 1720 near Dublin, Ireland, and immigrated to Pennsylvania around 1741. He settled near Carlisle. In the years before the French and Indian War he established a network of trading posts on the frontier. During the war he served with Washington and Braddock in their campaigns. In 1756 he was appointed deputy superintendent of northern Indian affairs by Sir William Johnson and served till 1772. He died near Philadelphia in 1782.

66. Known as Monacatoocha or Monacatootha and also known as Scarroyaddy, and earlier to 1748, as Skwoniatta. He was an Oneida chief of the Six Nations who in 1754 lived near the Ohio.

67. Virginia Regiment War Council, June 28, 1754, Proceedings, GWP.

68. A pirogue is a dugout canoe-shaped boat.

69. Founders Online, National Archives, http://founders.archives.gov/?q=jumonville&s=1111311111&r=15.

70. Lengel, *General George Washington*, 42–43.

71. Ibid., 43; Founders Online, National Archives, http://founders.archives.gov/?q=jumonville&s=1111311111&r=15.

72. Dr. James Craik would be the doctor who forty-five years later attended Washington on his deathbed. He was born in 1730 in Kirkbean, County of Kirkcudbright, Scotland, and died in Alexandria, Virginia, on February 6, 1814. He is buried in the graveyard behind the Old Presbyterian Meeting House (erected in 1775) at 321 South Fairfax Street, Alexandria, Virginia.

73. Edward Braddock was born in 1695 at Perthshire, Scotland, and died July 13, 1755, at Great Meadow, Pennsylvania. He was the son of Major General Edward Braddock. He joined the Coldstream Guards in 1710 and was appointed major general in 1754.

74. Fort Saint-Frédéric was at Crown Point, New York.

75. Robert C. Alberts, "STOBO, ROBERT," in *Dictionary of Canadian Biography*, vol. 3, 2015, http://www.biographi.ca/en/bio/stobo_robert_3E.html.

76. Lengel, *General George Washington*, 53–54.
77. Ibid., 54–56.
78. Thomas Gage was born in 1719 or 1720 and died on April 2, 1787. Born to an aristocratic family in England, he graduated from Westminster in 1736 and entered military service with the rank of ensign. Gage was promoted to captain in 1743, and saw action in the War of the Austrian Succession and in the Second Jacobite Uprising, which culminated in the 1746 Battle of Culloden. Gage was promoted to lieutenant colonel in March 1751.
79. Lengel, *General George Washington*, 57.
80. Dunbar's camp was at present-day State Route 2021 about three miles north of U.S. Route 40 at Jumonville, Pennsylvania.
81. Horace Walpole to Richard Bentley, September 30, 1755. *Correspondence of Horace Walpole with George Montagu, Vol. 1, 1735–1755* (London: Henry Coldburn, 1837), 299.
82. John A. Nagy, *Rebellion in the Ranks: Mutinies of the American Revolution* (Yardley, Pennsylvania: Westholme Publishing, 2007), 1.
83. John Forbes was born in Fifeshire, Scotland. He died on March 11, 1759, in Philadelphia. He is buried inside Christ the King Church in Philadelphia.
84. John Blair was born circa 1687–1689 in Scotland. He came to Williamsburg, Virginia, as a child and graduated from the College of William and Mary. He was on the Governor's Council (1745–1770), becoming its president in 1757. From the departure of Robert Dinwiddie on January 12, 1758, until the arrival of Francis Fauquier on June 5 that year, he was the acting governor of Virginia. He served as acting governor on four occasions. He died in 1771.
85. George Washington to John Forbes, April 23, 1758, Founders Online, National Archives, http://founders.archives.gov/documents/Washington/02-05-02-0102.
86. Lengel, *General George Washington*, 70–75.
87. Ibid., 75–77.
88. George Washington to Robert H. Morris, Governor of Pennsylvania, January 1, 1756, Series 2, Letterbook 3: 16–17.

2. Drinking, Flashing the Ladies, and Grave Robbing

1. The British had one soldier wounded at Lexington and three killed and eight or ten wounded at Concord. The other casualties occurred on the march back to Boston. Edward H. Peckham,

ed., *The Toll of Independence: Engagements and Battle Casualties of the American Revolution* (Chicago: University of Chicago Press, 1974), 3.

2. *Journals of the Continental Congress, 1774–1789* (Washington, DC: United States Government Printing Office, 1904–1937), 2:75–78, June 2, 1775.

3. The Pennsylvania State House, now known as Independence Hall, was completed without the tower in 1748. *JCC* 2:79–91, June 3–15, 1775.

4. *JCC* 2:91, June 15, 1775.

5. For the story of Thompson's Pennsylvania Riflemen's mutiny on September 10, 1775, see John A. Nagy, *Rebellion in the Ranks: Mutinies of the American Revolution* (Yardley, Pennsylvania: Westholme Publishing, 2007), 3–5.

6. George Washington at Cambridge, August 22, 1775, General Orders, GWP.

7. Varick Transcripts, Letterbook 1: 71–72, GWP.

8. George Washington at Cambridge, September 1, 1775, General Orders, GWP.

9. Ezekiel Price, *Diary of Ezekiel Price, 1775–1776*, in *Proceedings of the Massachusetts Historical Society 1863–1864* (Boston: Massachusetts Historical Society, 1864), 194.

10. A piece (five and one quarter inches long) of the elm tree under which George Washington took command of the American army on July 3, 1775, in Cambridge, Massachusetts, is in the McClung Museum of Natural History and Culture of the University of Tennessee at Knoxville. http://mcclungmuseum.utk .edu/elm-tree-specimen/accessed September 6, 2015.

11. John Leach was born in England and came to North America when he was twenty-seven. He ran a navigation school in Boston prior to the Revolution. His diary reports that Loring was recently made a sheriff. Therefore it was Joshua Loring Jr. who served as high sheriff in Suffolk County, Massachusetts, and was a deputy commissary of American prisoners of war in New York from 1777 until 1783. Joshua Loring Jr. was born in Hingham, Massachusetts, in December 1744 and died in Edgefield, England, in August 1789. He served as ensign (1761) and later lieutenant (1765) in the 15th Regiment of Foot. His wife, Elizabeth Lloyd (1744–1831), of Dorchester, Massachusetts, used her physical assets to advance her social position and her husband's military position. She became the mistress of General Howe, and her husband was then appointed to the very lucrative position of

commissary of prisoners. It was said she occasionally lost as much as 300 guineas in an evening of playing cards.

12. James Lovell was born in Boston on October 31, 1737, and died in Windham, Maine, July 14, 1814. He graduated from Harvard in 1756. He was held in the Boston jail until he was taken to Halifax, Nova Scotia. He was imprisoned there until he was exchanged.

13. "A Journal Kept by John Leach, During his Confinement by the British, in Boston Gaol, July 2 to July 17, 1775," *New England Historical and Genealogical Register* (1865), 19:256.

14. Ibid., 19:262.

15. Ibid., 19:256.

16. The record is written as Captain Symmes but there is no record of a Symmes having served during the Revolution. I found a Captain Richard Symes of the 52nd Regiment of Foot having served in 1775.

17. "A Journal Kept by John Leach, During his Confinement by the British, in Boston Gaol, August 13, 1775," *New England Historical and Genealogical Register* (1865), 19:259.

18. Ibid., 262.

19. Enoch Hopkins and his son were operating ferries in Boston in 1775. Enoch Hopkins married in 1746 and died in 1778. His was the busier of the ferries. Information provided by John L. Bell.

20. There are too many Goodwins in Charlestown to currently identify the owner. Information provided by John L. Bell.

21. Elizabeth Ellery Dana, *The British in Boston: The Diary of Lieutenant John Barke of the King's Own Regiment from November 15, 1774 to May 31, 1776* (Cambridge: Harvard University Press, 1924), 48–49.

22. George Washington to Continental Congress, July 20, 1775, Letterbook 7: 19, GWP.

23. On July 15, 1775, Washington paid someone $333.33. George Washington, July 1775, Revolutionary War Expense Account, Financial Papers, GWP.

24. Loammi Baldwin was born on January 10, 1744, in Woburn, Massachusetts. He was a pump maker and cabinetmaker. He also worked in the family stores. In 1771 he and his friend Benjamin Thompson, later Count Rumford, attended the lectures of Professor John Winthrop at Harvard College. Thompson was a British spy in 1775. Harvard awarded Baldwin an honorary Master of Arts degree in 1785. He died in Woburn on October 20, 1807.

25. It is believed that Dewksbury in Reed's letter is Andrew Tewksbury, who was one of a score of men who were paid £2 each for guarding Pullen Point from April 19 to May 16, 1775. Mellen Chamberlain, ed., *A Documentary History of Chelsea, Including the Boston Precincts of Winnisimmet, Rumsey Marsh, and Pullen Point, 1624–1824* (Boston: Massachusetts Historical Society, 1908), 2 vols.

26. John Carnes was born in Boston in 1723. He graduated from Harvard in 1742. He got his master's degree and became the minister at Stoneham in December 1746 and resigned in July 1757. In April 1759 he accepted the post of minister at First Church in Seekonk. Today that church is known as the Newman Congregational Church. In December 1764, at the Rev. John Carnes's request, the Seekonk congregation dismissed him from their pulpit.

27. A note indicates one of the enclosed letters was from Dr. Church. Joseph Reed to Laommi Baldwin, July 28, 1775, Series 2, Letterbook 7: 31, GWP.

28. Loammi Baldwin at Chelsea to George Washington, August 15, 1775, Boston Area Intelligence Report, General Correspondence, GWP.

29. Price, *Diary of Ezekiel Price, 1775–1776*, 204–5.

30. Carnes family tradition, if correct, said he was suspected by General Thomas Gage, had his house and papers searched, and was ordered to leave, which he did. Gage departed Boston on October 11, 1775. *American Ancestry: Embracing Lineages from the Whole of the United States, 1888–1898*, vol. 11 (Albany: Joel Munsell's Sons, 1898), 134.

31. Unknown at Boston to Unknown, August 14, 1775, General Correspondence, GWP. This letter is possibly from an attorney, as he indicates that he has taken a number of powers of attorney from people outside the city.

32. Entry on July 15, 1775, George Washington, July 1775, Revolutionary War Expense Account, Financial Papers, GWP.

33. Was the agent who went into Boston to set up the contact the woman who came from Boston on July 20 as reported by Ezekiel Price? Washington wrote in his entry "to enduce him." Washington might have written "him" in a generic sense. No proof has surfaced that can document who the agent was. Entry on July 15, 1775, George Washington, July 1775, Revolutionary War Expense Account, Financial Papers, GWP.

34. George Washington to New York Provincial Congress, August 8, 1775, Letterbook 9: 21–22, GWP.

35. Thomas Gage was born 1721 in Firle, Sussex, England, and died April 2, 1787, in England. He commanded all British forces in North America for more than ten years (1763–1774) and was military governor of Massachusetts (1774–1775).

36. Abraham Fuller was born in 1720. He was a teacher, a selectman from 1760 to 1767, and town clerk and treasurer from 1766 to 1792. He was a representative to the General Court for eighteen years, delegate to the Provincial Congress, senator, and judge. He died April 20, 1794, at seventy-five years of age. He is in plot 1113 of the Old East Parish Burying Ground, Newton, Middlesex County, Massachusetts. http://interment.net/data/us/ma /middlesex/oldeast/buryinglist.htm, accessed September 4, 2015. William Cowley's deposition, October 12, 1775, Papers of the Continental Congress, 1774–1789. Microfilm. National Archives and Records Service, General Services Administration, Washington, DC, 1971, reel 166, item 152, vol. 1, 237–39; reel 186, item 169, vol. 1, 98–100.

37. George Washington to Continental Congress, October 12, 1775, Attachment 5, Series 2, Letterbook 7:110–15, GWP; PCC.

38. Peter Force, *American archives: consisting of a collection of authentick records, state papers, debates, and letters and other notices of publick affairs, the whole forming a documentary history of the origin and progress of the North American colonies; of the causes and accomplishment of the American Revolution; and of the Constitution of government for the United States, to the final ratification thereof* (New York: Johnson Reprint Corp., 1972), 4th Series, vol. 2: 1003–4.

39. Samuel Graves was born April 17, 1713, and died March 8, 1787. He was the commander in chief, North American Station, from June 1774 to January 1776.

40. Governor's Island is now part of Logan International Airport and is buried in the area north of the south end of runway 14/32. It was owned by the Winthrop family from 1632 until 1808.

41. British Vice Admiral Samuel Graves to William Colfleet, Edmund Saunders, and Thomas Maples, September 15, 1775, Fishing Permit, General Correspondence, GWP. In Peter Force the story is correct but the number of fishermen on the permit is three, not four. Force, *American Archives*, 4th Series, vol. 2: 1003–4.

42. Boston population return, October 2, 1775, Thomas Gage Papers, American Series, William L. Clements Library, University of Michigan, Ann Arbor, vol. 136.

43. Letter from Boston, July 5, 1775, *A View of the Evidence Relative to the Conduct of the American War Under Sir William Howe, Lord*

Viscount Howe, and General Burgoyne; as Given Before a Committee of the House of Commons Last Session of the Parliament. To Which Is Added a Collection of the Celebrated Fugitive Pieces That Are Said to Have Given Rise to That Important Enquiry (London: Sold by Richardson & Urquhart, 1779), 73–74.

44. The report says the information came from Captain Dodge but the only Captain Dodge was Richard Dodge at Chelsea. Unknown Intelligence, August 1775, GPA, vol. 133.

45. General Gates to Council of Massachusetts, November 8, 1775, Force, *American Archives,* 4th Series, vol. 2: 1402.

46. Lemuel Cox was born in Boston, Massachusetts, in 1736, and died in Charlestown, Massachusetts, on February 18, 1806. In 1786 he built the first of several bridges.

47. Mrs. Cooke's deposition, September 1775, GPA, vol. 135.

48. HMS *Rose* was built in Hull, England, in 1757. The *Rose* was a sixth-rate ship, the smallest class of ship that would be commanded by someone holding the rank of captain.

49. John Adams at Philadelphia to Abigail Adams, June 20, 1775 (two letters), Adams Family Correspondence, Founding Families: Digital Editions of the Papers of the Winthrops and the Adamses, http://www.masshist.org/publications/apde2/ (Boston: Massachusetts Historical Society), 1:214–15, FF.

50. Continental Army War Council, August 3, 1775, Proceedings at Cambridge, Massachusetts, General Correspondence, GWP.

51. George Washington to Continental Congress, August 4, 1775, Letterbook 7:41–54, GWP.

52. William Wallace Atterbury, ed., *Elias Boudinot: Reminiscences of the American Revolution* (New York, 1894), 9.

53. Henry Knox was born July 25, 1750, in Boston, and died on October 25, 1806. He owned a bookstore in Boston. He was chief artillery officer of the Continental Army.

3. Desperate Times

1. Thomas Paine, *American Crisis II,* in *The American Crisis* (London: R. Carlile, 1819), 11.

2. Andrew Elliot was born November 1728 in Edinburgh, the son of Sir Gilbert Elliot, 2nd Baronet of Minto. He was a brother of Gilbert, John, and Jean Elliot. In 1763, he was appointed collector of the Port of New York and receiver general of New York. In 1764 he was appointed to the province of New York Executive Council. He died in 1797. Andrew Elliot at Perth Amboy, New

Jersey, to Sir Gilbert Elliot (his brother), March 25, 1776, Elliot Papers, New-York Historical Society, quoted from Catherine S. Crary, *The Price of Loyalty: Tory Writings from the Revolutionary Era* (New York: McGraw-Hill, 1973), 52–54.

3. William Livingston at Elizabeth Town to George Washington, August 21, 1776, Carl E. Prince, ed., *The Papers of William Livingston* (Trenton: New Jersey Historical Commission, 1979–1988), 1:120–21.

4. George Washington, July 2, 1776, General Orders, Varick Transcripts, Letterbook 1: 301–3, GWP.

5. William Livingston to Hugh Mercer, July 3, 1776, Prince, ed., *The Papers of William Livingston*, 1:62–63.

6. William Livingston to Hugh Mercer, July 3, 1776, ibid., 1:106–7.

7. Hugh Mercer to George Washington, July 14, 1776, General Correspondence, GWP.

8. Mercereau's name is also spelled Mersereau.

9. Hugh Mercer to George Washington, July 16, 1776, General Correspondence, GWP.

10. *JCC*, 5:653, August 14, 1776.

11. Benjamin Franklin to General Gates, August 28, 1776, in Peter Force, *American Archives*, 5th Series, vol. 1: 1193.

12. John Hancock to George Washington, August 16, 1776, Founders Online, National Archives, http://founders.archives.gov /documents/Washington/03-06-02-0033.

13. *JCC*, 5:654–55, August 14, 1776.

14. Lieutenant Colonel Harmon Zedwitz of the 1st New York Regiment was given the assignment of translating the resolve. Later he wrote to Royal Governor William Tryon of New York advising him of the resolutions and planned distribution. He also offered to be a spy for the British. For the story of Zedwitz's adventures and capture, see John A. Nagy, *Invisible Ink: Spycraft of the American Revolution* (Yardley, Pennsylvania: Westholme, 2010), 191–93, 339, footnote 15, 339n17; *JCC* 5:654–55, August 14, 1776.

15. Christopher Ludwick was born in Geissen, Germany, on October 17, 1720. He became a baker just like his father. He served in the military from 1737 to 1741. He became a sailor circa 1746 for seven years and then relocated to Philadelphia. In May 1777 he was appointed superintendent of bakers by Congress. He died on June 17, 1801, in Philadelphia. He is buried in St. Michael's Lutheran Churchyard, 6671 Germantown Avenue (Germantown Avenue and Phil Ellena Street), Germantown, Philadelphia.

16. Joseph Reed at New York to William Livingston, August 19, 1776, Prince, ed., *The Papers of William Livingston*, 1:119.

17. George Washington to John Hancock, August 26, 1776, Founders Online, National Archives, http://founders.archives.gov /documents/Washington/03-06-02-0116.

18. There appear to be at least four Abraham Egberts who could have been the spy. Egbert was a popular name on Staten Island and there is even an area called Egbertville. Abraham Egbert of Staten Island had been examined by Colonel Jacob Ford Jr. and the report was sent by William Livingston to Joseph Reed. Livingston suspected that Egbert had been turned and was now spying for the British. William Livingston to Joseph Reed, August 24, 1776, Prince, ed., *The Papers of William Livingston*, 1:125; Joshua Mersereau to William Livingston, February 20, 1777, ibid., 1:125, footnote 4.

19. A Lawrence Mascoll was paid on August 23. Warrant Book, August 23, 1776, Financial Papers, GWP.

20. William Livingston to Hugh Mercer, August 23, 1776, Prince, ed., *Papers of William Livingston*, 1:124.

21. George Washington to John Hancock, August 29, 1776, Founders Online, National Archives, http://founders.archives.gov /documents/Washington/03-06-02-0133.

22. The original journal is part of the Jungkenn Papers in the William L. Clements Library, Ann Arbor, Michigan. Bernhard A. Uhlendorf, trans. and annotator, *Revolution in America: Confidential Letters and Journals 1776–1784 of the Adjutant General Major Baurmeister of the Hessian Forces* (New Brunswick: Rutgers University Press, 1957), 41.

23. Mark Anthony Morgan at Staten Island to Morton Pitt, August 4, 1776; Lady Georgiana Chatterton, *Memorials, Personal and Historical of Admiral Lord Gambier, G.C.B.* (London: Hurst & Blackett, 1861), 1:10–101.

24. George Washington at New York to William Heath, August 23, 1776, Letterbook 10: 30–31, GWP.

25. George Washington to Major General William Heath, September 5, 1776, Founders Online, National Archives, http://founders .archives.gov/documents/Washington/03-06-02-0181.

26. Ibid.

27. Peckham, *Toll of Independence*, 26.

28. Uhlendorf, *Revolution in America*, 50.

29. Ibid., 51.

30. Ibid.

31. Washington confirmed Abraham Patten's service as a spy to Congress: "His family well deserves the generous notice of Congress. He conducted himself with great fidelity to our cause rendering services and has fallen a sacrifice in promoting her Interest. Perhaps a public act of generosity, considering the character he was in [spy], might not be so eligible as a private donation." George Washington to Continental Congress, June 13, 1777, two the same date, Varick Transcripts, Letterbook 2: 302–8, GWP.

32. D. T. Valentine, *Manual of the Common Council of the City of New York* (New York: Common Council, 1863), 635–36.

33. Washington used an interesting choice of words in his letter to Congress. He says that he was not informed how it happened but does not say that he does not know how it happened. George Washington to John Hancock, September 22, 1776, Varick Transcripts, Letterbook 1: 428, GWP.

34. George Washington to Jonathan Trumbull, September 23, 1776, Varick Transcripts, Letterbook 1: 306–9, GWP.

35. Colonel George Brewerton served in DeLancey's Brigade, a Loyalist unit established in September 1776.

36. Colonel Elias Boudinot in New York City, February 1778, in *Pennsylvania Magazine of History and Biography,* vol. 24 (Philadelphia: Historical Society of Pennsylvania, 1900), 453, 456, 461.

37. Alexander Flick incorrectly led some to believe that Nathan Hale, who is the spy referenced, had anything to do with the fire. There is no proof of his involvement. A person (Nathan Hale), who was arrested on the evening of the September 21 during interrogation, admitted to being a rebel spy, was executed on the 22nd at 11 a.m. in front of the artillery park. Today it would be at 66th Street and Third Avenue in Manhattan. Alexander C. Flick, *America Revolution in New York; Its Political, Social and Economic Significance* (Albany: State University of New York Press, 1926), 172.

38. James Hutson, *Nathan Hale Revisited: A Tory's Account of the Arrest of the First American Spy,* Library of Congress Information Bulletin, July/August, 2003.

39. Society of Gentlemen, *A new and complete dictionary of arts and sciences; comprehending all the branches of useful knowledge, with Accurate Descriptions as well of the various Machines, Instruments, Tools, Figures, and Schemes necessary for illustrating them, as of The Classes, Kinds, Preparations, and Uses of Natural Productions, whether Animals, Vegetables, Minerals, Fossils, or Fluids; Together with The Kingdoms, Provinces, Cities, Towns, and other remarkable Places throughout*

the World. Illustrated with above three hundred copper-plates, engraved by Mr. Jefferys, Geographer to His Majesty. The whole extracted from the best authors in all languages. By a society of gentlemen (London: W. Owen, 1763), second edition, vol. 2 of 4: 1780–1781.

40. George Washington to William Alexander, Lord Stirling, December 14, 1776, Varick Transcripts, Letterbook 2: 153–55, GWP.

41. William Gordon, *The History of the Rise, Progress, and Establishment, of the Independence of the United States of America: Including an Account of the Late War; and of the Thirteen Colonies, from Their Origin to That Period*, vol. 2 (London: Gordon, 1788), 391.

42. George Washington to John A. Washington, December 18, 1776, General Correspondence, GWP.

43. Ibid.

44. Mount Holly, New Jersey, was an early industrial town with a millrace, which was built in 1723. It had a two-bladed sawmill, fulling mill, gristmill, and an ironworks, which were all in operation by 1730. These were still in operation at the time of the Revolution and were producing much needed supplies for the Continental Army.

45. William S. Stryker, *The Battles of Trenton and Princeton* (Boston: Houghton Mifflin, 1898), 347.

46. Pennsylvania Supreme Executive Council, *Minutes of the Supreme Executive Council of Pennsylvania, from Its Organization to the Termination of the Revolution* (Harrisburg: T. Fenn, 1853), vol. 11, December 22, 1776.

47. William A. Slaughter, "Battle of Iron Works Hill at Mount Holly, New Jersey December 1776," in *Proceedings of the New Jersey Historical Society* (Newark: New Jersey Historical Society, 1919), New Series 1919, vol. 4, nos. 1–4, 25–26.

4. Pools of Blood

1. John Cadwalader was the son of Thomas Cadwalader and Hannah Lambert. He was born on January 10, 1742, in Trenton, New Jersey. The family moved to Philadelphia in 1750. He attended the Academy and College of Philadelphia from 1751 to 1758. He did not graduate from the college. He left to organize a successful mercantile business with his brother Lambert Cadwalader. He died in Kent County, Maryland, on February 10, 1786.

2. George Washington to John Cadwalader, December 12, 1776, Varick Transcripts, Letterbook 2: 145–46, GWP.

3. George Washington to James Ewing, December 12, 1776, Orders, General Correspondence, GWP.

4. George Washington to Philemon Dickinson, December 12, 1776, Orders, General Correspondence, GWP.

5. George Washington to John Cadwalader at Bristol, Pennsylvania, December 15, 1776, Varick Transcripts, Letterbook 2: 156–57, GWP.

6. Lewis's Mill was located on Black's Creek a short distance southeast of Bordentown. The mill was owned by Lieutenant Colonel William Lewis of the 1st Regiment of Burlington County militia.

7. Philemon Dickinson to George Washington, December 21, 1776, General Correspondence, GWP.

8. Philemon Dickinson to George Washington, December 24, 1776, General Correspondence, GWP.

9. John Cadwalader to George Washington, December 31, 1776, General Correspondence, GWP.

10. Richard Ketchum, *The Winter Soldiers: The Battles for Trenton and Princeton* (New York: Macmillan, 1999), 290.

11. Captain W. H. Wilkin, *Some British Soldiers in America* (London: Hugh Rees, Ltd., 1914), 223.

12. William Hooper was born on June 28, 1742, in Boston, Massachusetts. He graduated from Harvard in 1760. He moved to North Carolina in 1760 and in 1764 married Anne Clark. He was a lawyer, physician, politician, and member of the Continental Congress representing North Carolina from 1774 through 1777. Hooper was also a signer of the Declaration of Independence. He died on October 14, 1790.

13. William Hooper at Baltimore to Robert Morris, February 1, 1777, *Letters to Robert Morris, Collections of the New-York Historical Society for the Year 1878* (New York: New-York Historical Society, 1879), 415–19.

14. Referring to New Jersey as the Jerseys dates back to before 1702 when it was two colonies, East Jersey with its capital in Perth Amboy, and West Jersey with its capital at Burlington. The two colonies were united in 1702 as New Jersey with two capital cities. George Washington to William Heath, January 5, 1777, Varick Transcripts, Letterbook 2, 198–99, GWP.

15. Archibald Kennedy was a captain in the British navy in 1765. He owned a plantation called Horsimus at Pavonia adjacent to the fort at Paulus Hook, New Jersey. He also owned the house at One Broadway in New York City in 1776, which was used by American General Putnam as his headquarters.

16. Elias Boudinot with Frederick Bourquinn, ed., *Journal of Events in the Revolution* (Philadelphia: H. J. Bicking, 1894), 54–55, 199.
17. Ibid.
18. Alexander Graydon and John S. Littell, *Memoirs of His Own Time: With Reminiscences of the Men and Events of the Revolution* (Philadelphia: Lindsay & Blakiston, 1846), 212.
19. Harry M. Ward, *Major General Adam Stephen and the Cause of American Liberty* (Charlottesville: University of Virginia Press, 1989), 165.
20. Ibid., 165–66.
21. Major General Adam Stephen at Chatham, New Jersey, to George Washington, April 23, 1777, The Papers of George Washington Digital Edition, Revolutionary War Series, 9:254–55.
22. William Maxwell to Adam Stephen, April 10, 1777, Harry M. Ward, *General William Maxwell and the New Jersey Continentals* (Westport: Greenwood, 1997), 59, 197.
23. Alexander Hamilton at Middle Brook, New Jersey, to Nathanael Greene, April 1, 1779, Nathanael Greene, Papers of General Nathanael Greene (Chapel Hill: Published for the Rhode Island Historical Society by the University of North Carolina Press, 1976–2005), 3:376.
24. George Washington to William Alexander, Lord Stirling, February 4, 1777, Varick Transcripts, Letterbook 2: 265, GWP.
25. Nathaniel Sackett was born in Orange County, New York, on April 10, 1737, to Rev. Samuel Sackett and Hannah Hazard. He died in Sullivan County, New York, on July 28, 1805. William Duer was born in Devonshire, England, March 18, 1747; attended Eton College in England; in 1765 became aide-de-camp to Lord Clive, Governor General of India; immigrated to America in 1768 and settled in Fort Miller, New York; member of the New York Provincial Congress in 1776 and 1777; served in the State Senate in 1777; member of the Continental Congress in 1777 and 1778; assistant secretary of the treasury in 1789–1790; and died in New York City on April 18, 1799.
26. William Duer to George Washington, January 28, 1777, Founders Online, National Archives, http://founders.archives.gov/documents/Washington/03-08-02-0179.
27. George Washington to William Duer, February 3, 1777, Varick Transcripts, Letterbook 1: 409–11, GWP.
28. Ibid.
29. Some authors refer to Nathaniel Sackett as Washington's spymaster but that is incorrect, as Washington had other intelligence

assets working at the same time that Sackett would not have known about or been involved with. Sackett was a case officer controlling his group of spies. Other officers operated their spies independently of Sackett. George Washington at Morristown to Nathaniel Sackett, February 4, 1777, Varick Transcripts, Letterbook 2: 266, GWP; General Correspondence, GWP.

30. Nathanael Greene to George Washington, February 20, 1777, General Correspondence, GWP.

31. William Duer to George Washington, March 2, 1777, Founders Online, National Archives, http://founders.archives.gov /documents/Washington/03-08-02-0509.

32. George Washington, May–August 1777, Revolutionary War Expense Account, Financial Papers, 12, GWP.

33. George Washington to William Duer, March 6, 1777, Founders Online, National Archives, http://founders.archives.gov/documents /Washington/03-08-02-0546.

34. Nathaniel Sackett to George Washington, April 7, 1777, Founders Online, National Archives, http://founders.archives.gov /documents/Washington/03-09-02-0081.

35. George Washington at Morristown to Nathaniel Sackett at John Suffern's tavern at Suffern, April 8, 1777, Founders Online, National Archives, http://founders.archives.gov/documents /Washington/03-09-02-0096.

36. Washington's first-term inauguration took place on April 30, 1789.

37. Nathaniel Sackett to George Washington, April 7, 1777, Founders Online, National Archives, http://founders.archives.gov /documents/Washington/03-09-02-0081.

38. Ward, *Major General Adam Stephen and the Cause of American Liberty*, 167.

39. National Archives, Revolutionary War Pension and Bounty Land Warrant Application Files, microfilm, no. 1151, William Hadar's pension claim deposition, October 23, 1832. Hadar was born on September 1, 1762, in Hunterdon County, New Jersey.

40. Ibid.

41. *New Jersey Archives Series*, 1880–1950 (Trenton: New Jersey Bureau of Archives and History), 2nd series, vol. 4, newspaper extract, November 9, 1779, 54.

42. *Proceedings of the New Jersey Historical Society*, vol. 7, nos. 1 and 2 (Newark: New Jersey Historical Society, 1922), vol. 7, no. 2, 168, citing John Smith Hatfield at Public Record Office, Foreign Office 4/1.

43. *Proceedings of the New Jersey Historical Society*, vol. 7, no. 1, 26.

44. Lieutenant Colonel George Johnston to Adam Stephen, April 19, 1777, Varick Transcripts, Letterbook 3: 62, GWP.

45. Nathanael Greene to Catherine Greene, April 27, 1777, Greene, *Papers of General Nathanael Greene*, 2:60.

46. Nathanael Greene to General Benjamin Lincoln, April 27, 1777, Greene, *Papers of General Nathanael Greene*, 2:61.

47. The letter does not indicate which Colonel Spencer but the only Colonel Spencer at the time was Oliver. Adam Stephen at Chatham to George Washington, May 24, 1777, General Correspondence, GWP.

48. Bruce Burgoyne, compiler and editor, *Enemy Views: The American Revolutionary War as Recorded by the Hessian Participants* (Bowie, Maryland: Heritage Books, 1996), 141.

49. Alexander Graydon, *Memoirs of a Life, Chiefly Passed in Pennsylvania: Within the Last Sixty Years with Occassional Remarks upon the General Occurrences, Character and Spirit of That Eventful Period* (Harrisburg: John Wyeth, 1811), 257.

50. Frank Moore, *The Diary of the Revolution: A Centennial Volume Embracing the Current Events in Our Country's, History from 1775 to 1781 as Described by American, British, and Tory Contemporaries; Compiled from the Journals, Documents, Private Records, Correspondence, etc., of That Period, Forming an Interesting, Impartial, and Valuable Collection of Revolutionary Literature. Illustrated with Steel Engravings* (Hartford: J. B. Burr Publishing Company, 1876), 446.

51. Burgoyne, *Enemy Views*, 141.

52. Ibid., 141–42.

53. Ira D. Gruber, ed., *John Peebles' American War: The Diary of a Scottish Grenadier, 1776–1782* (Mechanicsburg, Pennsylvania: Stackpole, 1998), 53.

54. Washington sent a copy of the New York paper that mentioned Abraham Patten's execution. George Washington at Middle Brook to Continental Congress, June 13, 1777, Varick Transcripts, Letterbook 2: 307, GWP.

55. Ibid.

56. Major General Israel Putnam to George Washington, February 18, 1777, Founders Online, National Archives, http://founders.archives.gov/documents/Washington/03-08-02-03929.

57. I have been unable to locate a report of the court of inquiry. Putnam may not have held it prior to April 23, 1777, when the Woodwards and several others were accused by Thomas Forman, a justice of the peace in Upper Freehold, of conspiring to

"procure aid & assistance from the British Army, for the purpose of going to Freehold, and attacking the Militia, who were
embodied at that place." Deposition of Thomas Forman, Prince,
ed., *The Papers of William Livingston*, 1:310–11. See also Council
of Safety of New Jersey, *Minutes of the Council of Safety of the State
of New Jersey* (Jersey City: Printed by J. H. Lyon, 1872), 1:32.
Woodward Jr. denied the charges against him during an interrogation by the New Jersey Council of Safety on May 21, 1777.
On June 6, 1777, the council ordered the sheriff of Gloucester
County to arrest Woodward on charges of "maliciously & advis-
edly spreading such false rumours concerning the American
Forces, and the forces of the enemy as tend to alienate the affec-
tions of the people from the government." Ibid.; Prince, ed, *The
Papers of William Livingston*; and Council of Safety of New Jersey,
Minutes of the Council of Safety of the State of New Jersey, 1:50–51, 60;
George Washington at Morristown to Israel Putnam, February
20, 1777, Varick Transcripts, Letterbook 2: 307–9, GWP.

58. May 1777, George Washington, January–May 1777, Revolutionary
War Expense Account, Financial Papers, GWP.

59. James Bisset, April 16, 1777, Answers to Questions on British
Intelligence; Joseph Driver, April 16, 1777, Answers to Questions
on British Intelligence, General Correspondence, GWP.

5. Quaker Chicanery

1. George Washington to Israel Putnam, January 5, 1777, Varick
Transcripts, Letterbook 2: 197–98, GWP.

2. George Washington to Israel Putnam, February 22, 1777, two
same date, Varick Transcripts, Letterbook 2: 318–20, GWP.

3. George Washington to Thomas Mifflin, April 10, 1777, General
Correspondence, GWP.

4. Ibid.

5. George Washington, May–August 1777, Revolutionary War Expense Account, Financial Papers, Annotation June 1, 1777, GWP.

6. John Clark Jr. was born in Lancaster, Pennsylvania, in 1751. He
was appointed an aide to Major General Nathanael Greene on
January 14, 1777.

7. Major John Clark Jr. at York, Pennsylvania, to Nathanael Greene,
January 10, 177[7], Nathanael Greene, *Papers of General Nathanael
Greene* (Chapel Hill: Published for the Rhode Island Historical
Society by the University of North Carolina Press, 1976–2005),
2:249–51.

8. Robert F. Oaks, "Philadelphians in Exile: The Problem of Loyalty During the American Revolution," *Pennsylvania Magazine of History and Biography,* 96, no. 3 (July 1972): 302–3; John Sullivan to John Hancock, August 25, 1777, *JCC* 8:688–89. Congress received Sullivan's letter on August 28, and sent it to a committee. Sullivan led the American retreat from Canada in 1776. He was captured by the British at the Battle of Long Island and later exchanged.

9. Washington wrote, "I rec[eive]d yours of the 25th from Elizabeth Town by John Meeker." Abraham Clark wrote to William Livingston on November 13, 1777, that John Meeker was one of four people employed by Washington as spies working out of Elizabeth Town. From George Washington to Major John Clark Jr., September 29, 1777, Founders Online, National Archives, http://founders.archives.gov/documents/Washington/03-11-02 -0370.

10. *Pennsylvania Packet or General Advertiser* (Philadelphia, 1776–1781), September 10, 1776.

11. Tench Tilghman to Robert Morris, November 29, 1777, *Letters to Robert Morris, Collections of the New-York Historical Society for the Year 1878* (New York: New-York Historical Society, 1879), 432.

12. John Clark Jr. to George Washington, October 6, 1777, two same date, General Correspondence, GWP.

13. George Washington to John Armstrong, October 8, 1777, Varick Transcripts, Letterbook 4: 175–77, GWP.

14. Robert H. Harrison to John Clark Jr., October 23, 1777, Varick Transcripts, Letterbook 4: 222, GWP.

15. Major John Clark to George Washington, October 22, 1777, General Correspondence, GWP; *Minutes of the Supreme Executive Council of Pennsylvania,* 11:481–85.

16. Major John Clark Jr. at Whiteland, Pennsylvania, to George Washington, November 3, 1777, Founders Online, National Archives, http://founders.archives.gov/documents/Washington /03-12-02-0089.

17. The lower ferry is probably Gray's Ferry. Fort Island is the location of Fort Mifflin. Major John Clark Jr. to George Washington, November 3, 1777, Founders Online, National Archives, http:// founders.archives.gov/documents/Washington/03-12-02-0089.

18. George Washington to John Clark Jr., November 4, 1777, Varick Transcripts, Letterbook 4: 277–78 and footnote 11, GWP.

19. Philemon Dickinson to George Washington, November 1, 1777, General Correspondence, GWP.

20. The regiments aboard the ships were the 52nd, 36th, 7th, and the Light Dragoons. Philemon Dickinson to George Washington, November 2, 1777, General Correspondence, GWP.

21. George Washington to Philemon Dickinson, November 4, 1777, General Correspondence, GWP.

22. Ibid.

23. There would be a skirmish between Colonel Samuel Webb's regiment on November 27, 1777, with British troops near New Rochelle, New York. Edward H. Peckham, *The Toll of Independence: Engagements and Battle Casualties of the American Revolution* (Chicago: University of Chicago Press, 1974), 45.

24. George Washington to John Clark Jr., November 4, 1777, Varick Transcripts, Letterbook 4: 277–78, GWP.

25. Colonel Isaac Warner was from Lower Merion Township, Pennsylvania.

26. John Clark Jr. to George Washington, December 18, 1777, General Correspondence, GWP.

27. Ibid.

28. For the story of the Darraghs, see John A. Nagy, *Spies in the Continental Capital: Espionage Across Pennsylvania During the American Revolution* (Yardley, Pennsylvania: Westholme Publishing, 2011), x, xii, 48, 50–52, 191–92, 194n6, 209n7–9.

29. George Washington, December 18, 1777, General Orders, Varick Transcripts, Letterbook 2: 323–25, GWP.

30. George Washington to James Potter, December 21, 1777, Varick Transcripts, Letterbook 4: 352–53, GWP.

31. John Clark Jr. from General Potter's quarters to George Washington, December 22, 1777, two same date, General Correspondence, GWP.

32. James Varnum to George Washington, December 22, 1777, General Correspondence, GWP.

33. John Clark Jr. to George Washington, December 28, 1777, General Correspondence, GWP.

34. "Questions for Captain Allen McLane, 29 October 1777," Founders Online, National Archives, http://founders.archives.gov/documents/Washington/03-12-02-0043.

35. Unsigned, November 7, 1777, Allen McLane Papers on microfilm, New-York Historical Society, item 12.

36. Timothy Pickering to Allen McLane, November 15, 1777, Allen McLane Papers on microfilm, New-York Historical Society, item 13.

37. Receipt from Allen McLane, November 16, 1777, Allen McLane Papers on microfilm, New-York Historical Society, item 14.

38. Allen McLane to George Washington, November 20, 1777, General Correspondence, GWP.

39. Tench Francis Jr. (1730–1800) was an uncle of Lieutenant Colonel Tench Tilghman, who was aide-de-camp to George Washington. He was a lawyer and a merchant and lived in a two-story, five-bay brick house with green shutters and a curving driveway surrounded by trees on the north side of Girard Avenue between 29th and 30th Streets in Philadelphia.

40. Nathanael Greene to George Washington, November 28, 1777, Founders Online, National Archives, http://founders.archives .gov/documents/Washington/03-12-02-0424. *The Papers of George Washington*, Revolutionary War Series, vol. 12: 436–37, GWP.

41. Captain Charles Craig was the control agent for Lydia and William Darragh, American spies in Philadelphia. For more on the Darraghs, see Nagy, *Spies in the Continental Capital.* Captain Charles Craig to George Washington, November 28, 1777, Founders Online, National Archives, http://founders.archives.gov/documents /Washington/03-12-02-0420. *The Papers of George Washington*, Revolutionary War Series: 12: 433, GWP.

42. The Rising Sun Tavern was located at the north corner of Germantown Road and Old York Road (at one time called 12th Street). For a picture of the tavern, see Nagy, *Spies in the Continental Capital*, 49.

43. Allen McLane to George Washington, November 28, 1777, General Correspondence, GWP.

44. Harry Miller Lydenberg, ed., *Archibald Robertson, Lieutenant-General Royal Engineers: His Diaries and Sketches in America, 1762–1780* (New York: New York Public Library, 1930), 158.

45. Richard Kidder Meade to Allen McLane, December 4, 1777, Allen McLane Papers on microfilm, New York-Historical Society, item 24.

46. Gouverneur Morris to John Jay, February 1, 1778, Papers of John Jay, Columbia University, New York, columbia.jay.06961.

6. We Danced the Minuet

1. George Washington to Elias Dayton, July 26, 1777, Varick Transcripts, Letterbook 3: 406–8, GWP.

2. General Henry Clinton was born April 16, 1730, in Newfoundland, Canada, and died on December 23, 1795, in London, England. He was the son of Admiral George Clinton (c. 1685–1761) and grandson of Sir Francis Fiennes Clinton, 6th Earl of Lincoln. His father was governor general of Newfoundland, 1732–1741, and of New York, 1741–1751. By the 1770s he had reached the rank of colonel of the 12th Foot and served as a member of Parliament. In 1775 he accepted the post of third in command of the British forces in North America.

3. Dickinson's letter does not identify if the information came from Perth Amboy or South Amboy. It most likely came from Perth Amboy, as two American cannons and soldiers were stationed at St. Peter's Church to observe the British and Hessians on Staten Island. Philemon Dickinson to George Washington, May 27, 1778, General Correspondence, GWP.

4. George Washington to Philemon Dickinson, May 28, 1778, General Correspondence, GWP.

5. John Laurens was born on October 28, 1754, in Charleston, South Carolina, and died on August 27, 1782 (aged twenty-seven), at Combahee River, South Carolina. He is buried at Laurens Family Cemetery, Mepkin Abbey, Moncks Corner, South Carolina. He joined the Continental Army following the Battle of Brandywine in 1777. John Laurens, aide-de-camp to George Washington, to Allen McLane, May 27, 1778, from Historical Society of Pennsylvania, reproduced in Thomas Welch and Michael Lloyd, eds., *Allen McLane: Patriot, Soldier, Spy Port Collector* (Dover: Delaware Heritage Press, 2014), 104.

6. James McHenry to Allen McLane, May 31, 1778, General Correspondence, GWP.

7. Allen McLane to James McHenry, June 4, 1778, General Correspondence, GWP.

8. Allen McLane to James McHenry, June 6, 1778, General Correspondence, GWP.

9. George Washington to William Smallwood, June 1, 1778, General Correspondence, GWP.

10. Edward H. Peckham, *The Toll of Independence: Engagements and Battle Casualties of the American Revolution* (Chicago: University of Chicago Press, 1974), 51, June 3 and 6, 1778.

11. Ibid., 52, June 18, 1778.

12. George Washington to Continental Congress, June 18, 1778, three same date, Varick Transcripts, Letterbook 3: 347–48, GWP.

13. Gloucester Point, New Jersey, is south of the present-day Walt Whitman Bridge.

14. Philemon Dickinson was the brother of John Dickinson. He was born near Trappe, Talbot County, Maryland, on April 5, 1739. He graduated from the University of Pennsylvania at Philadelphia in 1759. He moved to Trenton in 1767 and was a delegate to the New Jersey Provincial Congress in 1776. He was commissioned brigadier general in 1776 and in 1777 major general commanding the New Jersey Militia, serving in the latter capacity throughout the Revolution. He was a member of the Continental Congress from Delaware (1782–1783). He died at his home, "The Hermitage," near Trenton, on February 4, 1809. He was buried in the Friends Meeting House Burying Ground, Trenton, New Jersey.

15. George Washington to Benedict Arnold, June 19, 1778, Varick Transcripts, Letterbook 5: 409–10, GWP; Continental Army, War Council, June 24, 1778, Varick Transcripts, Letterbook 2: 53–55, GWP.

16. Friedrich Wilhelm August Heinrich Ferdinand von Steuben was born on September 17, 1730, in Magdeburg, Duchy of Magdeburg. He joined the Continental Army on February 23, 1778, at Valley Forge. He died on November 28, 1794, in Utica, New York.

17. The Battle of Princeton was an American victory but the Americans had the larger force on the field of battle.

18. Elias Dayton was born on May 1, 1737, in Elizabeth, New Jersey, and died on October 22, 1807. He served in the New Jersey Militia during the French and Indian War. During the Revolution he commanded the 3rd New Jersey Regiment. Beginning in 1777 he was a case agent operating spies on Staten Island. He was promoted to brigadier general on January 8, 1783, and stayed in service until November 3, 1783. After the war he became the mayor of Elizabeth. He is buried in the First Presbyterian Churchyard in Elizabeth.

19. Asher Fitz Randolph was born in 1755 in Woodbridge, New Jersey, and died April 16, 1817, in Blazing Star (now Carteret), New Jersey. He was an ensign and a lieutenant in Captain Freeman's company, state troops. He was promoted to captain in Major Hayes's battalion. William S. Stryker, *Official Register of the Officers and Men of New Jersey in the Revolutionary War* (Trenton: William T. Nicholson, 1870), 406.

20. In 1750 Jane Emott married Thomas Bradbury Chandler (1726–1790), a prominent Loyalist Anglican clergyman. She died in 1801

in Elizabeth. He had been ordained in London, England, in 1751. He was granted D.D.'s from Oxford in 1766 and Columbia in 1767. Nelson R. Burr, *The Anglican Church in New Jersey* (Philadelphia: Church Historical Society, 1954), 595.

21. Jerry Kail, *Who Was Who During the American Revolution* (Indianapolis: Bobbs-Merrill, 1976), 196.

22. Cortlandt Skinner was born on December 16, 1727, in Perth Amboy, New Jersey, and died on March 15, 1799, in Bristol, England. He is buried in St. Augustine's Churchyard, Bristol. He was the last royal attorney general of New Jersey (1754–1776) and a brigadier general in the Loyalist forces during the American War of Independence.

23. William Skinner had been the clergyman at St. Peter's Church, Perth Amboy, from November of 1722 to his death in 1758.

24. Elizabeth Derbage was the wife of George Derbage, king's deputy surveyor for North America.

25. Hugh Edward Egerton, *The Royal Commission on the Losses and Services of American Loyalists, 1783 to 1785* (New York: Arno, 1969), li, 4–5, 33–34, 113, 156, memorial of George Derbage, November 18, 1783; William A. Whitehead, *Contributions to the Early History of Perth Amboy and Adjoining Country: With Sketches of Men and Events in New Jersey During the Provincial Era* (New York: D. Appleton & Company, 1856), 103–6.

26. William Livingston at Trenton to Mary Martin, February 16, 1778, Carl H. Prince, ed., *The Papers of William Livingston* (Trenton: New Jersey Historical Commission, 1979–1988), 2:212.

27. Squan in New Jersey can refer to Manasquan or Point Pleasant, New Jersey.

28. Abiah Parke to Christopher Sower, November 24, 1779, CP 77:7.

29. Christopher Sower, 1779, CP 82:54.

30. Coxestown most likely refers to Coxes Corner in Upper Freehold Township in Monmouth County. Named for Brigadier General James Cox (1753–1810), who had lived here at the family home of "Box Grove," it is at the juncture of County Routes 43 and 524. Patrick Garvey to Major John André, November 8, 1779, CP 74:17.

31. George Washington to Elias Boudinot, May 3, 1779, Varick Transcripts, Letterbook 1: 268–69, GWP.

32. Sir Hugh Plat, *The Jewel House of Art and Nature* (London: Elizabeth Alsop, 1653), 11–12, #8.

33. Ibid.

34. J. F. [John Falconer], *Rules for Explaining and Deciphering All*

Manner of Secret Writing, Plain and Demonstrative (London: Printed for Dan. Brown and Sam. Manship, 1692), 98–101.

35. John A. Nagy, *Invisible Ink: Spycraft of the American Revolution* (Yardley, Pennsylvania: Westholme Publishing, 2010), 30, 299, fn. 19; Lodewyk Bendikson, "The Restoration of Obliterated Passages and of Secret Writing in Diplomatic Missives," in *Franco-American Review* (New Haven: Friends of the Franco-American Review), vol. 1, no. 3 (December 1936), 253–355.

36. For detailed information on invisible ink used during the American Revolution, see Nagy, *Invisible Ink*, 27–41, and footnotes for chemical tests. George Washington to Benjamin Tallmadge, July 25, 1779, Varick Transcripts, Letterbook 9: 247–49, GWP.

37. For a description of the Pig Pen Cipher and others, see Nagy, *Invisible Ink*, 55–56.

38. George Washington to Benjamin Tallmadge, September 11, 1783, General Correspondence and Varick Transcripts, Letterbook 3: 184–86, GWP.

39. Morton Pennypacker, *General Washington's Spies on Long Island and in New York* (Garden City: Long Island Historical Society by Country Life Press, 1939), 35.

40. Lewis J. Costigan to George Washington, December 7, 1778, Intelligence Report; Signed "L" (actually "Z"), General Correspondence, GWP.

41. Richard Howell resigned on April 7, 1779. He was born in Newark, Delaware, on October 25, 1754, and died on April 22, 1802, in Trenton. He was buried in the Trenton Friends Burying Ground. He was the third governor of New Jersey (June 3, 1793–October 31, 1801). He had a twin, Lewis Howell. Lewis was a physician for the 2nd New Jersey Regiment and died during the Revolutionary War.

42. George Washington to Nathanael Greene, August 21, 1778, Varick Transcripts, Letterbook 1: 139–40, GWP.

43. George Washington to William Alexander, Lord Stirling, October 21, 1778, Varick Transcripts, Letterbook 6: 358–59, GWP.

44. Major Howell had sent an unnamed spy into New York for determining the destination of the ships. William Alexander, Lord Stirling at Perth Amboy and Elizabeth Town to George Washington, October 19, 1778, Intelligence from Richard Howell, General Correspondence, GWP; Richard Howell to William Alexander, Lord Stirling, November 3, 1778, General Correspondence, GWP.

45. George Washington at Morristown to General Samuel H. Parsons, December 13, 1779, General Correspondence; Varick Transcripts, Letterbook 10: 365, GWP.

46. Samuel Culper Jr. to John Bolton, December 27, 1779, General Correspondence, GWP.

47. Based upon the intelligence he received from Dayton, Washington would determine if Lord Stirling would attack. He notified Stirling the same day and the decision for the attack was his. General John Sullivan led an unsuccessful attack on Staten Island on August 22. George Washington to William Alexander, Lord Stirling, July 26, 1777, Varick Transcripts, Letterbook 3: 405–6, GWP.

48. George Washington to Elias Dayton, July 26, 1777, Varick Transcripts, Letterbook 3: 406–8, GWP.

49. George Washington to Elias Dayton, August 14, 1777, Varick Transcripts, Letterbook 4: 33–34, GWP.

50. Baker Hendricks was from Elizabeth Town. He had been arrested for counterfeiting and trading with the enemy. He died by 1798 and had at least three sons: Job, John, and Luther. Baker Hendricks Jr., deceased, had an inventory done on February 19, 1789, amounting to £162.30. Elmer T. Hutchinson, *Documents Relating to the Colonial History of the State of New Jersey, Calendar of New Jersey Wills, Volume IX, 1796–1800* (Trenton: MacCrellish & Quigley, 1944, rpt., Westminster, Maryland: Heritage Books, 2008), 171.

    Rev. James Caldwell wrote that Hendricks had been released from jail and completed an espionage mission. Reverend James Caldwell to William Livingston, July 7, 1777, Carl E. Prince, ed. (Trenton: New Jersey Historical Commission, 1979–1988), *The Papers of William Livingston*: vol. 2, 25. Baker Hendricks was held in the Newark jail. Council of Safety of New Jersey, *Minutes of the Council of Safety of the State of New Jersey* (Jersey City, New Jersey: J. H. Lyon, 1872), 74 and 264.

51. Council of Safety of New Jersey, ibid., 168.

52. Colonel Elias Dayton to George Washington, January 13, 1778, Founders Online, National Archives, http://founders.archives.gov/documents/Washington/03-13-02-0182.

53. George Washington to Elias Dayton, January 20, 1778, Varick Transcripts, Letterbook 4: 427, GWP.

54. George Washington to William Livingston, January 20, 1778, Founders Online, National Archives, http://founders.archives.gov/documents/Washington/03-13-02-0257.

55. William Livingston at Morristown to George Washington, January 26, 1778, Prince, ed., *The Papers of William Livingston*, 2: 193–95.

56. Essex County Grand Jury to William Livingston, August 13, 1777, Prince, ed., *The Papers of William Livingston*, 2:27.

57. William Livingston at Morristown to George Washington, January 26, 1778, Prince, ed., *The Papers of William Livingston*, 2:193–95.

58. George Washington to William Livingston, February 2, 1778, Varick Transcripts, Letterbook 2: 233–34, GWP.

59. Oyer and Terminer is the name of a court authorized to hear and determine all treasons, felonies, and misdemeanors; and, generally, is invested with other power in relation to the punishment of offenders. John Bouvier, *A Law Dictionary, Adapted to the Constitution and Laws of the United States of America and of the Several States of the American Union; with References to the Civil and Other Systems of Foreign Law* (Philadelphia: Childs & Peterson, 1856), 2:277.

60. John Vanderhovan to John Hendricks, July 26, 1780, General Correspondence, GWP.

61. Baker Hendricks to George Washington, October 18, 1780, Revolutionary War Accounts, Vouchers, and Receipted Accounts 2, Image 253, GWP.

62. Prince, ed., *The Papers of William Livingston*, 4:428–429; *JCC* 22:280–281.

63. W. Woodford Clayton, *History of Union and Middlesex Counties* (Philadelphia: Everts and Peck, 1882), 95, December 13, 1781.

64. Ibid., December 23, 1781.

65. Ibid., June 6, 1782.

66. Ibid., June 13, 1782.

67. For more on the case see Prince, ed., *The Papers of William Livingston*, 5:427 notes.

68. Prince, ed., *The Papers of William Livingston*, 4:428–429; *JCC* 22:280–281.

69. Prince, ed., *The Papers of William Livingston*, 4:428–429; *JCC* 22:280–281; *New Jersey Gazette*, Trenton, New Jersey, June 19, 1782, p. 3, col. 2.

70. Leonard Lundin, *Cockpit of the Revolution: The War for Independence in New Jersey* (Princeton: Princeton University Press, 1940), 377–78.

71. Convention army (the soldiers surrendered by British Major General John Burgoyne at Saratoga), November 1778, CP 47:15;

Quartermaster General's Department, Return of Vessels in and About New York, December 1, 1778, CP 47:21.

72. The *Ranger* was still at Princess Bay in 1781, Quartermaster General's Report, April 1, 1781, Frederick Mackenzie Papers, William L. Clements Library, University of Michigan, Ann Arbor, Michigan.

73. William Livingston to George Washington, April 4, 1778, Prince, ed., *The Papers of William Livingston*, 2:280–81.

74. Lundin, *Cockpit of the Revolution*, 379.

75. William Livingston to George Washington, November 22, 1777, Prince, ed., *The Papers of William Livingston*, 2:120–21; William Livingston to George Washington, January 12, 1778, Prince, ed., *The Papers of William Livingston*, 2:171–72.

76. Benjamin Tallmadge, *Memoir of Colonel Benjamin Tallmadge* (New York: Thomas Holman, Book and Job Printer, 1858; rpt., New York: New York Times & Arno Press, 1968), 50.

77. David Ramsey, *The History of the American Revolution in Two Volumes* (Philadelphia: R. Aitken & Son, 1789), 187–88.

78. An example was Joseph Wilson of Middletown, who was arrested in the fall of 1780 going from Sandy Hook to Shrewsbury for taking provisions to Staten Island. He was placed in the Trenton jail from which he escaped after nine weeks. He took three weeks to get to New York City, going by way of Little Egg Harbor. George Beckwith, *Information of Deserters and Others, October 1780–March 1781*, December 20, 1780, Emmett Collection, New York Public Library, New York, New York.

79. Lewis J. Costigan was made a first lieutenant in the 1st New Jersey Regiment on November 21, 1775. Samuel Tucker, President of New Jersey Provincial Congress, to the Chairman of the War and Ordnance Office, August 16, 1776, PCC, reel 82, i68: 207 and 211.

80. Lewis J. Costigan used the code name "Z" but some documents appear to be signed as coming from "L" because of Costigan's handwriting. Costigan spent money to procure information while in New York City. Colonel Matthias Ogden of the 1st New Jersey Regiment signed a document at Elizabeth Town on April 4, 1782, certifying Costigan's spy activities and that Costigan sent him "frequent and useful intelligence." Costigan spent money to procure information while in New York City. His bill for his spy activities was £65. Costigan's memorial to Washington for compensation for his spy activities, April 4, 1782, General Correspondence, GWP.

81. William Alexander, Lord Stirling to George Washington, December 25, 1778, General Correspondence, GWP.

82. Lewis J. Costigan also went secretly back into New York City in April 1779 for three days and nights to collect intelligence. Lewis J. Costigan to Samuel Holden Parsons, April 13, 1779, General Correspondence, GWP.

83. John Burgoyne to William Howe, May 14, 1777, CP 21:49.

84. Portuguese Johanneses were gold coins, 8 escudos (12,800 reis) in denomination; their name derived from the obverse of the coin, which bore the bust of Johannes V. They were minted in Brazil and Portugal. They were commonly known in the colonies as "Joes." The fractional denominations were 4 escudo and 2 escudo coins of the same origin. The 4 escudo (6,400 reis) coin, or "half Joe," was one of the most commonly used coins in the late colonial period. Ron Michener, University of Virginia, "Money in the American Colonies," on EH.net, Economic History Association, https://eh.net/encyclopedia/money-in-the-american-colonies/; Captain George Henry Preble, *Preble Family in America* (Boston: David Clapp & Son, 1868), 83.

85. William Howe to John Burgoyne, July 20, 1777, CP 22:4.

86. Philip Van Cortlandt was born in New York City on August 21, 1749. He graduated from King's College (later Columbia University) in 1768. He was a member of the Provincial Congress in 1775. He was a lieutenant colonel in the 4th New York Regiment and was promoted to colonel on November 21, 1776, of the 2nd New York Regiment. He was breveted a brigadier general on September 30, 1783. Francis B. Heitman, *Historical Register of Officers of the Continental Army During the War of the Revolution, April 1775, to December 1783*, 555. He died at Van Cortlandt Manor, Croton-on-Hudson, Westchester County, New York, on November 1, 1831, and was interred in Hillside Cemetery, Peekskill, New York.

87. Philip Van Cortlandt, *Autobiography of Philip Van Cortlandt, Brigadier General in the Continental Army, In Magazine of American History with Notes and Queries*, vol. 2, part 1 (New York: A. S. Barnes, 1878), 284; William Howe at New York to John Burgoyne, July 20, 1777, General Correspondence, GWP; Israel Putman at Peekskill to GW, July 24, 1777, General Correspondence, GWP; Henry Williams, July 24, 1777, Deposition on British Military Operations, General Correspondence, GWP; William Howe to John Burgoyne, July 20, 1777, nineteenth-century transcription,

General Correspondence, GWP; George Washington at Ramapo to Israel Putnam, July 25, 1777, Varick Transcripts, Letterbook 3: 398–99, GWP.

7. Double Agents

1. George Washington to Alexander McDougall, March 25, 1779, Varick Transcripts, Letterbook 8: 226–27, GWP.

2. William Livingston to Henry Lee Jr., November 24, 1779, Carl E. Prince, ed., *The Papers of William Livingston* (Trenton: New Jersey Historical Commission, 1979–1988), 3:230–31.

3. Bedford is in eastern Westchester County, New York, but is twelve miles north of Stamford, Connecticut. Elijah Hunter was a first lieutenant of the 4th New York Regiment, June 28, 1775. He was promoted to captain in January 1776. He declined a transfer to the 2nd New York Regiment on November 21, 1776. Lieutenant Colonel Frederick Weisenfels to Committee of Arrangement, December 2, 1776, informing of the resignation of Elijah Hunter, New York State, Department of State, *Calendar of Historical Manuscripts*, 4. Heitman, *Historical Register of Officers of the Continental Army*, 310. It is said Hunter was born in the town of New Castle in Courtlandt Manor in 1749. He operated a store in Bedford and his home was nearby. Robert B. Pattison, *The Books of the First Baptist Church of Ossining* in *The Quarterly Bulletin of the Westchester County Historical Society*, vols. 13–18 (White Plains: Westchester County Historical Society, New York, 1937), 26; Elijah Hunter to George Washington, March 11, 1783, General Correspondence, GWP.

4. John Bakeless, *Turncoats, Traitors and Heroes: Espionage in the American Revolution* (New York: J. B. Lippincott, 1959; rpt., New York: Da Capo, 1998), 241.

5. Elijah Hunter to Sir___ [probably William Tryon], February 27, 1779, marked intelligence, CP 53:11.

6. Alexander McDougall to John Jay, March 21, 1779, Jay ID #6829, John Jay Papers, Columbia University, New York.

7. George Washington to John Jay, September 7, 1779, Varick Transcripts, Letterbook 1: 334–38, GWP.

8. John Jay to George Washington, March 28, 1779, *Letters of Delegates to Congress: vol. 12, February 1, 1779–May 31, 1779* (Washington: Library of Congress, 1976–2000), 257.

9. George Washington to Alexander McDougall, March 25, 1779, Varick Transcripts, Letterbook 8: 226–27, GWP.

10. George Washington to Alexander McDougall, March 28, 1779, Varick Transcripts, Letterbook 8: 235–37, GWP.

11. Frederick Haldimand (1718–1791) was a native of Switzerland and served in the Swiss Guards and the Dutch army. William Tryon to Frederick Haldimand, March 13, 1779, General Correspondence, GWP.

12. George Washington to Alexander McDougall, March 28, 1779, Varick Transcripts, Letterbook 8: 235, GWP.

13. The docket for the manuscript is "In from G T Friend"—or, "In[telligence] from G[overnor] T[ryon's] Friend"; Elijah Hunter to William Tryon, April 2, 1779, CP 55:31.

14. P is probably Captain Jonathan Platt with whom Hunter had a conversation. Tuscarora probably means Tuscarora Mountain, which is a ridge of the Appalachians in central Pennsylvania. The mountain runs from northeast to southwest, extending from the Juniata River at Millerstown in the north to the end of Cove Mountain in the south. Elijah Hunter to Governor George Clinton, April 17, 1780, George Clinton, Public Papers of George Clinton, 10 vols. (New York and Albany: Wynkoop Hallenbeck Crawford Company, 1899–1914), 5:639–41; Elijah Hunter to William Tryon, April 2, 1779, CP 55:31.

15. Elijah Hunter to George Washington, May 21, 1779, General Correspondence, GWP.

16. Elijah Hunter, May 23, 1779, "Intelligence Report on British Military Plans," General Correspondence, GWP.

17. George Washington to Elijah Hunter, August 12, 1779, Varick Transcripts, Letterbook 9: 310–11, GWP.

18. George Washington to Elijah Hunter, August 12, 1779, Varick Transcripts, Letterbook 9: 312–13, GWP.

19. George Washington to Robert Howe, August 17, 1779, Varick Transcripts, Letterbook 9: 328–29, GWP.

20. Ibid.

21. George Washington to Robert Howe, August 20, 1779, two the same day, Varick Transcripts, Letterbook 9: 335–38, GWP.

22. Mary Campbell's report in Beckwith's handwriting, March 28, 1781, CP 151:7.

23. George Washington to Robert Howe, August 21, 1779, General Correspondence, GWP.

24. The fire occurred on July 11, 1779. The town of Bedford was

burned by Colonel Samuel Birch and 400 cavalrymen. Evelyne H. Ryan, *The Burning of Bedford Village History Re-examined* (Katonah, New York: Record Review, July 9, 2004, http://bedfordhistorical society.org/about_bedford_ny/pdfs/The_Burning_of_Bedford .pdf.

25. The many misspellings in his letter have been corrected for readability. Elijah Hunter to William Tryon, August 21, 1779, CP 66:21.

26. Elijah Hunter to John André, August 21, 1779, CP 66:20.

27. *Norwich Packet,* September 7, 1779, p. 3, col. 3.

28. George Washington to Robert Howe, August 28, 1779, Varick Transcripts, Letterbook 9: 373–74, GWP.

29. Ibid.

30. American Intelligence, 1779, British Ships in New York, General Correspondence, GWP.

31. George Washington to Robert Howe, September 5, 1779, Varick Transcripts, Letterbook 9: 403–4, GWP.

32. George Washington to Robert Howe, September 7, 1779, Varick Transcripts, Letterbook 9: 409–10, GWP.

33. John Jay to George Washington, August 25, 1779, *Letters of Delegates to Congress*: vol. 13, June 1, 1779–September 30, 1779 (Washington: Library of Congress, 1976–2000), 417.

34. Washington had given General McDougall 200 guineas with which to pay those who were used as secret agents. George Washington to Elijah Hunter, February 25, 1790, Varick Transcripts, Letterbook 22: 298, GWP; George Washington to John Jay, September 7, 1779, Varick Transcripts, Letterbook 1: 334–48, GWP.

35. James Holmes was a Native American who had a 273-acre farm and an African slave. He was a colonel of the 4th New York Regiment on June 30, 1775. The regiment wore a brown coat faced with scarlet. Francis B. Heitman reported that Holmes served until December 1775 when he renewed his obligation to Great Britain. He went within British lines in April 1778. He was captured in the fall of 1779 and held for twenty months in Poughkeepsie before escaping to the British. He joined Colonel James De Lancey's Corps of Loyal Refugees in August 1781 as a lieutenant colonel and served to the end of the war. He settled in St. John, New Brunswick, Canada. He died on July 8, 1824. His name was removed on account of promotion, resignation, or death from the list of officers raised in New York state for 1775. New York State, Department of State, *Calendar of Historical Manuscripts,*

Relating to the War of the Revolution, in the Office of the Secretary of State, Albany, N.Y. (Albany: Weed, Parsons & Company, Printers, 1868), 42–43. However, the New York State Library has his February 13, 1776, master rolls of the 4th New York Regiment in its Henry Livingston Collection, 1751–1833, SC19687, at the New York State Library. Francis B. Heitman, *Historical Register of the Officers of the Continental Army, During the War of the Revolution, April 1775, to December 1783,* 298; Peter Wilson Coldham, *American Migrations,* 1765–1799 (Baltimore Genealogical Publishing Co., 2000), 257.

36. Jonathan Platt was captain of the 4th New York Regiment on June 28, 1775. Heitman, *Historical Register of the Officers of the Continental Army,* 443.

37. Elijah Hunter at Bedford, N.Y., to Governor George Clinton, April 17, 1780, Clinton, *Public Papers of George Clinton,* 5:639–41.

38. The letter reads Mr. Naigts, which I believe is Mr. John Naight.

39. Major Richard Platte was 2nd lieutenant of the 1st New York Regiment on June 28, 1775; lieutenant of the 1st New York Regiment in November 1775; captain on November 21, 1776, but credited as of June 26, 1776; brigade major to General McDougall on August 12, 1776, to the end of the war. He died on March 3, 1830. Heitman, *Historical Register,* 443.

40. H.E.'s (Elijah Hunter's) report, June 6, 1779, CP 60:15.

41. Elijah Hunter to George Washington, April 12, 1781, General Correspondence, GWP.

42. Elijah Hunter to George Washington, March 11, 1783, General Correspondence, GWP.

43. John Bakeless, *Turncoats, Traitors and Heroes: Espionage in the American Revolution.* (New York: J. B. Lippincott, 1959; rpt., New York: Da Capo, 1998); 387 endnotes, say that E.H. is Elisha Holmes but that is incorrect as it is Elijah Hunter. Elijah Hunter to De Lancey, n.d., CP 228:32.

44. Elijah Hunter to George Washington, March 11, 1783, General Correspondence, GWP.

45. Ibid.

46. George Washington to Captain Elijah Hunter, June 11, 1783, General Correspondence, GWP.

47. George Washington to Elijah Hunter, December 1, 1783, Varick Transcripts, Letterbook 16: 358; draft, General Correspondence, GWP.

48. Elijah Hunter to George Washington, March 25, 1790, Series 2, Letterbook 22: 279, GWP.

49. William Maxwell to George Washington, February 9, 1777, General Correspondence, GWP.

50. William Maxwell to George Washington, August 31, 1778, General Correspondence, GWP; Harry M. Ward, *General William Maxwell and the New Jersey Continentals* (Westport: Greenwood, 1997), 108.

51. John A. Garraty and Mark C. Carnes, eds. *American National Biography,* (New York: Oxford University Press, 1999), 1:391.

52. Abraham Clark wrote to William Livingston on November 13, 1777, that John Morse Jr. was one of four people employed by Washington as spies working out of Elizabeth Town whose real intent was to trade with the enemy. Prince, ed., *The Papers of William Livingston*, 2:120–21; Council of Safety, January 10, 1778, *Minutes of the Council of Safety of the State of New Jersey* (Jersey City: John H. Lyon, 1872), 164, 186.

53. Morse is usually mentioned as Moss. George Washington to William Livingston, April 15, 1778, Varick Transcripts, Letterbook 2: 415–16, GWP; William Livingston to George Washington, April 11, 1778; Prince, ed., *The Papers of William Livingston*, 2:288.

54. Jacob Bankson (probably his father) was deeded land in Passyunk Township on June 20, 1755, from Sarah Stretch. There was also a release from Barbara Bankson and others to land in Moyamensing. Historical Society of Pennsylvania, Society Miscellaneous, Box 9B.

55. Alexander Hamilton to Stephen Moylan, April 3, 1778, General Correspondence, GWP.

56. William Livingston at Princeton to George Washington, April 9, 1778, Prince, ed., *The Papers of William Livingston*, 2:285–86.

57. Ibid.

58. John C. Fitzpatrick, ed., *The Writings of George Washington from the Original Manuscript Sources, 1745–1799* (Washington, DC: United States Government Printing Office, 39 vols., 1931–1944), vol. 1, George Washington's Accounts of Expenses While Commander-in-Chief of the Continental Army, 1775–1783.

59. William Livingston at Princeton to George Washington, May 17, 1778, written in Dutch, Prince, ed., *The Papers of William Livingston*, 2:333–34; William Livingston at Princeton to George Washington, May 17, 1778, written in English, ibid., 2:333.

60. Livingston identified him as an officer by the name of Bankson. The only officer named Bankson is Captain John Bankson of

the 2nd Pennsylvania Regiment. Heitman, *Historical Register of Officers in the Continental Army*, 85.

61. Articles 3 of the Articles of War, passed by Congress on June 30, 1775, levied fines (4 shillings lawful money) for soldiers and officers found guilty of swearing. *JCC* 2:112. William Livingston at Princeton to George Washington, May 23, 1778, Prince, ed., *The Papers of William Livingston*, 2:340–41.

62. Cornelius Hatfield Jr. of Elizabeth Town went to the British on Staten Island when they arrived in New Jersey in 1776. He claimed to have provided valuable intelligence. He was in London in 1785 (12/101/276; 13/96/426–27, 109/429–39). Coldham, *American Migrations, 1765–1799*, 403.

63. John Smith Hatfield had a forty-acre farm near Elizabeth Town and two vessels. In 1786 he was at St. John's. He had served as a guide and naval pilot. British National Archives, Kew, Richmond, Surrey, United Kingdom, Audit Office Papers, A013/22/120-122. Peter Wilson Coldham, *American Loyalist Claims* (Washington, DC: National Genealogical Society, 1980), 222.

64. Middle Town Point is now Matawan. George Washington to William Maxwell, December 20, 1778, Varick Transcripts, Letterbook 7: 197–98, GWP; George Washington to William Livingston, December 21, 1778, Varick Transcripts, Letterbook 2: 399–400, GWP.

65. William Maxwell to William Alexander, Lord Stirling, December 28, 1778, General Correspondence, GWP.

66. Prince, ed., *The Papers of William Livingston*, 563.

67. Rev. James Caldwell wrote that Hetfield (Hatfield) and Hendricks had been released from jail and completed an espionage mission. Rev. James Caldwell to William Livingston, July 7, 1777, Prince, ed., *The Papers of William Livingston*, 2:25.

68. Samuel H. Parsons to George Washington, December 16, 1779, General Correspondence, GWP.

69. Samuel Holden Parsons was born on May 14, 1737, in Lyme, Connecticut. He graduated Harvard in 1756. He practiced law in Lyme. He died on November 17, 1789, in western Pennsylvania.

70. George Washington to Samuel H. Parsons, December 23, 1779, two the same date, Varick Transcripts, Letterbook 10: 399–400, GWP.

71. George Washington to Moses Hatfield, Commissary of Hides, October 25, 1779, Varick Transcripts, Letterbook 10: 193, GWP;

George Washington to William Heath, January 12, 1780, Varick Transcripts, Letterbook 11: 29, GWP.

72. Moses Hazen was a lieutenant in the British army on half pay when he was appointed colonel of the 2nd Canadian Regiment on January 22, 1776. He died on February 3, 1893. George Washington to Moses Hazen, January 24, 1780, Varick Transcripts, Letterbook 11: 74–75, GWP; Heitman, *Historical Register*, 282.

73. George Washington to William Irvine, January 1, 1780, Varick Transcripts, Letterbook 11: 421, GWP.

74. George Washington to William Irvine, January 9, 1780, two the same date, Varick Transcripts, Letterbook 11: 18–19, GWP.

8. Traitors and Licensed Spies

1. Papers of the Continental Congress, 1774–1789 (Washington: National Archives and Record Service, General Services Administration, 1971), microfilm, vol. 7: 132–33, February 19, 1777.

2. George Washington to Benedict Arnold, March 3, 1777, Varick Transcripts, Letterbook 2: 335–36, GWP.

3. General Orders, May 28, 1778, Varick Transcripts, Letterbook 3: 220–22, GWP.

4. George Washington to Benedict Arnold, June 19, 1778, General Correspondence, GWP.

5. Resolve of Congress, February 15, 1779, *JCC* 13:184.

6. George Washington to Benedict Arnold, April 20, 1779, General Correspondence, GWP.

7. George Washington to Benedict Arnold, April 28, 1779, General Correspondence, GWP.

8. Rattoon's tavern was located at the north end of the road to Bordentown in South Amboy. Bordentown Road is now known as Main Street. The building was laid out in an east–west direction nearly parallel with the shoreline. The west side of the building was the original portion of the tavern and was two stories high. It was forty feet long and thirty feet deep. On the east side was a story-and-a-half addition that was fifty feet wide and twenty-five feet deep. The tavern had a dock that was located about a half mile across the salt marsh. "It was related of Rattoon that he was a man of infinite tact, and was able to entertain British and American officers in the house at the same time, locating them in the opposite ends without allowing either to

know of the presence of the other, and was 'hail fellow well met' with all." Rattoon's tavern is identified as the Railroad House Hotel (A. D. Vanpelt, Proprietor) on the Map of the County of Middlesex, New Jersey, by Smith Gallop & Co., published in 1861. W. W. Clayton, *History of Union and Middlesex Counties* (Philadelphia: Everts & Peck, 1882), 824.

9. The report is docketed on the back that it came from Mr. Ratton [*sic*] of South Amboy and was received by Colonel (Stephen) Moylan. There was also a Robert Rattoon. Ratton [John Rattoon], May 22, 1779, Intelligence Information on British Fleet Movements, General Correspondence, GWP.

10. To view an image of the July 15 letter in cipher with the British headquarters translation, see John A. Nagy, *Invisible Ink: Spycraft of the American Revolution* (Yardley, Pennsylvania: Westholme Publishing, 2010), 162. Moore [Benedict Arnold] to Captain John Anderson [John André] to be left at Mr. Odell's, Baltimore, July 15, 1780, Gold Star Box, William L. Clements Library, University of Michigan, Ann Arbor, Michigan.

11. Joshua Hett Smith's house was torn down in 1921.

12. George Washington to William Livingston, December 16, 1778, Varick Transcripts, Letterbook 2: 393–95, GWP.

13. *New Jersey Gazette*, Trenton, New Jersey, December 25, 1782, p. 3, cols. 1–3.

14. James Madison to Edmund Randolph, June 18, 1782, Founders Online, National Archives, http://founders.archives.gov/documents/Madison/01-04-02-0161.

15. Ibid.

9. Black Chambers and the Medicine Factory

1. Rebecca Burwell was born May 20, 1746, in Gloucester County, Virginia, and died August 5, 1806, in Richmond, Virginia.

2. William Donaldson at London to Peter N. B. Livingston at New York, September 6, 1775. This letter was intercepted by Mr. Todd, secretary to the Post Office, indicated by note, Alexander Gillon at New York to Edward Harthals, September 6, 1775, Historical Manuscript Commission, *Manuscripts of the Earl of Dartmouth, American Papers*, vol. 2, 14th report, Appendix, part 10, 1895 (Rpt., Boston: Gregg Press, 1972), 2:373.

3. On March 19, 1745, there were six members of the "Secret Office: Edward Hill, porter and messenger of the secret service; and five others, officers or pensioners, viz., Scholing, Bode, Zolman,

Edward Willes and William Willes." Money Book XLI: 466–67. "Treasury Books and Papers: March 1745," in *Calendar of Treasury Books and Papers*, vol. 5, 1742–1745, ed. William A. Shaw (London: His Majesty's Stationary Office, 1903), 672–79, http://www.british-history.ac.uk/cal-treasury-books-papers/vol5/pp672-679.

4. *JCC*, 3:368, November 24, 1775.

5. Ibid., 4:285–86.

6. Ibid., 288; and printed in the *Pennsylvania Evening Post*, April 18, 1776.

7. Elias Nexsen was born in New York in 1740, and died aged ninety-one years old. Nexsen owned the schooner *Harmony* before 1765. He became captain and supercargo, went abroad in his own vessel, and was a merchant when he reached New York. He lived in the house that formerly had been occupied by Christopher Fell until he died. It was opposite Robert Murray's. Occasionally he sold slaves. He was a member of the Marine Society in 1770.

8. Richmond Hill was built after 1767 on property leased from Trinity Church by Major Abraham Mortier, paymaster of the British army in the colony of New York. The house stood southeast of the modern intersection of Varick and Charlton Streets. It was a frame house five bays wide, with a tetrastyle Ionic portico, and three bays deep. It was raised on a high basement and approached by a flight of steps.

9. The Second River, or Watsessing River, in New Jersey is the second main tributary of the Passaic River when traveling upstream from its mouth at Newark. The name of the town of Second River was changed to Belleville in 1797.

10. By Walter Barrett [pseudonym], Clerk, for Joseph Alfred Scoville, *The Old Merchants of New York City* (New York: Carleton, 1863), 162.

11. The Rope Ferry was over the Niantic River in Waterford Township near New London, Connecticut.

12. Beverley Robinson was born January 11, 1721, in Middlesex County, Virginia, to John Robinson, president of the colony of Virginia. He married Susanna Philipse of New York, which brought him considerable wealth. He was commissioned colonel of the Loyal American Regiment. Often confused with his son Beverley, lieutenant colonel of the same regiment. Besides his command, he also performed secret service assignments.

After the war, he moved to Thornbury, near Bristol, England, where he died on April 9, 1792.

13. The second courier (Micah Townsend) to Colonel Samuel Wells was his son-in-law.

14. Samuel Wells was a judge of Cumberland County Court and a member of the Assembly of the Province of New York. He died August 6, 1786, and was fifty-five years old.

15. Black Point is south of Niantic, Connecticut, at the entrance to Niantic Bay.

16. David Gray was born in Lenox, Massachusetts. After the war he married in Pennsylvania and in 1823 was living in Vermont. David Gray, Gray Narrative (1825), 1–8.

17. Mr. Fish's first name appears in Moses Harris Jr.'s pension application. His name is on the October 1779 Saratoga District Tax List and he also signed a petition from the Saratoga and Cambridge Districts to New York governor George Clinton in 1778, http://www.saratoganygenweb.com/1778Petition.htm; *Public Papers of George Clinton,* First Governor of New York, 1777–1795, 1801–1804 (Albany: James B. Lyon, State Printer, 1900), 3:209–11.

18. Moses Harris Jr. was born November 8, 1745, in Dutchess County. His father had emigrated from Wales. At the start of the American Revolution he lived at Brayton Farm, about one mile south of Fort Ann village, and in early 1777 moved to Dutchess County and was living with his father and brothers Joseph and William. William L. Stone, "Schuyler's Faithful Spy," in *The Magazine of American History with Notes and Queries,* vol. 2, issue 2 (New York: A. S. Barnes, 1878), 415–19.

19. There was an Ensign Thomas Smith in the area on March 29, 1781. *Public Papers of George Clinton, First Governor of New York, 1777–1795, 1801–1804* (New York: State of New York, 1902), vol. 6: 772.

20. George Washington to George Clinton, April 15, 1781, Varick Transcripts, Letterbook 4: 119–20, GWP.

21. George Clinton to Philip Schuyler, April 16, 1781, *Public Papers of George Clinton, First Governor of New York, 1777–1795, 1801–1804* (New York: State of New York, 1902), vol. 6: 770–72; Philip Schuyler to George Clinton, May 4, 1781, ibid., 840–43.

22. Thomas Sherwood enlisted in the Corps of Loyal Rangers in 1777. He was born June 1, 1745, in Old Stratford, Connecticut, to Seth Sherwood and Sarah Pitcher. He married circa 1770 Annah Brownson (born on January 9, 1752, in New Milford,

Litchfield, Connecticut) in Ford Edward, New York. He died on December 10, 1826, in Brockville, Leeds, Ontario, Canada. Peter Wilson Coldham, *American Loyalist Claims* (Washington, DC: National Genealogical Society, 1980), 445; British Library, Additional Manuscripts, No. 21827, ff. 97–99, On-Line Institute for Advanced Loyalist Studies, http://www.royalprovincial.com/.

23. Philip Schuyler to George Clinton, May 4, 1781, *The Public Papers of George Clinton, First Governor of New York, 1777–1795, 1801–1804* (New York: State of New York, 1902), vol. 6: 840–43; Philip J. Schuyler to George Washington, May 4, 1781, General Correspondence, GWP.

24. George Washington to Philip J. Schuyler, May 14, 1781, General Correspondence, GWP.

25. The events described in the article "Schuyler's Faithful Spy" could not have occurred as recounted. General Schuyler did not know Moses Harris Jr. until 1781 and could not have been involved with Schuyler at the time of Burgoyne's descent in 1777. Stone, "Schuyler's Faithful Spy," 415–19.

26. William Shepherd in 1772 was working in New York City and moved to Albany before hostilities broke out. He and his wife, Jane, lived on the hill in Albany. He was a member and vestryman at St. Peter's. Beginning in 1775, he was paid by the Americans for making and repairing bayonets. In May 1776, he was identified as "notoriously disaffected" and the weapons in his possession were seized. He was confined but later released after posting bond. William Shepherd continued to make and fix bayonets, knives, and swords, for the American cause. At one time he captained a company of "armourers" under Philip Van Rensselaer. The life of William Shepherd is from Colonel Albany Project, biography no. 1155, extracted from Joel Munsell, *Annals of Albany* (Albany, New York: Joel Munsell, 1850–1859), 10:280. Shepherd also posted bond for two Loyalists, Richard Brooks on August 24, 1778, and Joseph Hawkins of Kingsbury, who was charged with being with the enemy, on August 29, 1780. Victor Hugo Paltsits, *Minutes of the Commissioners for Detecting and Defeating Conspiracies in the State of New York* (Albany: State of New York, 1909), 1:216, 2:573, 597.

27. Moses Harris Jr., Revolutionary War Pension Applications, microfilm (Washington, DC: United States National Archives).

28. John Taylor, lieutenant governor of New York, at Albany, New York, to ___, February 6, 1821, Moses Harris Jr., Revolutionary

War Pension Applications, microfilm (Washington, DC: United States National Archives).

29. Report from Frederick Haldimand, June 21, 1781, CP 160:6.

30. John Taylor, lieutenant governor of New York, at Albany, New York, to ____, February 6, 1821, Moses Harris Jr., Revolutionary War Pension Applications, microfilm (Washington, DC: United States National Archives).

31. John McKinstrey's name was also spelled McKinstry and McIstrey. He joined the New York State Militia in 1775. He was in the 8th Regiment of the Albany County Militia. New York State Comptroller, *New York in the Revolution as Colony and State*, vol. 71 (Albany: J. B. Lyon, Printers, 1904), http://dunhamwilcox.net /ny/ny_rev_levies_albany2.htm. Paltsits, *Minutes of the Commissioners for Detecting and Defeating Conspiracies in the State of New York*, 2:762, 767–68.

32. Benjamin Thompson at Woburn, Massachusetts, to Unknown in Boston, May 6, 1775, Gold Star Box at the Clements Library, University of Michigan, Ann Arbor, Michigan.

33. This letter has not been found. Tench Tilghman to James Tilghman, February 22, 1777, Oswald Tilghman, *Memoir of Lieutenant Colonel Tench Tilghman* (Albany, 1876), 151–53.

34. William Smith was born in New York City on June 18, 1728. He was the eldest child of William Smith and Mary Het. He married Janet Livingston on November 3, 1752, and they had eleven children. He died on December 6, 1793, in Quebec City. He graduated from Yale in 1745 and was a lawyer and historian. He was the Loyalist chief justice of the province of New York from 1780 to 1782, and chief justice of the province of Quebec, later Lower Canada, from 1786 until his death. Leslie Francis Stokes Upton, *The Loyal Whig: William Smith of New York and Quebec* (Toronto: University of Toronto Press, 1969), 225.

35. Silas Deane was born in Groton, Connecticut, the son of a blacksmith. He graduated from Yale in 1758. He practiced law for a short time outside Hartford before he became a merchant in Wethersfield, Connecticut. On September 26, 1776, he, along with Benjamin Franklin and Thomas Jefferson, was appointed commissioner to the court of France.

36. John Jay to Robert Morris, October 6, 1776, *Letters to Robert Morris, 1775–1782*, in *Collections of the New-York Historical Society for the Year 1878* (New York: New-York Historical Society, 1879), 401–4.

37. George Washington to Elias Boudinot, May 3, 1779, Varick Transcripts, Letterbook 1: 268–69, GWP.

38. George Washington to Benjamin Tallmadge, April 30, 1779, Varick Transcripts, Letterbook 8: 323, GWP.
39. Jonathan Odell to John André, May 31, 1779, CP 59:27.
40. George Washington to James Jay, April 9, 1780, Varick Transcripts, Letterbook 2: 41–42, GWP.
41. James Jay at Fishkill to George Washington, April 13 and 20, 1780, General Correspondence, GWP.
42. George Washington to James Jay, May 12, 1780, Varick Transcripts, Letterbook 3: 264–65, GWP; George Washington to Udny Hay, May 13, 1780, Varick Transcripts, Letterbook 11: 313–14, GWP.
43. James Jay at Fishkill to George Washington, September 19, 1780, General Correspondence, GWP.

10. Petite Guerre

1. George Washington to Philip J. Schuyler, February 23, 1777, Varick Transcripts, Letterbook 2: 322–24, GWP.
2. George Washington to William Heath, August 19, 1781, Varick Transcripts, Letterbook 14: 140–44, GWP.
3. George Washington to William Alexander, Lord Stirling, December 9, 1779, Varick Transcripts, Letterbook 10: 350–51, GWP.
4. George Washington to Marquis de Lafayette, May 19, 1780, Varick Transcripts, Letterbook 11: 336–38, GWP.
5. George Washington at Morristown to Benedict Arnold at Philadelphia, June 4, 1780, Varick Transcripts, Letterbook 11: 386, GWP.
6. The document said Mr. Claypole but the only match I found was David Claypoole.
7. Benedict Arnold to George Washington, June 7, 1780, Founders Online, National Archives, http://founders.archives.gov/documents/Washington/99-01-02-02021.
8. Carl Van Doren, *Secret History of the American Revolution* (New York: Viking, 1951), 263–64.
9. Ibid.
10. John C. Fitzpatrick, Editor of the *The Writings of George Washington from the Original Manuscript Sources, 1745–1799* (Washington, DC: United States Government Printing Office, 1931–1944), 18:476, believed that Mrs. Peggy Arnold provided the proclamation to the British. Arnold's letter states he left it with Stansbury and Stansbury's letter to British headquarters enclosed it. George Washington at Morristown to Benedict Arnold at Philadelphia,

June 4, 1780, Varick Transcripts, Letterbook 11: 386, GWP; British Transcripts, C. O. 5, vol. 100, fol. 243, Library of Congress; memorandum of Mrs. Arnold being paid, after the discovery of Arnold's treason, £350 for services in Henry Clinton's Papers, in the William L. Clements Library, University of Michigan, Ann Arbor, Michigan.

11. Alexander Hamilton was an aide-de-camp to Washington from 1777 to 1781.

12. Nathanael Greene to George Washington, June 22, 1780, at five o'clock, Founders Online, National Archives, http://founders .archives.gov/documents/Washington/99-01-02-02196.

13. Ibid., 10 p.m.

14. MD [Daniel Martin] to Baron Wilhelm von Knyphausen, June 17, 1780, CP 105:5.

15. Bryant's Tavern was located in the present-day vicinity of Broad Street and Route 24 in Summit, New Jersey.

16. After Orders and General Orders, Head Quarters, Short Hills, June 18, 1780, Varick Transcripts, Letterbook 5: 56–61, GWP; John H. Hawkins, *John H. Hawkins' First Pennsylvania Orderly Book, June 16–18, 1780*; Samuel Hazard, *Pennsylvania Colonial Records* (Harrisburg: T. Fenn, 1838–1853), Series 2, vol. 11.

17. MD [Daniel Martin] to Baron Wilhelm von Knyphausen, June 17, 1780, CP 105:5.

18. DM [Daniel Martin] at Paramus to SHC, July 3, 1780, CP 108:36.

19. Intelligence summary, March 18, 1781, CP 150:15.

20. The Shrewsbury Inlet reopened again in 1830 and stayed open in varying degrees for five years.

21. Ernest W. Mandeville, *The Story of Middletown—The Oldest Settlement in New Jersey* (Middletown, New Jersey: Christ Church, 1927; rpt., Academy Press, 1972), 60.

22. Robert Townsend in his intelligence report of November 27, 1779, reported that the warships at Sandy Hook took on water. Morton Pennypacker, *General Washington's Spies on Long Island and in New York* (Garden City: Long Island Historical Society by Country Life Press, 1939), 262.

23. William Livington at Morristown to Henry Laurens, August 22, 1778, Carl E. Prince, ed., *The Papers of William Livingston* (Trenton: New Jersey Historical Commission), 2:423.

24. Lieutenant Enos Reeves's letterbook, December 14, 1780, *Pennsylvania Magazine of History and Biography* (Philadelphia: Historical Society of Pennsylvania), vol. 20, 1896, 471.

25. Garrett's Hill is at latitude 40.4078863 and longitude -74.0779183.

26. William S. Hornor, *This Old Monmouth of Ours* (Freehold, New Jersey: Moreau Brothers, 1932; rpt., Baltimore: Genealogical Publishing Co., 1990, 1999, 2009), 9.

27. John Stillwell to David Forman, June 16, 1780; John Stillwell, June 18, 1780, British Naval Positions; John Stillwell to David Forman, July 16, 1780; John Stillwell to David Forman, November 11, 1780, sent to George Washington on November 12; John Stillwell to David Forman, November 18, 1782; John Stillwell to David Forman at Freehold, December 15, 1781, Intelligence, all the above in General Correspondence, GWP.

28. Shoal Harbor is now known as Port Monmouth. Martha was the wife of American Major Thomas Seabrook. With Thomas off to war, she opened the house as an inn and today it is known as the Spy House.

29. George Washington to John Mercereau at Elizabeth Town, April 13, 1780, Varick Transcripts, Letterbook 11: 270–71, GWP; William A. Whitehead, *Contributions to the Early History of Perth Amboy and Adjoining Country: With Sketches of Men and Events in New Jersey During the Provincial Era* (New York: D. Appleton & Company, 1856), 85.

30. Historians sometimes attribute the nickname "Black David" to General David Forman but it belongs to his cousin Sheriff David Forman. Hornor, *This Old Monmouth of Ours*, 216.

31. William Bernard Gifford was born in Ireland on December 25, 1751, and died on February 1, 1814, on Staten Island. He is buried at the Reformed Church Cemetery, Port Richmond, Staten Island, New York.

32. Francis B. Heitman, *Historical Register of Officers of the Continental Army During the War of the Revolution, April 1775, to December 1783* (1914), 247.

33. Abraham Buskirk to Sir Thomas Stirling, January 16, 1780, CP 109:16. During the raid, they burned the Presbyterian meeting house, the courthouse, and De Hart's house (which was used by the American pickets).

34. Rev. James Caldwell at Springfield, New Jersey, to Nathanael Greene, January 30, 1780, *Papers of General Nathanael Greene* (Chapel Hill: Published for the Rhode Island Historical Society by the University of North Carolina Press, 1976–2005), 5:329–30.

35. New York State, *Names of Persons for Whom Marriage Licenses Were*

Issued by the Secretary of the Province of New York Previous to 1784 (Albany, 1860), 440.

36. William Bernard Gifford at New Utrecht, Long Island, to Oliver De Lancey, November 10, 1780, CP 129:18.

37. William Bernard Gifford to Oliver De Lancey, November 28, 1780, CP 131:35.

38. Thomas Hughes was the son of Major William Hughes. There were a number of Lieutenant Browns in the British army in North America, and it's not possible to determine which one was at the tavern without more information. Worthington Chauncey Ford, *British Officers Serving in the American Revolution, 1774–1783* (Brooklyn: Historical Printing Club, 1897), 98.

39. William Bernard Gifford to Oliver De Lancey, December 7, 1780, CP 132:44; Thomas Hughes; R. W. David, ed., *A Journal by Thos. Hughes for His Amusement: & Designed Only for His Perusal by the Time He Attains the Age of 50 If He Lives So Long (1778–1789)* (Cambridge [England]: University Press, 1947), 101–2.

40. There is an intelligence report marked "G," which might be Gifford or Gould, CP 133:21, before December 12, 1780. William Bernard Gifford to Oliver De Lancey, December 7, 1780, CP 132:44.

41. Francis Barber was born in 1750 and died on February 11, 1783. On the way to his quarters, he came upon some soldiers in the act of cutting down trees. As he rode toward them, one large tree "struck him on the head, and killed him in a minute." The tree is described as being very tall, and the root being "some distance from the path . . . the soldiers did not see him till he was directly opposite; they cried out, he stopped sudden, and began to turn round his horse, but before he got round he received the fatal stroke." Some sources say he was on the way to dine with Washington in Newburgh, New York. *New Jersey Gazette*, 1782.

42. George Washington to Lieutenant Colonel Francis Barber, December 13, 1780, Varick Transcripts, Letterbook 12: 402, GWP.

43. Lieutenant Colonel Francis Barber at Pompton, New Jersey, to George Washington, December 11, 1780, Varick Transcripts, Letterbook 12: 402, GWP.

44. William Bernard Gifford to Oliver De Lancey, January 18, 1781, CP 141:25.

45. George Washington at New Windsor to Lieutenant Colonel Francis Barber, January 21, 1781, Varick Transcripts, Letterbook 13: 80–88, GWP.

46. William Bernard Gifford to Oliver De Lancey, January 20, 1781, CP 141:35.
47. *Oliver De Lancey's Journal* (ten-page copy), CP 144:12, reproduced in John A. Nagy, *Rebellion in the Ranks: Mutinies of the American Revolution* (Yardley, Pennsylvania: Westholme Publishing, 2007), Appendix C, 304–10, January 21, 1781.
48. Hughes, *A Journal by Thos. Hughes*, 107.
49. Samuel Mabbot may be from Dutchess County, New York. His name sometimes appears as Mabbet and Mabbit. William H. W. Sabine, ed., *Historical Memoirs of William Smith, 1778–1783* (New York: New York Times & Arno Press, rpt., 1971), 209, January 5, 1780.
50. Ibid., 379, January 23, 1781.
51. Ibid., 379–80 and note, January 23, and 24, 1781.
52. Ibid., 381, January 25, 1781.
53. William McMichael was commissioned a lieutenant on February 7, 1776. Heitman, *Historical Register of Officers of the Continental Army*, 374.
54. Elias Dayton to George Washington, April 7, 1781, General Correspondence, GWP.
55. Thomas Ward to Commanding Officer at Elizabeth Town, April 9, 1781, Historical Society of Pennsylvania. L. S. Thomas Ward quoted from the On-Line Institute for Advanced Loyalist Studies, http://www.royalprovincial.com/military/rhist/lrv/lrvlet4.htm.
56. Washington acknowledged a letter of Dayton's of April 10 but Dayton's letter was dated April 7, 1781. George Washington to Elias Dayton, April 11, 1781, Varick Transcripts, Letterbook 13: 271–72, GWP.
57. Ibid.
58. Elias Dayton to George Washington, April 14, 1781, General Correspondence, GWP.
59. Dr. John Connolly was born circa 1741–1750 and raised near Wright's Ferry, Pennsylvania. Lord Dunmore commissioned him a lieutenant colonel in the Queen's Royal Rangers in November 1775. He had proposed attacks on Fort Pitt in 1775. He was captured near Hagerstown, Maryland, jailed in York, Pennsylvania, then Philadelphia, and exchanged in 1780.
60. McMichael was still operating as a spy in New York City for Dayton until circa August 4, 1782. David Humphreys to Elias Dayton, August 4, 1782, Varick Transcripts, Letterbook 15: 237–38, GWP; Elias Dayton to George Washington, April 20, 1781, General Correspondence, GWP.

61. Connolly, on March 15, 1781, was living at 40 Upper Marybone Street in New York City. John Connolly at Flatbush to Henry Clinton, April 20, 1781, CP 152:48.

62. Henry Clinton to Charles Cornwallis, June 9, 1781, CP 158:12.

63. George Washington to Elias Dayton, May 1, 1781, Varick Transcripts, Letterbook 13: 328–29, GWP.

64. Ibid.

65. Donald Jackson and Dorothy Twohig, eds., *The Diaries of George Washington*, vol. 3: 1771–75, 1780–81 (Charlottesville: University of Virginia Press, 1978), 375. Hereinafter *DGW*.

66. George Washington to Elias Dayton, May 11, 1781, Varick Transcripts, Letterbook 13: 360–61, GWP.

67. Elias Dayton to George Washington, May 9, 1781, General Correspondence, GWP.

68. *DGW*, 3:362, May 11, 1781.

69. George Washington to Jean B. Donatien de Vimeur, Comte de Rochambeau, May 11, 1781, Varick Transcripts, Letterbook 1: 256–57, GWP.

70. George Washington to Continental Congress, May 11, 1781, Varick Transcripts, Letterbook 6: 51, GWP.

71. *DGW*, 3:362, May 12, 1781.

72. Ibid., 3:365, May 15, 1781.

73. The Watering Place was at the northeast corner of Staten Island.

74. Elias Dayton at Chatham to George Washington, May 16, 1781, General Correspondence, GWP.

75. Ibid.

76. Ibid.

77. George Washington to Elias Dayton, May 28, 1781, General Correspondence, GWP.

78. George Washington to Elias Dayton, June 14, 1781, Varick Transcripts, Letterbook 14: 7–8, GWP.

79. Colonel Elias Dayton even while he was stationed with his men, 159 of the 1st New Jersey and 182 of the 2nd New Jersey Regiments, at Dobbs Ferry, New York, was case officer for a spy operating out of Newark, and providing intelligence for Washington. Elias Dayton to George Washington, June 25, 1781; Elias Dayton, July 13, 1781, New Jersey Brigade; Elias Dayton to George Washington, July 14, 1781; Elias Dayton to George Washington, July 23, 1781; Elias Dayton to George Washington, July 28, 1781, all the above in General Correspondence, GWP.

80. George Washington at Rocky Hill, New Jersey, to Major General

Alexander McDougall, October 15, 1783, Gilder Lehrman Collection, GLC-01106, New-York Historical Society.

11. Deception Battle Plan: The Objective

1. One thousand two hundred fifty infantry and 67 artillerymen were given a discharge, and 1,150 men were given a furlough to March or April. For more on the Pennsylvania Line Mutiny, see John A. Nagy, *Rebellion in the Ranks: Mutinies of the American Revolution* (Yardley, Pennsylvania: Westholme Publishing, 2007), 77–166, 304–10.

2. David Humphreys writing for George Washington to William Heath, January 21, 1781, Varick Transcripts, Letterbook 11: 78-79, GWP.

3. George Washington to Robert Howe, January 22, 1781, Varick Transcripts, Letterbook 13: 83–84, GWP.

4. United States Naval Observatory, Sun and Moon Data for Saturday January 27, 1781, at Pompton, New Jersey, http://aa.usno.navy.mil/data/docs/AltAz.php.

5. Sources are not consistent with Tuttle's first name. It is recorded as John, Israel, "J," and "I." For more detail on the New Jersey Line Mutiny and other mutinies, see Nagy, *Rebellion in the Ranks*.

6. George Washington to John Laurens, April 9, 1781, Varick Transcripts, Letterbook 2: 208–12, GWP.

7. Joseph Paul, Marquis de Grasse Tilly, Comte de Grasse was born on September 13, 1722, at Le Bar-sur-Loup, Provence, France. His father was François de Grasse Rouville, Marquis de Grasse. He died on January 11, 1788, at Tilly, Île-de-France, France, and is buried at the Church of Saint-Roch, Paris.

8. The Webb House was built by Joseph Webb, merchant, in 1752 following his marriage to Mehitabel Nott in 1749. He hired Judah Wright to frame a three-and-a-half-story house and shop with a massive gambrel roof that provided upper-floor storage for Joseph's trade goods. When Joseph Webb died in 1761, the property was inherited by his son, Joseph Webb Jr., who married Abigail Chester in 1774.

9. *DGW*, 3:369, May 22, 1781.

10. George Washington to Marquis de Lafayette, May 31, 1781, Varick Transcripts, Letterbook 13: 396–97, GWP.

11. Jacques-Melchior Saint-Laurent, Comte de Barras, was born in 1719 and died in 1793.

12. William H. W. Sabine, ed., *Historical Memoirs of William Smith, 1778–1783* (New York: New York Times & Arno Press, rpt., 1971), 426, July 4, 1781.

13. William B. Willcox, *Portrait of a General: Sir Henry Clinton in the War for Independence* (New York: Alfred A. Knopf, 1964), 398.

14. Ibid., 405–6, 443.

15. James Moody, *Lieut James Moody's Narrative of His Exertions and Sufferings in the Cause of Government, Since the Year 1776; Authenticated by Proper Certificates* (London: Richardson & Urquhart, 1783), 2nd ed., 40–42.

16. Ibid.

17. Sabine, ed., *Historical Memoirs of William Smith, 1778–1783*, 421, June 15, 1781.

18. Frederick Mackenzie was born around 1731, probably in Dublin, Ireland. He was the only son of Scottish merchant William Mackenzie and Mary Ann Boursiquot, who was of French Huguenot descent. In 1745 he received a commission in the 23rd Regiment of Foot, also known as the Royal Welch Fusiliers. Fought in the War of the Austrian Succession and in the European theater of the Seven Years's War. Went with his regiment in August 1774 to Boston. He was promoted to captain and after the British evacuation of Boston to Halifax served as major of brigade under General William Howe. He served as deputy adjutant-general for the army under Henry Clinton from 1778–1782 (commissioned a major in 1780) and Guy Carleton from 1782–1783. In 1787, he became lieutenant colonel of the 37th Regiment of Foot, and in 1794, he raised the 1st Exeter Volunteers. He later became secretary of the Royal Military College. He died in 1824 in Teignmouth, Devon, England. Frederick Mackenzie, *Diary of Fredrick Mackenzie* (Cambridge: Harvard University Press, 1930), 2:536.

19. Sabine, ed., *Historical Memoirs of William Smith, 1778–1783*, 421, June 15, 1781.

20. Benjamin Franklin Stevens, *The campaign in Virginia, 1781: an exact reprint of six rare pamphlets on the Clinton-Cornwallis controversy, with very numerous important unpublished manuscript notes by Sir Henry Clinton, K.B., and the omitted and hitherto unpublished portions of the letters in their appendixes added from the original manuscripts; with a supplement containing extracts from the journals of the House of Lords, a French translation of papers laid before the House, and a catalogue of the additional correspondence of Clinton and*

Cornwallis, in 1780–81: about 3456 papers relating to the controversy or bearing on affairs in America in two volumes (London, 1888), 1:381.

21. George Washington at New Windsor to Dr. John Baker at Philadelphia, May 29, 1781, intercepted mail, Gold Star Box, William L. Clements Library, University of Michigan, Ann Arbor, Michigan.

22. Sabine, ed., *Historical Memoirs of William Smith, 1778–1783*, 423, June 23, 1781.

23. René Chartrand and Francis Back, *The French Army in the American War of Independence* (London: Osprey, 1991).

24. Jean-Baptiste Donatien de Vimeur, Comte de Rochambeau, was born July 1, 1725, in Vendôme, Orléanais, France, and died on May 30, 1807, at Thoré, Loir-et-Cher, France. He is buried at Thoré Cemetery, Thoré-la-Rochette.

25. Ezra Birch's pay abstract for a company of teams, July 20, 1781, before Jabez Botsford, justice of the peace at New Town, August 10, 1781, Private Collection.

26. The widow Sarah Bates's house is known as the Odell House. It is at 425 Ridge Road, Hartsdale, New York. It was named after Colonel John Odell, who purchased the house in 1785. It was a two-room, shingled, framed tenant house of the Philipsburg Manor. It was built in 1732 by John Tompkins with two rooms and an attic with random-width red pine flooring. Gilbert Bates added an east wing between 1760 and 1765 and doubled the size of the house. The French forces camped on the tenant farm of Gilbert Bates. Bates had been captured by the British and died in captivity. Jini Jones Vail, *Rochambeau: Washington's Ideal Lieutenant: A French General's Role in the American Revolution* (Tarentum, Pennsylvania: Word Association Publishers, 2011), 133.

27. Henry Clinton to George Brydges Rodney, June 28, 1781, CP 160:44. See also Admiral Samuel Hood to Henry Clinton, August 4, 1781, CP 169:7.

28. Nagy, *Rebellion in the Ranks*, 181–82.

29. *DGW*, 3: August 14, 1781.

30. *La Concorde* was a thirty-two-gun fifth-rate frigate. She was launched in Rochefort on September 3, 1777. She was captured by HMS *Magnificent* in 1783. George Washington and Jean B. Donatien de Vimeur, Comte de Rochambeau, to François-Joseph Paul, Comte de Grasse, August 17, 1781, Varick Transcripts, Letterbook 1: 319–23, GWP.

12. Deception Battle Plan: Enemy Assumptions

1. The province of Quebec at this time included Ontario.
2. Howard H. Peckham, *The Toll of Independence Engagements and Battle Casualties of the American Revolution* (Chicago: University of Chicago Press, 1974), 88–89.
3. Henry Clinton's comments after the American Revolution on Rochambeau's book, CP 241:47.
4. John Mauritius Goetschius was born on July 1, 1751, at Schraalenburg, Bergen County, New Jersey. He died on October 16, 1821, at Franklin, Franklin County, Ohio.
5. The Newark Mountains, on the western part of Newark, in 1780 had their name changed to Orange. Today that would be the area of East Orange, Orange, South Orange, and West Orange. The name Orange adopted, June 7, 1780. David Lawrence Pierson, *History of the Oranges to 1921: Reviewing the Rise, Development and Progress of an Influential Community* (Orange, New Jersey: Lewis Historical Publishing Company, 1922), 1:155; George Beckwith to Oliver De Lancey, August 21, 1781, CP 171:14.
6. Ira D. Gruber, ed., *John Peebles American War: The Diary of a Scottish Grenadier, 1776–1782* (Mechanicsburg, Pennsylvania: Stackpole, 1998), 467, August 23, 1781.
7. Johann Carl Philipp von Krafft, 1752–1804; Thomas H. Edsall, ed., *Journal of John Charles Philip von Krafft . . . 1776–1784* (New York: Printed for private distribution, 1888), 147. Accessed on March 27, 2016 at https://archive.org/stream/cu31924032740114 /cu31924032740114 djvu.txt.
8. Ibid.
9. Kakiat is now New Hempstead, Rockland County, New York. Jacob Brower, Property Confiscations, *New Jersey Gazette*, Trenton, December 16, 1778. Muster Roll of Captain Joseph Crowell's Company, September 11, 1780, National Archives of Canada, RG 8, "C" Series, vol. 1852, 83, cited from On-Line Institute for Advanced Loyalist Studies, http://www.royalprovincial.com /military/musters/lnjv/njvcrowell1.htm.
10. Robert Greene in *33 Strategies of War* (New York: Viking, 2007) calls it Misperception Strategies.

13. Deception Battle Plan: Method

1. George Washington to Noah Webster, July 31, 1788, Letterbook 15: 195–96, GWP.

2. Ibid.

3. James Thacher, *A Military Journal During the American Revolution from 1775 to 1783 . . . by James Thacher, M.D., Late Surgeon in the American Army* (Boston: Cottons & Barnard, 1827), 262.

4. The British had a total of 30 ten-foot pontoon bridge sections. It took 118 horses to move the thirty sections. The bridgemaster, a captain in the artillery, was responsible for the pontoons. Return of Pontoons, March 13, 1779, CP 54:2.

5. The Descendants of Jean Mousnier de la Montagne (1595–1670) website reports that the courier was Benjamin Montayne. He was born on January 13, 1745, in New York City and died on December 25, 1825, in New Vernon, Orange County, New York. He was a blacksmith in New York City and was raised in the Reformed Dutch Church. At the outbreak of the war he relocated to Fishkill where he became a courier for the army. Family tradition says he was the courier of the intercepted mail. The name is close to the one provided by other sources. The website got its information from Florence Rose King's Daughters of the American Revolution application for membership, #141450, in 1919, http://wc.rootsweb.ancestry.com/cgi -bin//igm.cgi?db=delamontagne&id=I504&op=GET&style =TABLE. I searched William Buell Sprague's *Annals of the American Pulpit*, which lists most but not all ministers. I did not find anyone named Montayne or Montagnie. Benson John Lossing appears to be the first person to tell the story in 1852. He said he received it from a Mr. Pierson, who says he received it directly from Montagnie. Lossing said Mrs. Elizabeth Oakes Smith received it from Mr. P[ierson], who was eighty-seven years old at the time. She recorded the name as Montagner in Elizabeth Oakes Prince Smith, *The Salamander: A Legend for Christmas Found Amongst the Papers of the Late Ernest Helfenstein* (New York: George P. Putnam, 1848), 16; Benson John Lossing, *The Pictorial Field Book of the Revolution; Or, Illustrations by Pen and Pencil, of the History, Biography, Scenery, Relics, and Traditions of the War for Independence* (New York: Harper and Brothers, 1851–1860), 1:213–14.

6. Don R. Gerlock, "Philip Schuyler and the New York Frontier in 1781," *New York-Historical Society Quarterly,* 53 (1960): 347–50. There are several copies of the letter, one in the Haldimand Papers and another in the Henry Huntington Library. The Huntington Library copy has the additional annotation: "Copy of a Letter Calculated to Mislead the Enemy with respect to Gen.

Washington's Intentions July 15, 1781 Directed to the Gen[era]l but carried to the Enemy etc."

7. *DGW*, 3:411, August 19, 1781.

8. Ibid., 3:413, August 19, 1781.

9. Baron Ludwig von Closen, *The Revolutionary Journal of Baron Ludwig von Closen, 1780–1783* (Chapel Hill: Published for the Institute of Early American History and Culture at Williamsburg, Virginia, by the University of North Carolina Press, 1958), 104.

10. William B. Willcox, *The American Rebellion* (New Haven: Yale University Press, 1954), 326.

11. To protect the French bakery, Dayton would have needed to block Hobart Gap, a strategic pass through the Watchung Mountains. Today it is New Jersey Route 124. George Washington to Elias Dayton, August 19, 1781, Varick Transcripts, Letterbook 14: 145, GWP; *DGW*, 3:411.

12. William H. W. Sabine, ed., *Historical Memoirs of William Smith, 1778–1783* (New York: New York Times & Arno Press, rpt., 1971), 433, August 20, 1781.

13. *DGW*, 3:413, August 21, 1781.

14. Sabine, ed., *Historical Memoirs of William Smith, 1778–1783*, 423, June 22, 1781.

15. Smith to William Tryon, draft, August 18–25, 1781, Sabine, ed., *Historical Memoirs of William Smith, 1778–1783*, 430–33.

16. Cornelius Harbrouck on November 8, 1781, stated to New York governor Clinton that Issac Ogden was employed by Cortlandt Skinner to provide intelligence. Hugh Hastings, ed., *Public Papers of George Clinton, First Governor of New York, 1777–1795, 1801–1804* (New York: State of New York, 1899–1914), 7:493.

17. Alexander Hamilton to William Livingston, April 29, 1777. Carl E. Prince, ed., *The Papers of William Livingston*, 1:316.

18. Isaac Ogden to Oliver De Lancey, August 16, 1781, CP 170:29.

19. Otto Huefeland, *Westchester County During the American Revolution, 1775–1783* (White Plains: Westchester County Historical Society, 1926), 40.

20. Sabine, ed., *Historical Memoirs of William Smith, 1778–1783*, 426–27, July 11, 1781.

14. Deception Battle Plan: The Sting—Executing the Plan

1. George Washington, August 5, 1781, General Orders, Varick Transcripts, Letterbook 5: 359–61, GWP.
2. George Washington, August 13, 1781, General Orders, Varick Transcripts, Letterbook 5: 369–70, GWP.
3. George Washington, August 15, 1781, General Orders, Varick Transcripts, Letterbook 5: 370–72, GWP.
4. *DGW*, 3:411, August 19, 1781.
5. William H. W. Sabine, ed., *Historical Memoirs of William Smith, 1778–1783* (New York: New York Times & Arno Press, rpt., 1971), 433, August 20, 1781.
6. George Washington, August 20–27, 1781, General Orders, Varick Transcripts, Letterbook 5: 376–78, GWP.
7. Jonathan Trumbull, *Journal of Jonathan Trumbull, Proceedings of the Massachusetts Historical Society* (Boston: J. Wilson & Son, 1876), 332, August 21, 1781.
8. Jean Edmund Weelan, *Rochambeau, Father and Son* (New York: H. Holy and Company, 1936), 224–25.
9. The Arthur Kill in the eighteenth century was sometimes known as the Raritan Sound. Connecticut Farms is located in Union Township, present-day Union County, New Jersey. George Washington to Benjamin Lincoln, August 24, 1781, Varick Transcripts, Letterbook 14: 150–52; and General Correspondence, GWP. But the following is crossed out: "I have put Colo[nel] Seely who commands the [New] Jersey Militia in the vicinity of Dobbs ferry under your orders, it will be proper therefore to direct him to march for Hackensack on the same day you march for Acqua Kanack [Aquackanonk], and for Connecticut Farms the day you march for Springfield where or in that neighbourhood he is [to] remain, keeping constant patrols to the sound as far as [Perth] Amboy till the French Army has Pssed Princeton and then act under the orders he may receive from Governor Livingston."
10. George Washington to Sylvanus Seely, August 26, 1781, Varick Transcripts, Letterbook 14: 147–48, GWP.
11. George Washington to Elias Dayton, August 24, 1781, Varick Transcripts, Letterbook 14: 154–55, GWP.
12. Ibid.
13. George Washington to Philip J. Schuyler at Poughkeepsie,

New York, June 19, 1781, Varick Transcripts, Letterbook 14: 16–17, GWP.

14. Philip J. Schuyler at Albany, New York, to George Washington, July 21, 1781, General Correspondence, GWP.

15. *DGW*, 3:402–3 and footnote 4, July 29, 1781.

16. Wappinger Creek is sometimes spelled as Wappings and Wappingers Creek. It is thirty-eight miles long and enters the Hudson River at Wappinger Falls. Ibid., 404, August 1, 1781.

17. George Washington to Brigadier General William Smallwood in Maryland, August 24, 1781, Varick Transcripts, Letterbook 14: 153–54, GWP. George Washington to Major General Arthur St. Clair at Philadelphia, August 24, 1781, Varick Transcripts, Letterbook 14: 148–49, GWP.

18. George Washington to Brigadier General David Forman, August 24, 1781, Varick Transcripts, Letterbook 14: 154, GWP.

19. George Washington to Sylvanus Seely, August 25, 1781, General Correspondence, GWP.

20. Guillaume Deux-Ponts, *My Campaigns in America, A Journal Kept by Count William de Deux-Ponts, 1780–81* (Boston: K. Wiggin & P. Lunt, 1868), 125, August 27, 1781, while camped at Whippany, New Jersey.

21. Alexander McDougall to George Washington, July 10, 1781, Founders Online, National Archives, http://founders.archives.gov /documents/Washington/99-01-02-06354.

22. George Washington to Alexander McDougall, August 18, 1781, Varick Transcripts, Letterbook 14: 139, GWP.

23. "Diary entry: 21 August 1781," Founders Online, National Archives, http://founders.archives.gov/documents/Washington /01-03-02-0007-0004-0015.

24. John Dods Tavern is located at 8 Chapel Hill Road, Lincoln Park, New Jersey. It was built circa 1770. Timothy Pickering to George Washington, August 21, 1781, General Correspondence, GWP.

25. George Washington to Benjamin Lincoln, August 24, 1781, General Correspondence, GWP.

26. George Washington to Philip Van Cortlandt, August 25, 1781, Varick Transcripts, Letterbook 14: 156–57, GWP.

27. Samuel Ogden's Iron Works were founded around 1770 on a six-acre tract along the Rockaway River, near Boonton.

28. Tench Tilghman at Chatham to Philip Van Cortlandt, August 27, 1781, Varick Transcripts, Letterbook 14: 160, GWP.

29. Philip Van Cortlandt to George Washington, August 28, 1781, Founders Online, National Archives, http://founders.archives .gov/documents/Washington/99-01-02-06820.

30. George Washington to Samuel Miles, August 27, 1781, Varick Transcripts, Letterbook 14: 160–62, GWP.

31. Bruce E. Burgoyne, trans., *Journal of the Hesse-Cassel Jaeger Corps* (Bowie, Maryland: Heritage Books, 2005), 161.

32. Donatien-Marie-Joseph de Vimeur, Vicomte de Rochambeau's name is one of the 660 names inscribed under the Arc de Triomphe in Paris.

33. Jean François de Beauvoir, Marquis de Chastellux, was born in 1734 in Paris and died October 24, 1788, in Paris. He was a general who served on Rochambeau's staff. He spoke fluent English and was liaison officer between the French commander in chief and George Washington.

34. Sabine, ed., *Historical Memoirs of William Smith, 1778–1783*, 434, August 23, 1781.

35. Villemanzy traveled from Brest, France, to North America with Rochambeau and Ternay in the *L'Ardent,* a seventy-four-gun ship of the line. He is sometimes referred to as Comte de Ville-manzy, but he was not made a comte until August 15, 1809. *L'Ardent* (ex-British *Ardent,* captured 1779) was recaptured by the British in the Battle of the Saintes in April 1782 and was added to the British navy as the HMS *Tiger* and was sold in 1784. List of Ships of the Line of France, https://en.wikipedia.org /wiki/List_of_ships_of_the_line_of_France.

36. Ludwig von Closen says the bricks were collected on the left bank of the Raritan and the men were fired upon by the advance works at Paulus Hook (the upper New York Bay side of present-day Jersey City), which is incorrect as neither the Raritan Bay, River, nor Sound is anywhere near that location. Ludwig von Closen, *The Revolutionary Journal of Baron Ludwig von Closen* (Chapel Hill: Published for the Institute of Early American History and Culture at Williamsburg, Virginia, by the University of North Carolina Press, 1958), 109. The only British battery near the location was at the Christopher Billopp House. The area the battery would threaten is present-day Smith and Front Streets in Perth Amboy. Weelan, *Rochambeau, Father and Son*, 224–25.

37. *DGW*, 3:414, August 29, 1781.

38. Ibid., August 30, 1781.

39. Trumbull, *Journal of Jonathan Trumbull*, 332, August 21, 1781.

40. Oliver De Lancey to Major Thomas Ward at Bergen Neck, August 21, 1781, CP 83:9.

41. Major Thomas Ward to Oliver de Lancey, August 24, 1781, CP 172:13.

42. Intelligence, CP 174:20, and envelope to Isaac Ogden, September 14, 1781, CP 174:29.

43. Sources disagree as to whether his arrival in Philadelphia was the 30th or 31st.

44. *DGW*, 416.

45. Ibid., 418; and Closen, *The Revolutionary Journal of Baron Ludwig von Closen, 1780–1783*, 123.

15. Deception Battle Plan: Exploitation

1. Henry Clinton to Charles Cornwallis, August 27, 1781, William B. Willcox, *The American Rebellion* (New Haven: Yale University Press, 1954), 562.

2. Sir Edmund Affleck to Henry Clinton, September 5, 1781, CP 173:36; Charles Cornwallis to Henry Clinton, September 4, 1781, Stevens, *The Campaign in Virginia, 1781: An Exact Reprint of Six Rare Pamphlets on the Clinton-Cornwallis Controversy* (London, 1888), 2:151; Willcox, *The American Rebellion*, 330.

3. James Moody, *Lieut. James Moody's Narrative of His Exertions and Sufferings in the Cause of Government, Since the Year 1776; Authenticated by Proper Certificates* (London: Richardson & Urquhart, 1783, 2nd ed.), 41.

4. William Heath to George Washington, September 7, 1781, General Correspondence, GWP.

5. Marks's report does not provide Lockwood's first name but a Millington Lockwood of Greenwich, Connecticut, served on the gunboats. In Sibil Lockwood's widow's petition, William Peck, on August 4, 1789, completed a sworn affidavit that he knew Millington Lockwood, and he had been sent out by the army to gather intelligence during the war. Peter Wilson Coldham, *American Migrations, 1765–1799* (Baltimore: Genealogical Publishing Co., 2000), 20; Nehemiah Marks to Oliver De Lancey, September 4, 1781, CP 173:35.

6. Nehemiah Marks to Oliver De Lancey, September 18, 1781, CP 175:4.

7. Knox was not approved to receive the pay until a resolve of Congress on September 24, 1779; John Jay to George Knox, July 27, 1779, Paul Hubert Smith and Ronald M. Gephart, eds., *Letters of*

Delegates to Congress, 1774–1789 (Washington: Library of Congress, 1976–2000), vol. 13: 297–98; *JCC* 14:890, July 26, 1779; *JCC* 15:1102, September 24, 1779.

8. British Spy Reports, report on George Knox, September 5, 1781, Gilder Lehrman Collection, GLC-05224.

9. William H. W. Sabine, *Historical Memoirs of William Smith, 1778–1783* (New York: New York Times & Arno Press, rpt., 1971), 442–43, September 14, 1781.

10. Morris House is the Morris-Jumel Mansion Museum at 65 Jumel Terrace between 160th and 162nd Streets in New York City. The house is a five-bay, two-story structure. It was built in 1765 by Colonel Robert Morris on 130 acres.

11. Ludwig Marquard to Oliver De Lancey, September 22, 1781, CP 175:20.

12. Ludwig Marquard to Oliver De Lancey, September 24, 1781, CP 176:10.

13. Henry Clinton's Notes, September 30, 1781, CP 177:1.

14. George Washington to William Heath at Dobbs Ferry, August 19, 1781, Varick Transcripts, Letterbook 14: 140–44, GWP.

15. Report from South Amboy, New Jersey, September 24, 1781, CP 176:1.

16. Accusations against Van Wagoner, October 6, 1781, CP 178:18; Captain Ward's report on the activities of Jacob Van Wagoner and on page 2 of the document are the activities of Garret Frealin, October 1781, CP 181:7.

17. James Lovell to George Washington, September 21, 1781, Founders Online, National Archives, http://founders.archives.gov/documents/Washington/99-01-02-06994.

18. The brig *Sea Nymph* is not the *Sea Nymph* that was captured by the British in October 1775, which was renamed *Hope*.

19. Mordecai Gist to George Washington, September 24, 1781, General Correspondence, GWP.

20. George Washington to James Lovell, October 6, 1781, Varick Transcripts, Letterbook 6: 139, GWP.

21. George Washington to James Lovell, October 12, 1781, Varick Transcripts, Letterbook 6: 141, GWP.

22. James Lovell to George Washington, October 14, 1781, General Correspondence, GWP.

23. David Kahn, *The Code Breakers* (New York: Macmillan, 1967, 1972), 182.

24. Ibid., 183.

25. Richard Peters (June 22, 1744–August 22, 1828) was an attorney from Philadelphia who served as a register of admiralty from 1771 to 1776, and was secretary of the Board of War from June 1776 to December 1781. He served as a delegate to the Continental Congress from November 1782 to November 1783. George Washington in April 1792 appointed Peters judge of the United States District Court for Pennsylvania, a position that he held until his death. Peters and Washington shared an interest in scientific agriculture, about which they corresponded after the war. Philander D. Chase et al., eds., *The Papers of George Washington. Revolutionary War Series* (Charlottesville: University of Virginia Press, 1985–present), vol. 8: 263–64.

26. Anne-César de La Luzerne was born on July 15, 1741, in Paris. He joined the French army and served during the Seven Years' War reaching the rank of major general in 1762. He served as second French minister to the United States from 1779 to 1784. He died on September 14, 1791, at Southampton, England.

27. Catherine S. Crary, "The Tory and the Spy: The Double Life of James Rivington," *William and Mary Quarterly* 16, no. 1 (January 1959): 68.

28. McLane arrived in Virginia in early February 1781, retired in February, and stayed in Virginia to an undetermined date, but by June he was back in Philadelphia. The first meeting occurred before July 1781 when McLane embarked on the privateer *Congress* and went to the Caribbean. He returned to Philadelphia on September 18, 1781, when the Continental Army was in Maryland.

29. McLane Papers, New-York Historical Society, 41.

30. Colonel Allen M'Lane, *A Relic of the American Revolution, A Journal of Eight Years Hard Fighting During the War for Our Independence, The Knickerbocker* (New York: William Osborn, 1838), vol. 11, no. 1, January 1838, 177–79.

31. Richard Peters to George Washington, October 19, 1781, Founders Online, National Archives, http://founders.archives.gov/documents/Washington/99-01-02-07208.

32. George Washington to Allen McLane, December 31, 1781, Varick Transcripts, Letterbook 14: 345, GWP.

33. The first set of signals bore Admiral Mariot Arbuthnot's name. He was commander in chief on the North American Station from 1779 to July 1781.

34. Richard Peters to George Washington, October 19, 1781,

Founders Online, National Archives, http://founders.archives
.gov/documents/Washington/99-01-02-07208.

35. George Washington to Continental Congress War Board [Richard
Peters], October 27, 1781, two the same date, Varick Transcripts,
Letterbook 6: 153–54, GWP.

36. George Washington to Anne-César, Chevalier de La Luzerne, October 29, 1781, Varick Transcripts, Letterbook 1: 392, GWP. The
original is in the Paris Archives, Aff. Etrang., Mems. et Does.,
E.U., vol. 6.

37. James Innes to Governor Benjamin Harrison V, February 11,
1782, Dr. William P. Palmer, ed., *Virginia Calendar of State Papers
and Other Manuscripts* (Richmond, 1883; rpt., New York: Kraus
Reprint Corp., 1968), 3:58–59.

38. George Washington to Marquis de Lafayette, July 13, 1781, Varick Transcripts, Letterbook 14: 74–76, GWP.

39. George Washington to Marquis de Lafayette, July 30, 1781, two
the same date, Varick Transcripts, Letterbook 14: 108–11, GWP.

40. There is a tombstone for Charles Morgan in the Morgan Meeting House Cemetery, Clay, Onondaga County, New York, that
was established in 1840, thirty-seven years after his death. The
tombstone reads, "Charles Morgan, Revolty Spy, One Of The
Captors Of Major Andre, Capt. Wm. Gifford's Co., Col. Dayton's 3rd N.J. Reg., 1745–1803." Charles Morgan was from Monmouth County, New Jersey. He operated as a spy in Virginia at
Yorktown in 1781. The original story comes from Dr. James
Thacher's *Military Journal* in 1781. Morgan was a private and is
said to usually have been called Charlie. His descendants were
in Onondaga County, New York, in 1848, so it is most likely the
same person. An article in *Spirit of '76 Magazine*, vol. 11 (New
York: Louis H. Cornish, 1902), page 126, reports that Charles
Morgan's grave had been recently discovered "on the Moyer
farm near Liverpool." His body was apparently moved circa
1902 to the Morgan Meeting House Cemetery. The article further reports, "Morgan is said to have been one of the spies who
captured [John] Andre [*sic*] and the original of Fenimore Cooper's 'The Spy.'" In addition, "Twenty revolutionary soldiers
were buried on the Moyer farm." Morgan was not the source of
Cooper's *The Spy*. The question is, why would twenty Revolutionary War soldiers be buried on a remote farm in upstate New
York, north of Syracuse? There was no battle fought there. Those
who captured André were not spies. This 1902 article further
reports, "The Onondaga Historical Society is to place a suitable

marker about the grave of Charles Morgan." The three captors of John André are well known and Morgan is not one of them. The information on the tombstone appears to come from someone who recalled that Morgan was said to have been a spy but got his/her stories mixed up. The local historical society appears to have believed the tale, a good one, but with no proof.

41. Lafayette to George Washington, August 25, 1781, Founders Online, National Archives, http://founders.archives.gov/documents /Washington/99-01-02-06792.

42. The *London* was launched on May 24, 1766, at Chatham Dockyard. She was later increased to ninety-eight guns when she had eight 12-pounders installed on her quarterdeck. The *London* was Sir Thomas Graves's flagship and was broken up in 1811.

43. HMS *Charon* was launched in 1778 and destroyed by a French ship on October 10, 1781.

44. Thomas B. Allen, *George Washington, Spymaster: How the Americans Outspied the British and Won* (Washington, DC: National Geographic Society 2004), 149, http://www.mountvernon.org/george -washington/the-revolutionary-war/spying-and-espionage /george-washington-spymaster/.

16. Conclusion

1. Landon Carter to George Washington, October 7, 1755, General Correspondence, GWP.

2. Dave R. Palmer, *George Washington's Military Genius* (Washington, DC: Regnery, 2012), 224.

3. Ibid.

4. The two serpents were Burgoyne's and Cornwallis's armies. Benjamin Franklin to John Adams, November 26, 1781, *The Papers of Benjamin Franklin* (New Haven: Yale University Press, 1959–present), 36:113–16.

BIBLIOGRAPHY

Manuscript Collections

Adams Family Correspondence, Founding Families: Digital Editions of the Papers of the Winthrops and the Adamses, http://www.masshist .org/publications/apde2/. Boston: Massachusetts Historical Society.

British Transcripts, Colonial Office, C.O. 5, Library of Congress.

Clinton, Henry. Papers. William L. Clements Library, University of Michigan, Ann Arbor, Michigan.

Colonial Office Papers. British National Archives, Kew, Richmond, Surrey, United Kingdom.

Emmett Collection. New York Public Library, New York, New York.

Founders Online. National Archive. http://founders.archives.gov/.

Gage, Thomas. Papers, American Series. William L. Clements Library, University of Michigan, Ann Arbor, Michigan.

Gilder Lehrman Collection. New-York Historical Society, New York, New York.

Gold Star Box. Papers. William L. Clements Library, University of Michigan, Ann Arbor, Michigan.

Jay, John. Papers. Columbia University, New York, New York.

Livingston, Henry. Collection, 1751–1833, SC19687. New York State Library, Albany, New York.

Mackenzie, Frederick. Papers, William L. Clements Library, University of Michigan, Ann Arbor, Michigan.

McLane, Allen. Papers. New-York Historical Society, New York, New York.

Papers of the Continental Congress, 1774–1789 (Washington, DC: National Archives and Records Service, General Services Administration, 1971), microfilm.

Society Miscellaneous, Box 9B. Papers. Historical Society of Pennsylvania, Philadelphia, Pennsylvania.

Washington, George. Papers. Library of Congress, Washington, DC.

Published Material

Allen, Thomas B. *George Washington, Spymaster: How the Americans Outspied the British and Won.* Washington, DC: National Geographic Society, 2004.

American Ancestry: Embracing Lineages from the Whole of the United States, 1888[–1898], vol. 11. Albany: Joel Munsell's Sons, 1898.

Atterbury, William Wallace, ed. *Elias Boudinot: Reminiscences of the American Revolution.* New York, 1894.

Bakeless, John. *Turncoats, Traitors and Heroes: Espionage in the American Revolution.* New York: J. B. Lippincott, 1959; rept., New York: Da Capo, 1998.

Bendikson, Lodewyk. "The Restoration of Obliterated Passages and of Secret Writing in Diplomatic Missives," *Franco-American Review.* New Haven: Friends of the Franco-American Review, vol. 1, no. 3 (December 1936).

Biographical Directory of the United States Congress. http://bioguide.congress.gov/biosearch/biosearch.asp.

Boudinot, Elias, with Frederick Bourquinn, ed. *Journal of Events in the Revolution.* Philadelphia: H. J. Bicking, 1894.

Bouvier, John. *A Law Dictionary, Adapted to the Constitution and Laws of the United States of America and of the Several States of the American Union; with References to the Civil and Other Systems of Foreign Law,* vol. 2. Philadelphia: Childs & Peterson, 1856.

Burgoyne, Bruce, compiler and ed. *Enemy Views: The American Revolutionary War as Recorded by the Hessian Participants.* Bowie, Maryland: Heritage Books, 1996.

———, trans. *Journal of the Hesse-Cassel Jaeger Corps.* Bowie, Maryland: Heritage Books, 2005.

Burr, Nelson R. *The Anglican Church in New Jersey.* Philadelphia: Church Historical Society, 1954.

Chamberlain, Mellen, ed. *A Documentary History of Chelsea, Including the Boston Precincts of Winnisimmet, Rumsey Marsh, and Pullen Point, 1624–1824,* 2 vols. Boston: Massachusetts Historical Society, 1908.

Chartrand, René, and Francis Back. *The French Army in the American War of Independence.* London: Osprey, 1991.

Chatterton, Georgiana, Lady. *Memorials, Personal and Historical of Admiral Lord Gambier, G.C.B.,* vol. 1. London: Hurst & Blackett, 1861.

Chernow, Ron. *Washington: A Life.* New York: Penguin, 2010.

Clayton, W. Woodford. *History of Union and Middlesex Counties.* Philadelphia: Everts & Peck, 1882.

Clinton, George. *Public Papers of George Clinton,* 10 vols. New York and Albany: Wynkoop Hallenbeck Crawford Company, 1899–1914.

Closen, Baron Ludwig von. *The Revolutionary Journal of Baron Ludwig von Closen, 1780–1783.* Chapel Hill: Published for the Institute of Early American History and Culture at Williamsburg, Virginia, by the University of North Carolina Press, 1958.

Coldham, Peter Wilson. *American Loyalist Claims.* Washington, DC: National Genealogical Society, 1980.

———. *American Migrations, 1765–1799.* Baltimore: Genealogical Publishing Co., 2000.

Collections of the New-York Historical Society for the Year 1878. New York: New-York Historical Society, 1879.

Congress, Letters of Delegates to Washington, DC: Library of Congress, 1976–2000. February 1, 1779–May 31, 1779, and vol. 13, June 1, 1779–September 30, 1779.

Council of Safety of New Jersey. *Minutes of the Council of Safety of the State of New Jersey.* Jersey City: J. H. Lyon, 1872.

Crary, Catherine S. *The Price of Loyalty: Tory Writings from the Revolutionary Era.* New York: McGraw-Hill, 1973.

———. "The Tory and the Spy: The Double Life of James Rivington." *William and Mary Quarterly* 16, no. 1 (January 1959).

Dana, Elizabeth Ellery. *The British in Boston: The Diary of Lieutenant John Barke of the King's Own Regiment from November 15, 1774 to May 31, 1776.* Cambridge: Harvard University Press, 1924.

Daughters of the American Revolution application for membership #141450 in 1919. http://wc.rootsweb.ancestry.com/cgi-bin/igm.cgi?db=delamontagne&id=I504&op=GET&style=TABLE.

Deux-Ponts, Guillaume. *My Campaigns in America, A Journal Kept by Count William de Deux-Ponts, 1780–81.* Boston: K. Wiggin & P. Lunt, 1868.

Dictionary of Canadian Biography, vols. 3 and 4. Toronto: University of Toronto/Université Laval, 2003–.

Dinwiddie, Robert. *Official Records of Robert Dinwiddie, Lieutenant Governor of the Colony of Virginia, 1751–1758,* vol. 1. Richmond: Virginia Historical Society, 1883.

Doren, Carl van. *The Secret History of the American Revolution.* New York: Viking, 1951.

Egerton, Hugh Edward. *The Royal Commission on the Losses and Services of American Loyalists, 1783 to 1785.* New York: Arno, 1969.

F. [Falconer], J. *Rules for Explaining and Deciphering All Manner of Secret Writing, Plain and Demonstrative.* London: Printed for Dan. Brown and Sam. Manship, 1692.

Fairfax Land Grant. http://www.lva.virginia.gov/public/guides /opac/lonnabout.htm.

Fitzpatrick, John C., ed. *The Writings of George Washington from the Original Manuscript Sources, 1745–1799,* 39 vols. Washington, DC: United States Government Printing Office, 1931–1944.

Flexner, James Thomas. *George Washington.* Boston: Little, Brown, 1968.

Flick, Alexander C. *America Revolution in New York: Its Political, Social and Economic Significance.* Albany: State University of New York Press, 1926.

Force, Peter. *American Archives: consisting of a collection of authentick records, state papers, debates, and letters and other notices of publick affairs, the whole forming a documentary history of the origin and progress of the North American colonies; of the causes and accomplishment of the American Revolution; and of the Constitution of government for the United States, to the final ratification thereof.* New York: Johnson Reprint Corp., 1972.

Ford, Worthington Chauncey. *British Officers Serving in the American Revolution, 1774–1783.* Brooklyn: Historical Printing Club, 1897.

Franklin, Benjamin. *The Papers of Benjamin Franklin.* New Haven: Yale University Press, 1959–present.

Garraty, John A., and Mark C. Carnes, eds. *American National Biography,* vol. 1. New York: Oxford University Press, 1999.

Gerlock, Don R. "Philip Schuyler and the New York Frontier in 1781." *New-York Historical Society Quarterly,* 53 (1960).

Gist, Christopher; William J. Darlington, ed. *Christopher Gist's Journals with Historical, Geographical and Ethnological Biographies of His Contemporaries.* Pittsburgh: J. R. Weldin, 1893.

Gordon, William. *The History of the Rise, Progress, and Establishment, of the Independence of the United States of America: Including an Account of the Late War; and of the Thirteen Colonies, from Their Origin to That Period,* vol. 2. London: Gordon, 1788.

Gray, David. Gray Narrative, 1825.

Graydon, Alexander. *Memoirs of a Life, Chiefly Passed in Pennsylvania: Within the Last Sixty Years with Occasional Remarks upon the General Occurrences, Character and Spirit of That Eventful Period.* Harrisburg: John Wyeth, 1811.

Graydon, Alexander, and John S. Littell. *Memoirs of His Own Time: With Reminiscences of the Men and Events of the Revolution.* Philadelphia: Lindsay & Blakiston, 1846.

Greene, Nathanael. *Papers of General Nathanael Greene.* Chapel Hill: Published for the Rhode Island Historical Society by the University of North Carolina Press, 1976–2005.

Greene, Robert. *33 Strategies of War.* New York: Viking, 2007.

Gruber, Ira D., ed. *John Peebles' American War: The Diary of a Scottish Grenadier, 1776–1782.* Mechanicsburg, Pennsylvania: Stackpole, 1998.

Hawkins, John H. *John H. Hawkins' First Pennsylvania Orderly Book, June 16–18, 1780.*

Hazard, Samuel. *Pennsylvania Colonial Records.* Harrisburg, Pennsylvania: T. Fenn, 1838–1853.

Heitman, Francis B. *Historical Register of Officers of the Continental Army During the War of the Revolution, April 1775, to December 1783.*

Historical Manuscript Commission. *Manuscripts of the Earl of Dartmouth, American Papers,* vol. 2, 14th report, appendix, part 10, 1895. Rpt., Boston: Gregg Press, 1972.

Historical Society of Pennsylvania. *Pennsylvania Magazine of History and Biography.* Philadelphia: Historical Society of Pennsylvania.

Hornor, William S. *This Old Monmouth of Ours.* Freehold, New Jersey: Moreau Brothers, 1932; Rpt., Baltimore: Genealogical Publishing Co., 1990, 1999, 2009.

Huefeland, Otto. *Westchester County During the American Revolution, 1775–1783.* White Plains: Westchester County Historical Society, 1926.

Hughes, Thomas; R. W., David ed. *A Journal by Thos. Hughes for His Amusement: & Designed Only for His Perusal by the Time He Attains the Age of 50 If He Lives So Long (1778–1789).* Cambridge [England]: University Press, 1947.

Hutchinson, Elmer T. *Documents Relating to the Colonial History of the State of New Jersey, Calendar of New Jersey Wills, Volume IX,*

1796–1800. Trenton: MacCrellish & Quigley, 1944; Rpt., Westminster, Maryland: Heritage Books, 2008.

Hutson, James. *Nathan Hale Revisited: A Tory's Account of the Arrest of the First American Spy*. Library of Congress Information Bulletin, July/August, 2003.

Jackson, Donald, and Dorothy Twohig, eds. *The Diaries of George Washington*, vol. 1, 1748–65; vol. 3, 1771–75, 1780–81. Charlottesville: University of Virginia Press, 1976, 1978.

Journals of the Continental Congress, 1774–1789. Washington, DC: United States Government Printing Office, 1904–1937.

Kahn, David. *The Code Breakers*. New York: Macmillan, 1967, 1972.

Kail, Jerry. *Who Was Who During the American Revolution*. Indianapolis: Bobbs-Merrill, 1976.

Ketchum, Richard, *The Winter Soldiers: The Battles for Trenton and Princeton*. New York: Macmillan, 1999.

Krafft, Johann Carl Philipp von, 1752–1804; Edsall, Thomas H., ed. *Journal of John Charles Philip von Krafft . . . 1776–1784* (New York: Printed for private distribution, 1888), 147. Accessed on March 27, 2016, at https://archive.org/stream/cu31924032740114 /cu31924032740114 djvu.txt.

Lengel, Edward G. *General George Washington: A Military Life*. New York: Random House, 2005.

List of Ships of the Line of France. https://en.wikipedia.org/wiki /List_of_ships_of_the_line_of_France.

Lossing, Benson John. *The Pictorial Field Book of the Revolution; Or, Illustrations by Pen and Pencil, of the History, Biography, Scenery, Relics, and Traditions of the War for Independence*, vol. 1. New York: Harper and Brothers, 1851–1860.

Lundin, Leonard. *Cockpit of the Revolution: The War for Independence in New Jersey*. Princeton: Princeton University Press, 1940.

Lydenberg, Harry Miller, ed. *Archibald Robertson, Lieutenant-General Royal Engineers: His Diaries and Sketches in America, 1762–1780*. New York: New York Public Library, 1930.

Mackenzie, Frederick. *Diary of Fredrick Mackenzie*, vol. 2. Cambridge: Harvard University Press, 1930.

Mandeville, Ernest W. *The Story of Middletown—The Oldest Settlement in New Jersey*. Middletown, New Jersey: Christ Church, 1927; Rpt. Middletown, New Jersey: Academy Press, 1972.

Michener, Ron. "Money in the American Colonies." On EH.net,

Economic History Association. https://eh.net/encyclopedia
/money-in-the-american-colonies/.

M'Lane, Colonel Allen. *A Relic of the American Revolution, A Journal of Eight Years Hard Fighting During the War for Our Independence, The Knickerbocker.* New York: William Osborn, 1838.

Moody, James. *Lieut. James Moody's Narrative of His Exertions and Sufferings in the Cause of Government, Since the Year 1776; Authenticated by Proper Certificates.* London: Richardson & Urquhart, 1783; 2nd ed.

Moore, Frank. *The Diary of the Revolution: A Centennial Volume Embracing the Current Events in Our Country's History from 1775 to 1781 as Described by American, British, and Tory Contemporaries; Compiled from the Journals, Documents, Private Records, Correspondence, Etc., of That Period, Forming an Interesting, Impartial, and Valuable Collection of Revolutionary Literature. Illustrated with Steel Engravings.* Hartford: J. B. Burr Publishing Company, 1876.

Nagy, John A. *Invisible Ink: Spycraft of the American Revolution.* Yardley, Pennsylvania: Westholme Publishing, 2010.

———. *Rebellion in the Ranks: Mutinies of the American Revolution.* Yardley, Pennsylvania: Westholme Publishing, 2007.

———. *Spies in the Continental Capital: Espionage Across Pennsylvania During the American Revolution.* Yardley, Pennsylvania: Westholme Publishing, 2011.

National Archives. Revolutionary War Pension and Bounty Land Warrant Application Files. Microfilm, no. 1151.

New England Historical Genealogical Society. *The New England Historical and Genealogical Register,* vol. 19. Boston: New England Historical Genealogical Society, 1874–.

New Jersey Archives Series, 1880–1950. Trenton: New Jersey Bureau of Archives and History, 2nd series, vol. 4.

New York State. *Names of Persons for Whom Marriage Licenses Were Issued by the Secretary of the Province of New York Previous to 1784.* Albany, 1860.

New York State, Department of State. *Calendar of Historical Manuscripts, Relating to the War of the Revolution, in the Office of the Secretary of State, Albany, N.Y.* Albany: Weed, Parsons & Company, Printers, 1868.

On-Line Institute for Advanced Loyalist Studies. http://www
.royalprovincial.com.

Paine, Thomas. *American Crisis II*, in *The American Crisis*. London: R. Carlile, 1819.

Palmer, David R. *George Washington's Military Genius*. Washington, DC: Regnery, 2012.

Palmer, Dr. William P., ed. *Virginia Calendar of State Papers and Other Manuscripts*. Richmond: 1883; Rpt., New York: Kraus Reprint Corp., 1968.

Paltsits, Victor Hugo. *Minutes of the Commissioners for Detecting and Defeating Conspiracies in the State of New York*, 2 vols. Albany: State of New York, 1909.

Pattison, Robert B. *The Books of the First Baptist Church of Ossining in The Quarterly Bulletin of the Westchester County Historical Society*, vols. 13–18. White Plains, New York: Westchester County Historical Society, 1937.

Peckham, Edward H., ed. *The Toll of Independence: Engagements and Battle Casualties of the American Revolution*. Chicago: University of Chicago Press, 1974.

Pennsylvania Supreme Executive Council. *Minutes of the Supreme Executive Council of Pennsylvania, from Its Organization to the Termination of the Revolution*. Harrisburg: T. Fenn, 1853.

Pennypacker, Morton. *General Washington's Spies on Long Island and in New York*. Garden City: Long Island Historical Society by Country Life Press, 1939.

Pierson, David Lawrence. *History of the Oranges to 1921: Reviewing the Rise, Development and Progress of an Influential Community*, vol. 1. Orange, New Jersey: Lewis Historical Publishing Company, 1922.

Plat, Sir Hugh. *The Jewel House of Art and Nature*. London: Elizabeth Alsop, 1653.

Preble, Captain George Henry. *Preble Family in America*. Boston: David Clapp & Son, 1868.

Price, Ezekiel. *Diary of Ezekiel Price, 1775–1776*. In *Proceedings of the Massachusetts Historical Society, 1863–1864*. Boston: Massachusetts Historical Society, 1864.

Prince, Carl E., ed. *The Papers of William Livingston*. Trenton: New Jersey Historical Commission, 1979–1988.

Proceedings of the New Jersey Historical Society, vol. 7, nos. 1 and 2. Newark: New Jersey Historical Society, 1922.

Ramsey, David. *The History of the American Revolution in Two Volumes*. Philadelphia: R. Aitken & Son, 1789.

Rose, Alexander. *Washington's Spies: The Story of America's First Spy Ring.* New York: Bantam, 2006.

Ryan, Evelyne H. *The Burning of Bedford Village History Re-examined.* Katonah, New York: Record Review, July 9, 2004. http://bedfordhistoricalsociety.org/about_bedford_ny/pdfs/The _Burning_of_Bedford.pdf.

Sabine, William H. W., ed. *Historical Memoirs of William Smith, 1778–1783.* New York: New York Times & Arno Press, rpt., 1971.

Slaughter, William A. *Battle of Iron Works Hill at Mount Holly, New Jersey December 1776.* In *Proceedings of the New Jersey Historical Society.* New Jersey Historical Society, 1919, New Series 1919, vol. 4, nos. 1–4.

Smith, Elizabeth Oakes Prince. *The Salamander: A Legend for Christmas Found Amongst the Papers of the Late Ernest Helfenstein.* New York: George P. Putnam, 1848.

Society of Gentlemen. *A new and complete dictionary of arts and sciences; comprehending all the branches of useful knowledge, with Accurate Descriptions as well of the various Machines, Instruments, Tools, Figures, and Schemes necessary for illustrating them, as of The Classes, Kinds, Preparations, and Uses of Natural Productions, whether Animals, Vegetables, Minerals, Fossils, or Fluids; Together with The Kingdoms, Provinces, Cities, Towns, and other remarkable Places throughout the World. Illustrated with above three hundred copper-plates, engraved by Mr. Jefferys, Geographer to His Majesty. The whole extracted from the best authors in all languages. By a society of gentlemen* (London: W. Owen, 1763), second edition, vol. 2 of 4: 1780–1781.

Spirit of '76 Magazine, vol. 11. New York: Louis H. Cornish, 1902.

Stevens, Benjamin Franklin. *The campaign in Virginia, 1781: an exact reprint of six rare pamphlets on the Clinton-Cornwallis controversy, with very numerous important unpublished manuscript notes by Sir Henry Clinton, K.B., and the omitted and hitherto unpublished portions of the letters in their appendixes added from the original manuscripts; with a supplement containing extracts from the journals of the House of Lords, a French translation of papers laid before the House, and a catalogue of the additional correspondence of Clinton and Cornwallis, in 1780–81: about 3456 papers relating to the controversy or bearing on affairs in America in two volumes.* London: 1888.

Stryker, William S. *The Battles of Trenton and Princeton.* Boston: Houghton Mifflin, 1898.

————. *Official Register of the Officers and Men of New Jersey in the Revolutionary War.* Trenton: William T. Nicholson, 1870.

Tallmadge, Benjamin. *Memoir of Colonel Benjamin Tallmadge.* New York: Thomas Holman, Book and Job Printer, 1858; Rpt., New York: New York Times & Arno Press, 1968.

Thacher, James. *A Military Journal During the American Revolution from 1775 to 1783 . . . by James Thacher, M.D., Late Surgeon in the American Army.* Boston: Cottons & Barnard, 1827.

Tilghman, Oswald. *Memoir of Lieutenant Colonel Tench Tilghman.* Albany, 1876.

Trumbull, Jonathan. *Journal of Jonathan Trumbull, Proceedings of the Massachusetts Historical Society.* Boston: J. Wilson & Son, 1876.

Uhlendorf, Bernhard A., trans. and annotator. *Revolution in America: Confidential Letters and Journals, 1776–1784 of the Adjutant General Major Baurmeister of the Hessian Forces.* New Brunswick, New Jersy: Rutgers University Press, 1957.

United States Naval Observatory, Astronomical Applications Department. http://aa.usno.navy.mil/cgi-bin/aa_phases.pl?year=1754 &month=5&day=20&nump=50&format=p.

Upton, Leslie Francis Stokes. *The Loyal Whig: William Smith of New York and Quebec.* Toronto: University of Toronto Press, 1969.

Vail, Jini Jones. *Rochambeau: Washington's Ideal Lieutenant: A French General's Role in the American Revolution.* Tarentum, Pennsylvania: Word Association Publishers, 2011.

Valentine, D. T. *Manual of the Common Council of the City of New York.* New York: Common Council, 1863.

Van Cortlandt, Philip. *Autobiography of Philip Van Cortlandt, Brigadier General in the Continental Army.* In *Magazine of American History with Notes and Queries*, vol. 2, part 1. New York: A. S. Barnes and Co., 1878.

Van Doren, Carl. *Secret History of the American Revolution.* New York: Viking, 1951.

A View of the Evidence Relative to the Conduct of the American War Under Sir William Howe, Lord Viscount Howe, and General Burgoyne; as Given Before a Committee of the House of Commons Last Session of the Parliament. To Which Is Added a Collection of the Celebrated Fugitive Pieces That Are Said to Have Given Rise to That Important Enquiry. London: Richardson & Urquhart, 1779.

Walpole, Horace. *Horace Walpole: Correspondence of Horace Walpole with George Montagu, vol. 1, 1735–1755.* London: Henry Coldburn, 1837.

———. *Memoirs of the Reign of King George the Second,* 3 vols. London: H. Colburn, 1847.

Ward, Harry M. *General William Maxwell and the New Jersey Continentals.* Westport: Greenwood, 1997.

———. *Major General Adam Stephen and the Cause of American Liberty.* Charlottesville: University of Virginia Press, 1989.

Washington, George. Philander D. Chase et al., eds. *The Papers of George Washington. Revolutionary War Series.* Charlottesville: University Virginia Press, 1985–present.

Weelan, Jean Edmund. *Rochambeau, Father and Son.* New York: H. Holy & Company, 1936.

Weems, [Mason Locke] Parson. *The Life of Washington the Great.* Augusta, Georgia: George P. Randolph, 1806.

Welch, Thomas, and Michael Lloyd, eds. *Allen McLane: Patriot, Soldier, Spy Port Collector.* Dover: Delaware Heritage Press, 2014.

Whitehead, William A. *Contributions to the Early History of Perth Amboy and Adjoining Country: With Sketches of Men and Events in New Jersey During the Provincial Era.* New York: D. Appleton & Company, 1856.

Wilkin Captain W. H., *Some British Soldiers in America.* London: Hugh Rees, Ltd., 1914.

Willcox, William B. *The American Rebellion.* New Haven: Yale University Press, 1954.

———. *Portrait of a General: Sir Henry Clinton in the War for Independence.* New York: Alfred A. Knopf, 1964.

Newspapers

New Jersey Gazette, Trenton, New Jersey, 1782.

Norwich Packet, Norwich, Connecticut, September 7, 1779.

Pennsylvania Packet or General Advertiser, Philadelphia, Pennsylvania, 1776–1781.

INDEX